T0343505

Gentrification is Inevitable and Other Lies

Gentrification is Inevitable and Other Lies

Leslie Kern

VERSO
London • New York

This edition published by Verso 2022
First published by Between the Lines, Toronto, Ontario, 2022
© Leslie Kern, 2022

The moral rights of the author have been asserted

1 3 5 7 9 10 8 6 4 2

Verso
UK: 6 Meard Street, London W1F 0EG
US: 388 Atlantic Avenue, Brooklyn, NY 11217
versobooks.com

Verso is the imprint of New Left Books

ISBN-13: 978-1-83976-754-8
ISBN-13: 978-1-83976-757-9 (US EBK)
ISBN-13: 978-1-83976-756-2 (UK EBK)

British Library Cataloguing in Publication Data
A catalogue record for this book is available from the British Library

Library of Congress Cataloging-in-Publication Data
A catalog record for this book is available from the Library of Congress

Text design by DEEVE
Printed and bound by CPI Group (UK) Ltd, Croydon, CR0 4YY

In loving memory of my father, a gentle and generous man

CONTENTS

Thank you to Amanda Crocker, my editor at Between the Lines, for your constant encouragement and insightful feedback at every stage of this project. Leo Hollis at Verso has also been tremendously supportive and thoughtful about the orientation of this book. A huge thanks to the staff of both of these independent presses, who do amazing work behind the scenes in design, editing, and marketing. Nadine Ryan provided outstanding copyediting services, and any remaining errors are my own.

Thank you to the Mi'kmaq on whose lands I have been a guest since 2009. I am honoured to have had the opportunity to live, work, and learn in the territory of Mi'kma'ki during the writing of this book.

I am grateful for colleagues (who I also consider friends) such as Winifred Curran, whose own research and willingness to collaborate have uplifted this and other projects of mine. Michael Fox took a chance on hiring a non-geographer into a geography department and fought to keep me there. Roberta Hawkins has patiently waited for my work on this book to end so I can return to our work together.

My friends have been my biggest cheerleaders and despite distance, a pandemic, and the roller coaster of life, they remain a great joy in my life: Jennifer Kelly, Kris Weinkauf, Katherine Krupicz, Sarah Gray, Cristina Izquierdo, Michelle Mendes, Katie Haslett, Jane Dryden, Shelly Colette, and Lisa Dawn Hamilton.

Thank you to my family for always encouraging me to go far in my career and in life: Dale Kern, Ralph Kern, Josh Kern, Geof Dunn, Kathy Saunders, Charmaine Peters, and my grandparents, aunts, uncles, and cousins.

My daughter Maddy continues to inspire me to (hopefully) inspire her. My partner Peter keeps me grounded with his unfailing love and care. Thank you all.

ACKNOWLEDGEMENTS

1

GENTRIFICATION IS . . .

I used to live in a west-end Toronto neighbourhood called the Junction. Carved up and isolated at the "junction" of intersecting railroads, its industrial history was tangible in the sounds and smells drifting from rubber, paint, and meatpacking factories. Today, on a hot afternoon, some of those smells might waft along, but they are competing with the scents emanating from upscale cafés and vegan bakeries. I know it is a cliché to talk about how gritty your neighbourhood once was, but there is a reason why we are all tired of this narrative: so many of our neighbourhoods are being remade before our very eyes.

What I witnessed in the Junction is part of a set of changes to the places and communities that have, historically, made cities special, made them interesting, made them sites of protest and progress. These changes have come to be called gentrification, and this is a book about the struggle to keep gentrification from steamrolling over everything many of us hold dear about city life.

Despite having lived in and around Toronto for over twenty years, I had never heard of the Junction before I moved there in 2000. It was an odd place: a dry (no alcohol served) neighbourhood from 1904 to 1998, its location next to Toronto's historic stockyards had attracted immigrants from Malta, Italy, and Poland to work in the meat industry. Active industrial sites and meat processing plants sat next to abandoned factories and vacant lots, just blocks from the decidedly utilitarian offerings along the main commercial strip. Blockbuster Video, a discount grocery store, and the post office were some of the only retail spaces that I, as a graduate student and new mom, was likely to access. The pawn shops and strange overabundance of upholstery repair places were less appealing destinations.

What we did have were higher than average rates of air pollution, parks with discarded needles, and a largely forgotten working-class, low-income, immigrant population. I say largely forgotten because unlike other Toronto neighbourhoods stigmatized for drug use, homelessness, sex work, or crime, the Junction rarely made the news. It was not a place imagined as "other" or frightening. It was not imagined at all by those who lived outside the railroad triangle. When I was looking for affordable apartments, all of the Junction listings called the area "High Park North," evoking the stately neighbourhood and beautiful park to the south. It was a creative piece of nomenclature designed to mask the fact that High Park, it was not.

Still, there were lots of young families, good schools, and decent little green spaces dotted throughout the residential areas. After all, this is still a Canadian city we are talking about, where levels of public investment in urban infrastructure have rarely plummeted so low as to create deeply unlivable places. Although my mouse-infested basement apartment left a lot to be desired, I soon met other moms with kids my daughter's age and found a supportive local community. The first few years offered up occasional signs of change: an interesting new business, a local event. But few seemed to stick. It was a little bit artsy, but far from hip.

That all started to change in the mid-2000s, when a critical mass of new retail and restaurant spaces defied the trend and brought widespread attention to the neighbourhood. Suddenly, the Junction was "up-and-coming." Toronto's newest "hot 'hood." Trendy. Bringing old and new together. A destination. Toronto news media featured Junction events, bars, stores, and restaurants in weekly "what to do" and "where to eat" sections. The hyperbole reached new heights in 2009 when the *New York Times* online travel section ran a story on the Junction under the headline, "Skid Row to Hip in Toronto."[1]

The article encapsulated a Cinderella narrative that, like the fairy tale, relies on a contrast between the before and after. In this and other articles like it, the "old" Junction was described as withered, a grimy skid row, a toxic wreck, too shitty to fix, stuck in the past, declining. These adjectives certainly set a writer up to tell a compelling story of metamorphosis. They also serve another purpose. By portraying the neighbourhood as damaged, abandoned, and dirty, the changes brought by gentrification come to seem necessary, good, and welcome. Describing the neighbourhood as a place in need of saving makes gentrification into a hero.

The *New York Times* travel writer tells readers that the "young and artsy are taking advantage of still-cheap real estate to tiptoe into the Junction's empty storefronts and low-slung houses." These heroes are doing good work, it seems: "Block by block, they are transforming this stretch of Dundas Street West from a grimy skid row into a bright enclave filled with quirky bookstores, vegan restaurants and organic cafés. . . . Instead of porn shops, Dundas Street West is now lined with wholesome and organic food purveyors."[2] The shadow of grime, poverty, and pornography is dispersed by the sunlight of books, vegan cafés, and organic food.

In the midst of the hype about the Junction's redemption, few seemed concerned about the fate of those who might no longer be welcome or who would be priced out of their community. A scroll through the comment sections on local blogs revealed little sympathy for these residents. In fact, commenters seemed sure that once the greasy spoons, grimy donut shops, and vacant lots disappeared, the "freak show," as one person described the presence of people experiencing mental illnesses, homelessness, and disabilities, would be leaving town.³

Was the Junction's shift from a working-class, industrial area to a hip, wholesome neighbourhood simply a natural phase in the cycle of urban development? Is it a matter of basic economics driving an unavoidable upward swing after decades of decline? Was there something culturally desirable about the Junction that young hipsters felt inexorably drawn toward? And as gentrification rolls ever onwards, what, if any, harms have been done? The answers to these and other questions about neighbourhoods like the Junction become the stories we tell about how and why gentrification happens. These stories, each with their share of heroes and villains, conflicts and twists, plot holes and underdeveloped characters, are the subject of this book.

If, like me, the stories you hear about gentrification leave you feeling a mixture of frustration, helplessness, confusion, outrage, anger, and empathy, this book is for you. Not that long ago, the term gentrification was academic jargon rarely heard outside of scholarly debates. Now, more people than ever want to understand what is happening in their neighbourhoods and to make sense of their own relationships to gentrification. But just when you think you have it figured out, gentrification seems to manifest itself in a frightening new way. This book offers a foundation for understanding gentrification's past, but more importantly, provides a framework for understanding how, where, and why gentrification is happening now.

It digs into thorny questions of accountability, responsibility, and power. It also foregrounds issues that are often sidelined in discussions about gentrification, such as race, colonialism, gender, and sexuality. Most crucially, though, this book will remind us that there are lots of examples of successful resistance to gentrification. No matter your position with respect to gentrification, there are ways to act in solidarity with these struggles right now.

Each chapter zooms in on a different way of looking at and understanding gentrification; different stories, if you will, that offer partial perspectives on an unwieldy topic. I explore what these stories reveal and conceal, what they include and exclude, what they focus on and ignore. I take this approach because I believe stories matter. They frame how we perceive the past and the present, shape our capacity for empathy with others, and most critically, mould the range of potential outcomes that we both desire and imagine. I am especially interested in whether the stories we concoct about gentrification offer a vision, even a glimmer of possibility, of a city where gentrification is not believed to be inescapable.

ORIGINS

In the late 1990s I lived and worked in north London, unknowingly adjacent to the borough that had originally inspired the term gentrification. Islington, as I recall it, was full of signature rows of Georgian terrace houses and had a bustling high street with shops, pubs stuffed with Arsenal Football Club supporters, and plenty of cafés and restaurants. Council estates (public housing) and Pentonville Prison were part of the mix in what seemed to me like a typical north London neighbourhood.

Not only had I not heard of gentrification at this point, I had no idea Islington was once an overcrowded, unsanitary, and poverty stricken zone. In the mid-nineteenth century, many poor residents of inner London were displaced by massive public works projects like the construction of the London Underground system. Pushed north, they crowded into small flats inside Islington's once fashionable bourgeois homes. By the mid-twentieth century, it was one of several areas considered deeply blighted by urban poverty. The destruction wrought by enemy bombing in the Second World War meant that large areas of damaged terrace housing could be replaced by council housing estates, offering some improvement in living conditions.

Toward the 1960s, however, the remaining Georgian homes, somewhat run-down but solid enough to have survived the war, were gradually attracting middle-class residents. London-based sociologist Ruth Glass noticed this slow influx of middle-income families moving into "shabby, modest mews and cottages."[4] The families gradually renovated and restored the rotting terraces through sweat equity: their own physical labour. Over time, the homes rose remarkably in value. In 1964, Glass coined the term gentrification to describe this economic and demographic change. The word itself signals what she considered the most important aspect of the process: class change. The "gentry" were steadily remaking the neighbourhood in their own image, to match their own tastes and preferences.

Right from the start, Glass foregrounded displacement as a hallmark, though often debated, feature of gentrification. In her own words: "Once this process of 'gentrification' starts in a district, it goes on rapidly until all or most of the original working class occupants are displaced, and the whole social character of the district is changed."[5] Glass called this process an "invasion" and noted that it had already transformed parts of Notting Hill, which was a crowded, west London working-class community of Caribbean immigrants. The importance of displacement and the idea that the "whole social character" of a neighbourhood could be transformed are still central to what we talk about when we talk about gentrification.

Middle- and upper-class people have probably always taken space and remade it to suit their own needs and desires. What seemed noteworthy in Islington was that this was happening in a dense, urbanized, working-class area, to homes that Glass noted had an inverse relationship between their current social status and their value and size. In other words, their social status was high, while their value was low and their size was small. These middle-class folks were not moving out of the city or looking for bigger and newer dwellings. Instead, they were either staying in or coming back to the city and seeking something other than modern spaces and suburban quiet. Just what they were seeking remains an area of debate. But in contrast to trends like suburbanization, gentrification seemed to be driven by a different set of hopes and fears.

The displacement of working-class, immigrant, and racialized communities from urban neighbourhoods was certainly nothing new in England or many other countries at that point. So-called "blighted" or "slum" areas had been targeted by governments for urban renewal projects designed to clear these communities out and replace them with other land uses like freeways or shopping malls or different communities entirely. Unlike urban renewal, though, the process of gentrification—at least as Glass observed it at the time—was not a top-down, state-funded enterprise; nor did it involve the demolition of previous neighbourhoods.

Instead, middle-class and white residents were trickling into what seemed like less-desirable areas of their own volition and making gradual changes to the physical environment through renovations and landscaping. While urban renewal and gentrification are undoubtedly connected, as we will explore later in the book, gentrification seemed different enough to deserve its own moniker.

Since 1964, however, gentrification as Glass defined it has taken on different forms and trajectories. In some cases, processes that are considered gentrification do not look at all like the scenario seen in Islington several decades ago.

NOT YOUR PARENTS' GENTRIFICATION

After a year or so in north London, I returned to Toronto in late 1999 accompanied by a small person in a stroller. Trying to navigate busy city streets is hard enough, but I found myself stuck in tight bottlenecks as construction sites gobbled up sidewalk space all over downtown. I swerved the stroller through a slalom course of sandwich boards, each announcing the imminent arrival of a shiny condominium tower sure to be the "ultimate in modern living."[6] I was annoyed but admittedly intrigued by this building craze that made my hometown the construction crane capital of the world for a time.

While I did not yet know anything about gentrification, I did not need to be an urban researcher to notice who condominiums were being marketed to. After all, I was veering around their grinning, young, white faces at least once a block. These were the faces of people that apparently had no problem paying hundreds of thousands of dollars to live in one-room cubes in the sky above a freeway. It was a couple more years before I had enough knowledge to make the link myself, but something connected those colourful mews in Islington to the steel and glass behemoths now looming over my city.

Although the kind of house-by-house gentrification described by Glass still occurs, it has been eclipsed by many other types of change that produce total social transformations. These are not limited to the property buying practices of individual households, nor even to the residential realm. They are bigger, faster, and arguably more dangerous. After all, ten condominium buildings with three hundred units each are going to feel more like an asteroid hit the neighbourhood than the slow climate change brought on by a few households slowly renovating old housing stock.

Gentrification is being facilitated by forces much more powerful than your average middle-class homeowner: city governments, developers, investors, speculators, and distant digital platforms that create new ways to profit from urban space. The old-school gentrification of the 1960s seems almost quaint compared to the juggernaut of processes that are bearing down on our neighbourhoods right now.

Today, we are attuned to different symbols of gentrification than those that Glass pointed out in 1964. Locked key boxes, for example, clutter railings outside of apartment buildings, marking the likely presence of short-term rental units. The sound of rolling suitcases rattling over cobblestones is an auditory trace of tourism-based gentrification, one that residents of a historic Amsterdam neighbourhood identify as a rather annoying sign of change.[7] Old factory buildings are no longer indicators of urban decline but rather the hip residences of everyone from artists to stockbrokers. Even public housing projects receiving physical upgrades can warn of gentrification, as these "regenerations" typically include space for market-rate units out of the reach of public housing residents.

All of this suggests that there are a lot of different ways for gentrification to happen these days. It is not enough to pay attention to the choices of individual homebuyers, although questions of middle-class tastes and preferences remain relevant. It seems more urgent now to home in on the increasingly active role that governments and corporations are playing to both facilitate and profit from gentrification. Cities are now quite deliberately sparking middle-, upper-, and even investor-class reinvestment in the city, while promoting policies that smooth the path for particular kinds of real estate and commercial developments.

Some elements of the recipe are so predictable that we see them in cities from San Francisco to Shanghai. From waterfront revitalization projects to pedestrianized shopping districts to new green spaces to arts and culture projects, cities are following remarkably similar blueprints for what they hope will be the right kinds of amenities to attract people with the necessary combination of financial and cultural resources. Although not all such efforts are accurately described as gentrification, they are often part of a suite of interventions and spatial changes that allows cities and neighbourhoods to be marketed in new ways, for a new demographic.

At the same time, local governments have found ways to partner with the private sector to accelerate the pace of change throughout downtown areas and beyond. For example, incentives for developers like tax breaks help to encourage massive new residential development projects, as do opportunities for private developers to "renew" crumbling public housing projects for a share of new market housing in the area. In some cases, it is the state itself that embarks upon urban redevelopment projects that deliberately scatter the poor and destroy informal housing in order to make space for the kinds of properties that will draw in wealthy investors and a new middle class.

Given the expanded set of tactics used by the powerful agents in gentrification, is gentrification even the right term anymore? As early as 1984, researchers such as Damaris Rose worried that it had become a "chaotic concept,"[8] stretched so far beyond its original definition that it had lost meaning. Unfortunately, the alternative words that have bubbled up out of planning and policy discourse are designed to hide displacement and hierarchies of power.

Revitalization, reurbanization, renewal, revival, and regeneration comprise the vocabulary of choice for pro-development city planners, politicians, developers, real estate agents, mortgage lenders, and others who promote large-scale, city- and developer-led initiatives designed to spark reinvestment (another "r" word). These terms avoid the troublesome notion of class change captured by Glass's creative word. If we want to be able to talk about injustice when we talk about gentrification, we might do well to keep it for now.

HOW GENTRIFICATION AFFECTS PEOPLE

Talking about injustice and the ways people are affected by gentrification is a crucial part of appreciating what gentrification is on a human level. Whether people have been physically displaced (pushed out of their neighbourhoods) or not, many feel as though gentrification has had a significant impact on their quality of life and their sense of belonging. For those who have been unwillingly relocated via evictions, rent increases, demolitions, or modern-day "urban renewal," the effects can be devastating and may reverberate through generations. It is easy to recognize the trauma of forced displacement for refugees from war and natural disaster. It seems much harder, however, to acknowledge the harm of the everyday dislocations that occur all across our cities.

Although many researchers and policymakers disagree about the degree of displacement caused by gentrification, people all over report changes in their neighbourhoods that have made them less diverse, less affordable, and less welcoming. The effects are varied. Scholars have drawn connections between gentrification and ongoing racial wealth gaps, the dismantling of public housing, increased policing, and disparities in access to quality schools, green spaces, clean water, and public services. The gradual loss of public space in favour of privatized, patrolled, and surveilled spaces organized around consumption is also linked to gentrification.

When we talk about the effects of gentrification, especially displacement, we are actually talking about a lot of different things. Physical displacement can occur for many reasons, including rent increases, property tax increases, evictions, demolitions, and the closure of public housing. However, physical displacement is not the only troubling effect of gentrification. Describing gentrification as a form of violence, Atlanta organizer Da'Shaun Harrison writes about the pain of feeling displaced in your own neighbourhood:

> People with whom I've built community are struggling more and more to pay their rent that doesn't seem to stop rising; Black kids being met with looks of terror and detest by white folks clutching the handle of their babies' strollers and tightly holding on to their dogs' leashes as they jog around our neighborhoods.[9]

Even if residents do not have to actually move, they can experience a loss of community, belonging, and sense of place as their neighbours, local businesses, and built environment change in ways that leave them feeling—and even treated—like outsiders.

The ways that gentrification affects people vary not only from place to place, but from group to group. It probably goes without saying that some people benefit a great deal from gentrification, though we will not be overly concerned with their feelings in this book. When we talk about those who experience displacement, loss, exclusion, and violence, we must pay attention to differences that terms such as "the working class" or "minorities" can gloss over. The specific consequences of gentrification depend on how people are positioned in relation to systems of power such as gender, race, sexuality, age, and ability. For example, women feel the effects of gentrification in ways that reflect their position as primary caregivers, their higher likelihood of being single parents, their longer lifespans, and the consequences of the gendered wage gap.

BEYOND CLASS CHANGE

Class is not the only lens through which we can comprehend the logic of gentrification. While the fight to keep class-based displacement in the story has been a necessary one, gender, race, colonialism, ability, age, and sexuality have too often been relegated to secondary character roles. Thanks to the hard work of activists, scholars, writers, artists, and critical planners, however, gentrification is increasingly seen as a process that draws on all sorts of power relations to accomplish the tasks of displacement and place transformation.

For example, author and journalist Ta-Nehisi Coates connects gentrification in American cities to the historical and ongoing theft of wealth and resources from Black Americans, from slavery through Jim Crow, redlining (a form of racist housing policy), and gentrification today. As he remarked in an interview in 2019: "Gentrification is a cute word for theft. The solution is pretty easy: Stop stealing. That's one. And return what you stole. That's two."[10] This perspective pushes us to move beyond a class-focused narrative to understand how racial inequality is a driving force in the story of gentrification—a topic we will explore in more depth throughout the book.

The role of gender also deserves greater attention. Feminist urban geographer Winifred Curran argues that gender relations are not incidental to gentrification.[11] Rather, gender actively shapes how, when, and where gentrification happens. Women's changing rates of labour force participation throughout the late twentieth century had a major impact on the kinds of spatial arrangements that women and their families sought out. For many, living in the city offered an improvement over the suburbs, where juggling paid and unpaid work with a lack of transportation was all but impossible. For others, gentrification has exacerbated long-standing gender inequalities in housing, leading to displacement, homelessness, and a heightened risk of violence.

The pressing past and present of colonialism also signals that it is time to rewrite the story, from the ground up. Terms like frontier, pioneer, invasion, settler, jungle, and colonizer have long been staples of gentrification writing. Yet, few urban geographers have paused to consider how gentrification and other modes of urban development are non-metaphorical extensions of colonization as they buttress the historical displacement of Indigenous peoples through colonial city-building and ongoing practices of marginalization and dispossession in urban space today.

American studies scholar and Indigenous resistance activist Nick Estes includes gentrification as one of many urban processes that are explicitly "anti-Indian" in settler colonial cities where "Natives off the reservation represent the unfinished business of colonialism."[12] The property-centred logics of gentrification reinforce settler control of space while gentrification-induced displacement attempts to eliminate Indigenous presence and shore up the idea that Indigenous people have no claims to city spaces.

Understanding intersecting forces such as race, gender, and colonialism is not a distraction. Not only is an intersectional analysis likely to help clarify the outcomes of gentrification, such as displacement, it also offers hope for intervention. As Curran asks, if the point of all this writing about gentrification is to in fact stop it, or to improve the lives of people affected by it, should we not be paying close attention to all forms of inequality? If so, it is imperative to ask: What are we *not* talking about when we talk about gentrification?

AN UNSTOPPABLE FORCE?

In her evocative book *Hollow City*, self-described city lover Rebecca Solnit laments the impacts of gentrification on San Francisco:

> What is happening here eats out the heart of the city from the inside: the infrastructure is for the most part being added to rather than torn down, but the life within it is being drained away, a siphoning off of diversity, cultural life, memory, complexity. What remains will look like the city that was—or like a brighter, shinier, tidier version of it—but what it contained will be gone.[13]

Solnit's concerns will be familiar to anyone who has watched and worried over the changes happening in their cities. With dire warnings and heart-wrenching eulogies, city writers have asked us to confront the emptiness left in gentrification's wake. It is hard to hold on to hope. Good news stories are difficult to find.

For some, gentrification has come to seem unavoidable. I sympathize with the sense of exhaustion and despair that witnessing gentrification entails. However, the story of inevitability plays too neatly into the hands of those who benefit from gentrification. It keeps us isolated and frustrated in our own bubbles, unaware that alternatives exist or that community struggles can bear fruit.

From direct action practices like squatting and occupying vacant spaces to collaborating with the city on community land trusts (CLTs), there are many examples of successful actions to secure housing and weaken the grip of gentrification. Social movements including Black Lives Matter, anti-domestic violence movements, and urban environmental justice movements all incorporate anti-gentrification platforms, understanding that precarious housing, displacement, and violence are all linked. I want to make sure that when we talk about gentrification, we talk about resistance as well as alternative models of neighbourhood investment and development that do not rely on displacement.

AND OTHER LIES

The purpose of this book is to take a closer look at a number of stories (seven, to be exact) about how to understand gentrification. I do not believe that any of these are literally lies. Some, however, are dangerous narratives that strangle the possibility of change or justice. Others are not so much wrong as they are incomplete or hampered by the privileging of certain perspectives over others. My hope is that each story gives you at least one way of thinking about gentrification that you had not considered before. The final chapter shares a set of principles and practices that you can take as starting points for reflection and action.

While I do not presume that my version of events is the best story or even the truest story, I do think this book offers a glimmer of hope that we can change the story of gentrification's inevitability. By the end, I hope you will agree.

2

I love following Instagram accounts dedicated to historical photos of my hometown, Toronto, and I especially enjoy before-and-after images contrasting the old (anything before 1990, these days) and the new. It is fascinating to see how much has changed, and even more interesting, what is simply layered over the remnants of the past.

In being drawn into these images, one could be forgiven for interpreting the changes as part of a natural growth process, one that seems organic and perhaps even predetermined by some kind of urban DNA. The city spreads out, it grows upward, it becomes increasingly dense, it moves more quickly. Like the growth of any organism, it seems to be fulfilling its natural destiny. Indeed, the idea of the city as organism is an attractive one, allowing us to superimpose its beating heart, nerve centres, arteries, and veins over our own.

Unfortunately, the transfer of concepts from the natural

world to built environments can mask the all-too-human foundations of the places we call home. Evoking natural processes feels like a useful way to make sense of a complicated beast like a city, but it is also an effective way to make power relations invisible.

The first story about gentrification in this book, then, is one that has done a lot of damage and requires pushback. Thus, I counter the idea that gentrification is a natural (read: expected, inevitable, normal) process by asking, who wins and who loses when we say, "but isn't it just natural?"

It is not hard to understand why it is so tempting to grasp at evolution, the laws of physics, and anthropomorphism (attributing human characteristics) to help us get a handle on how cities change. Humans are fond of metaphor. For one thing, metaphors let us make connections between different sorts of objects and ideas and allow us to see them in new ways. As a writer, I cannot argue against metaphor. But a metaphor is not the same thing as an explanation, and this is where things start to get slippery when we talk about, for example, cities as evolving organisms.

Evolution is a powerful theory that helps us explain—to make sense of—the dizzyingly complex and dynamic living world. There is comfort in an explanation. It gives a measure of stability, predictability, and certainty. The "laws" of evolution bring a perception of order to a constantly changing environment. It is no wonder we are eager to apply these laws to other elaborate systems, including our cities.

In an informal way, we will often the use the word "evolve" as a synonym for change. However, evolve, in its casual use in English at least, also connotes some kind of positive or desirable change, such as an increase in complexity (of organisms), efficiency (of technology), or knowledge and wisdom (human emotional growth). In other words, it is not a neutral signifier. Perhaps more importantly, though, it is inextricably connected to the theory of how species change and adapt in response to their environments. The theory of evolution has been applied to cities, and to gentrification processes in particular, in ways that go well beyond synonym and metaphor.

Proponents of this way of thinking are not necessarily subtle about it. "Gentrification is a natural evolution" was a 2014 headline in the *Guardian* for a piece in which opinion writer Philip Ball drew on the work of scholar Sergio Porta to argue that "troubled" London neighbourhoods like Brixton and Battersea were undergoing an evolutionary process, taking them from crime- and drug-ridden to bohemian and trendy.[1] Ball describes cities as "natural organisms" and the gentrification of "edgy" London areas as "almost a law of nature." Porta and colleagues, writing in the peer-reviewed and intriguingly named journal *Physics and Society*, claim to have found a formula that predicts gentrification.

Focusing on physical attributes of a neighbourhood, they claim that the likelihood of gentrification can be quantified by calculating the geometry of the street grid and its connectedness to major thoroughfares. The argument is that cities obey certain natural laws and these take primacy over the intentional interventions of planners, politicians, and developers: "Looked at this way, the researchers are studying city evolution much as biologists study natural evolution—almost as if the city itself were a natural organism."[2] Based on these assumptions, Porta concludes that gentrification is actually healthy for cities, suggesting "it's a reflection of their ability to adapt, a facet of their resilience."

Long-time Brixton and Battersea residents might view their resiliency in a different way, as a facet of their ability to survive against a wave of changes that have threatened these Black, multicultural, and working-class boroughs in different ways across decades. Indeed, the language of evolution and healthy adaptation is particularly galling given the racialized context, where people of colour are being displaced by and for white gentrifiers.

Residents and local businesses fear rising rents and displacement as multimillionaire foreign investors buy up spaces like Brixton Market and blanket Battersea in luxury high-rise developments.[3] Brixton market store owner Folashade Akande told the *New York Times*: "All the local people, ethnic minorities, are being driven away [. . .] I'll try to stay as long as I can." In the much-lauded (by conservative politicians) Vauxhall-Nine Elms-Battersea "opportunity" area, luxury flats owned by speculative buyers sit empty while those in the "affordable" buildings and shared ownership units enter their flats through segregated "poor doors" and face "the noise and dust of the construction site for London's new 'super-sewer.'"[4]

The "gentrification is natural adaptation" story assumes that the actual people in these neighbourhoods matter less than the physical environment—or perhaps not at all. It is as if the changes happening are driven by laws of location, street configuration, and building type rather than by decisions made by real people, and that these changes are experienced in an abstract, spatial way rather than by human beings whose daily lives and physical and mental well-being are threatened.

Despite the protestations of those fighting displacement, there is a lure to the natural evolution story, a way in which it appeals to a deep-seated cultural need to reduce what we observe to a set of cause-and-effect relationships guided by immutable laws that we have no control over. It makes things so much simpler! After all, what is the point in trying to challenge the physics of the city? Might as well defy gravity.

What is interesting to me is the work this story does. I find it helpful to keep the effects, intended or otherwise, of "natural law" claims at the front of mind. First, these claims absolve us of responsibility. If something like gentrification is just a law of physics, then it is no one's fault, and no one should feel responsible for trying to do anything to change it. Second, the word "natural" tends to connote good and right. So not only are these changes inevitable, they are beneficial in the long term. In western worldviews, change itself is seen as progress, and progress is good, always moving us toward a better future. Third, these claims release us back into the comforting arms of the status quo. We can be reassured that the way things are happening is the way they should be happening.

THE ECOLOGICAL CITY

Naturalizing the city extends back much further than accounts of gentrification. It is not hard to find writers comparing cities to organisms, as living entities with beating hearts, nerve centres, circulatory networks, waste and digestive systems, and cycles of growth and decay. Influential planning critic Jane Jacobs' ideas about emergent urban change arising from complex, everyday urban processes are often characterized as holding to an organic view of the city in contrast to top-down, master-planned modernist visions.[5]

Long before Jacobs' writing in the 1960s, nineteenth-century thinkers like Patrick Geddes were interested in applying biological concepts like evolution to both society and the city. Geddes believed that town planning would put into practice the insights drawn from understanding how "man" interacted with his environments. He also used metaphors of "surgery" and "weeding" to describe his approach to slum preservation, wherein the worst of the houses would be surgically weeded out to allow more light and air into the remaining tenements and courtyards.[6]

Famous twentieth-century urbanist Lewis Mumford, who was heavily influenced by Geddes' work, used organicist metaphors to make his case that unchecked technological- and economic-driven urban growth was destructive and required a regional conception of planning that understood cities and their surroundings as interconnected organic entities. Mumford likened the ideal city to a cell, which would form a new central nucleus and new cell rather than grow too large or exceed its ability to function as designed.[7]

If you are going to look at the city like a body or part of a body, you are probably going to talk about what can go wrong in that body. Thus, disease and medical metaphors are common. Unchecked growth might be likened to a tumour, while lack of growth could be a sign of decay or latent disease. Disease and similar medical metaphors are regularly used to talk about social problems, and social problems are all-too-readily mapped onto urban geographies.

Communications scholar Júlia Todolí writes about the use of disease metaphors in urban planning to justify certain kinds of urban interventions targeting poor and working-class communities.[8] In a case study of a redevelopment project in Valencia, Spain, in the early 2000s, Todolí found that architects and planners used phrases like operation, major surgery, sanitizing, amputation, metastasis, killing the patient, and performing surgical operations to describe what "needed" to be done to complete the project.

Todolí argues this use of language forms a smokescreen of metaphors to hide the true purposes and effects of city plans. It also helps to frame and define a problem that presupposes a certain kind of solution. After all, if something is diseased or infected, it requires some combination of sanitization, surgery, or even amputation. Planners and architects symbolically take on the authority of surgeons, who have a higher social standing and public trust.

Some of the most influential urban scholars of the first half of the twentieth century, in what came to be known as the Chicago school, borrowed the language of evolution to portray the city as a kind of natural system. Indeed, the Chicago school is also known as the ecological school. Working out of the University of Chicago's sociology department from about 1915 to 1935, researchers such as Ernest Burgess and Robert E. Park, among many others, were keenly attentive to patterns of demographic change along lines of class, and to a lesser extent race, in their largely blue-collar, immigrant-rich city.[9] They rejected hypotheses that suggested people's life chances were determined by personal characteristics or genetics. Instead, they focused on social structures and the environment as the critical factors shaping things like criminality and social mobility.

Burgess's theory of urban growth made use of many concepts drawn from the increasingly accepted theory of evolution popularized by Charles Darwin's *On the Origin of Species* in the late nineteenth century. He suggested that major cities, like Chicago, experienced growth through the outward expansion of concentric circles or zones that included different social classes. The central zone of business was surrounded by "slums" (or "transition") areas, then "workingmen's homes," residential areas, and finally bungalow or commuter areas.

In general, the size, cost, and quality of housing improved as one moved outward through each zone. Burgess suggested that as communities achieved some longevity and upward mobility in the city, they moved outwards, replaced by newer immigrant groups. For example, Italians and Jews who once crowded the area known as the Near West Side eventually made their way to suburban zones such as Cicero, Berwyn, Oak Park, Evanston, and Highland Park.

The processes through which these zones interacted and groups shifted were described with terms like invasion and succession. The metabolism of the city powered these changes as the city evolved and adapted. Because the city was an ecosystem, the principles of ecology dictated that issues in one place or one system—for example a failure of educational institutions—had consequences for other parts of the city or the system. This more holistic approach to understanding the city and its challenges was a departure from mainstream views that preferred to locate urban problems within the moral, racial, or genetic failings of individuals and groups.

This brief explanation is obviously a simplification of the work of dozens of scholars over many decades. My aim is not to suggest that Chicago school members were themselves reductionist or seeking to simplify urban processes into neat biological categories. They clearly recognized that the "natural forces" they discussed were very much human-driven. However, the legacy of a biologically informed urban discourse has outlasted the finer nuances of their contributions. Indeed, a biology-laced understanding of cities has gone well beyond metaphor and worked its way into actual policy and practice. For example, in the 1990s several US cities adopted a program called "Weed and Seed," which aimed to "weed out" crime and "seed" favourable economic development activities.

Geographer Tim Cresswell argues that the program's use of ecological and bodily metaphors worked to denote some groups of people as "out of place" in ways that then serve to justify their displacement.[10] Cresswell writes,

> The "Weed and Seed" program referred also to the government's prescriptive goal of ridding problem areas of undesirable inhabitants (weeds) and planting them with the proper inhabitants (community centers, job schemes, and police stations). This connotation of out-of-place people is attended by a host of other less obvious implications based on the characteristics of weeds. These out-of-place people may be viewed as weak but cunning, as reproducing quickly, as "fugitives" always on the move. All of these reinforce a representation of "aliens" invading the proper order of the American city.[11]

Here, the notions of invasion and succession are mobilized through the everyday metaphor of the weed. Who has not battled a weed? When framed in this way, we know what the solution must be: you pull up the weeds and plant good seeds. This is a long way from the theories of the Chicago school, but within it we can hear the distorted echoes of their work.

Justifying displacement by naturalizing it as part of ecological and/or evolutionary processes contributes to the overall naturalization of gentrification. Although gentrification had once seemed counterintuitive (and perhaps unnatural), because of the well-established, outward-moving model put forth by the Chicago school, terms like succession and invasion were readily applied to gentrification when it was first named and described in the 1960s and beyond. Casting gentrification as an ecological process, with a little evolutionary flavour built in around competition for urban resources, works well to foster the idea that the displacement of certain groups is to be expected and that the normal trajectory of urban development is toward increasing concentrations of wealth.

COLONIZATION AND NATURALIZATION

When I leave my small university town and make my way to bigger cities nearby, like Halifax, Nova Scotia, I do not have to be particularly attuned to Indigenous issues to notice markers of Indigenous presence around me: a vibrant mural on the local Friendship Centre;[12] Indigenous place names on street signs; the flags of local Indigenous Nations flapping in the breeze; an empty plinth where a statue of a violent colonial ruler once stood. But in many cities around the world, any acknowledgement or celebration of an ongoing Indigenous presence was once (and in many cases, continues to be) much harder to find.

Urbanization in settler colonial societies did an exceptional job of not only dispossessing and displacing Indigenous peoples, but of wiping Indigenous history off the urban map.[13] This erasure is widely reflected in the lack of attention to Indigenous peoples, issues, and settler colonialism in urban geography. Too often, colonization metaphors are used without reflecting on the actual, continuous practice of colonization happening in those very same places.[14]

As biological and ecological researcher Silvano Onofri explains,

> Widely used in ecological sciences, biological colonization describes the: occupation of a habitat or territory by a biological community or of an ecological niche by a single population of a species [. . .] Biological colonization is a dynamic process that begins when unoccupied habitats, territories, or niches become available, or when organisms acquire the ability to survive and reproduce under environmental conditions of new niches, by a process of adaptation.[15]

It would be naive to think, however, that when used as a metaphor it can be detached from the historical and ongoing human processes that bear its name. This intertwining of the natural and the political puts us in very dicey territory indeed.

Arguably, European colonialism itself and its long-lasting effects have benefited from the naturalization of human processes of colonization. If ecological invasion, establishment, replacement, and dominance are natural, then why not view human versions the same way? Is it not just natural that stronger species will invade and conquer weaker ones? This logic has been part and parcel of both historic and recent justifications for colonialism and imperialism.

It should go without saying that applying logics that govern plant species to human societies is more than a little problematic. If we lean into the metaphor, we end up casting some societies as inherently superior and others as inherently inferior. It establishes a natural "right" for those cast as superior to invade, conquer, and occupy other peoples' territories, and to eliminate or drastically reduce the population of the conquered group. In other words, it grounds colonization in some kind of natural, biologically based system.

The naturalization of colonization was also aided by depictions of Indigenous people as "savages." Portrayed as primitive and animalistic, Indigenous people were not viewed as fully developed humans by Europeans who marked their own civilizational development as superior. The concept of *terra nullius*, or empty earth, was also significant. By refusing to recognize Indigenous ways of using and occupying land, colonizers saw the land as uncultivated, still in a "natural" state. Without markers of European-style domestication, the land was deemed empty and available for capture.

Gentrification writers have regularly utilized the discourse of colonization. Jim Stratton's 1977 book *Pioneering in the Urban Wilderness* is a notable example.[16] Writing about the trend toward reclaiming factory spaces for loft living, Stratton describes "urban pioneers" moving into "the dilapidated and under-used spaces of America's urban disaster areas." Terms like settler, settled, urban jungle, frontier, occupation, tamed, and wild are staples of gentrification writing.

Critics of this language, like geographer Neil Smith, note that it positions the working class in much the same way as Indigenous people were positioned in art and literature: as a natural element of their physical surroundings, rather than as part of the social world.[17] Ironically, however, this particular critique appears in his book called *The New Urban Frontier*. Smith misses the opportunity to acknowledge that this representation of Indigenous peoples is not merely historical, and to acknowledge that gentrification is a continuation of colonization in many cities today.

In response to activist declarations that "gentrification is the new colonialism," Indigenous people have responded that there is no "new colonialism" because the "old colonialism" is not over. The Last Real Indians Media Movement reminds anti-gentrification activists who use such slogans that colonialism is still alive and well, and that "saying gentrification is the new colonialism in any way is an act of anti-native violence."[18] Recalling an encounter with anti-gentrification activists in Seattle, writer Wakínyaŋ Waánataŋ told them that the city they were in was part of the

> lands, waterways and resources in which [the Duwamish] had occupied for tens of thousands of years and had been systematically, and forcibly, been removed and keep from. That is colonialism and that system of settler colonialism continues to exist and plague our collective Tribal communities and homelands to this day.

It is incumbent upon all those critical of gentrification to reflect on how our own ways of talking about gentrification reproduce colonial ways of thinking and being on the land even as we are attempting to disrupt other forms of naturalization.

SURVIVAL OF THE FITTEST

It is not surprising that naturalization is so prevalent in urban writing and research. After all, western society has a tendency to naturalize all capitalist economic processes. Charles Darwin might be dismayed to find his careful observations about the unique adaptations of isolated species in particular environments reduced to simplistic justifications for craven profiteering. For example, the capitalist idea that competition drives innovation is seemingly justified by similar principles of evolution. "The survival of the fittest" is a very convenient concept for naturalizing the great disparities in wealth and well-being produced under capitalism, and for normalizing individualism, selfishness, and a desire for profit-making and resource hoarding.

However, these assertions are based on highly selective and reductionist readings of evolutionary theory. They conveniently ignore and underplay the role of cooperation in the adaptation and survival of species. They also misread "survival of the fittest" as survival of the strongest and most powerful individuals, rather than the survival of those populations best adapted to their environments.

In *The End of Capitalism (As We Knew It)* feminist geographer J. K. Gibson-Graham argues that a good deal of capitalism's power derives from it having convinced us that there is no alternative, no "outside" that we can point to.[19] Gibson-Graham claims that an essentialist view of the economy as a singular system that subsumes and controls all aspects of social, cultural, and economic life is a trap. It leaves no room to generate anti-capitalist or non-capitalist practices, spaces, or imaginings. Naturalization feeds into this essentialist, and, as Gibson-Graham puts it, capitalocentric, perspective. Decentring and denaturalizing capitalism itself is crucial to challenging gentrification, because under capitalism, gentrification will always be read as success.

The problem is not that we use metaphors to help us make sense of how the world works. A good metaphor reveals or clarifies something about a complex phenomenon and allows people to make interesting connections. But a metaphor also has the power to shape the way we perceive something, and thus, what we might do about it. The risk with biology-based metaphors is that in encouraging us to see a process as natural, they limit how we understand it and whether or not we think we can act to change it.

It is also important to note that biology itself is not a neutral, objective framework for knowing the world. It and its practitioners are influenced by social and economic forces that shape the questions they ask, the theories they formulate, and the language they use.

Our task is not necessarily to find the better metaphor, but to resist the limitations a metaphor can impose. Naturalization sets up a sense of inevitability, normalcy, and value neutrality. For those of us concerned about gentrification, this leaves little room to challenge either what drives it or to propose a way to stop it. Naturalizing gentrification aligns all too comfortably with the status quo. It plays very well into the hands of powerful developers and growth boosters who see their desired kind of change as the right "evolution" for cities.

So, we need to look to other stories, other explanations. Ones that do not strip human agency out of the discussion. Ones that do not ignore power, context, or politics. Ones that—whatever other limitations they possess—do not foreclose the possibility of alternatives.

3

GENTRIFICATION IS ABOUT TASTE

There are few things simpler than a bowl of cereal. Faster to prepare than even a piece of buttered toast, cereal gets millions of people, children especially, fed and out the door as quickly as possible each morning. But what if cereal could be so much more? This was the question apparently asked and answered by Alan and Gary Keery, two Belfast brothers who opened the Cereal Killer Café in London's Shoreditch neighbourhood in 2014.

Until the coronavirus pandemic came along, you could walk into one of the poorest boroughs in London and buy one of the city's most expensive bowls of cereal at their Brick Lane counter.[1] Not surprisingly, their £3.20 bowl of corn flakes served just steps away from one of the country's lowest-income public housing projects made the café into an international symbol of gentrification.

The cereal café and other businesses like it, ones that fetishize and upscale simple, nostalgic foods or experiences, point toward another kind of story about gentrification. This one focuses on the tastes of a white, urban middle class as markers—or harbingers—of neighbourhood transformation. As potent symbols, these businesses often become targets of anti-gentrification activism.

In September 2015, Cereal Killer was vandalized with paint and the word "scum" during a protest against the gentrification of London's working-class neighbourhoods.[2] In Chicago's mostly Latinx Pilsen neighbourhood, gourmet café Bow Truss was repeatedly vandalized in 2015, with the message "White People Out of Pilsen" on a sticker of the Chicago city flag.[3] The strong reaction to these and other sites that cater to the preferences of "outsiders" suggests that one of the primary drivers of gentrification is the cultural desires of potential gentrifiers.

The case of Cereal Killer and its ilk reinvigorates questions that have been plaguing observers of gentrification for decades. In the 1970s, as reports of a "back to the city movement" among young people emerged in the media, many drew contrasts between these hip urbanites and their suburban counterparts. Speculation abounded. Was this trend being driven by disaffected suburban housewives? A taste for historic preservation? A rejection of the lawnmower? It bears noting that the people being wondered about were white, middle-class families, who were suddenly doing something that seemed counter to the "natural laws" of outward residential movement of the middle and upper classes.

The intervening decades have not so much provided an answer as entrenched a story about gentrification that centres its less tangible elements: a protest against the normative suburban dream; a set of tastes, styles, and aesthetics; and a desire for a particular kind of urban lifestyle.

Indeed, we are still dancing with a lot of the same questions. How much does individual taste and preference really shape urban dynamics? Are places like Cereal Killer attracting gentrification or are they a sign that it is already well underway? How much power do groups that embrace and exemplify new cultural trends—groups like artists, students, young people, and even small business owners—really have in the city today? What responsibilities do people who want an organic avocado on toast for breakfast have to their neighbours, their community, and their city? And does it make sense to position these trends as markers of class distinction that can somehow be disentangled from whiteness, male dominance, colonialism, and heteronormativity?

Peeling back the layers of this gentrification story reveals lingering questions about power and identity. The role of taste is an important one, but I do not think any of us believe that banning fancy coffee, vegan donuts, Mac laptops, or dark-rimmed glasses is the answer to what ails the city. Still, cultural power has material effects that contribute to the remaking of neighbourhoods in substantial ways. There are, however, parts of this story that are taken for granted and other parts that are overlooked. Let us begin, then, with one of the most influential prophets of the cultural lure of cities, Jane Jacobs.

DESIRING DIFFERENT

Shortly after my birth in 1975, my parents moved my family out of an apartment in downtown Toronto into a small townhouse in what was then a far-flung suburb with more cows than people. We were not destined to be one of the young, upwardly mobile families who would soon be gentrifying Toronto neighbourhoods like Cabbagetown and the Annex.

Jane Jacobs was, by then, a resident of the Annex and had already made her mark locally through her participation in the campaign to stop the construction of the Spadina Expressway. This project would have permanently ruptured the fabric of many of the city's most cherished neighbourhoods—Chinatown, Kensington Market, the Garment District—and greatly increased car traffic through the city. Just as she had in Manhattan, Jacobs fought for the preservation of old urban neighbourhoods against the mega-projects of planners and politicians concerned with connecting the booming suburbs to downtown business districts.

Her advocacy for a form of city life that she saw as threatened by modernist planning was fully laid out in her 1961 book,

The Death and Life of Great American Cities. Although Ruth Glass had not even coined the term gentrification yet, *Death and Life* explained exactly what it was that people like those Islington mews-buyers, and people like Jacobs herself, two thousand miles away in Greenwich Village, valued about urban life. As she railed against the urban renewal visions of the likes of New York City's planning czar Robert Moses, Jacobs also offered a fine-grained account of the everyday embodied and emotional life of the city, a life that was in danger of being stamped out by modernist design, car culture, and suburbanization.

The qualities that Jacobs lauded, such as mixed-use streetscapes, historical character, diversity, and neighbourhood connections, were the opposite of the prevailing planning and urban development ethos of the day. These were also the very qualities named by the "back to the city" upstarts who appeared to be swimming against the class- and race-propelled currents of white flight to the suburbs.

Jacobs captured something about the spirit of city life that resonated with many people. Decades of suburbanization had not produced domestic bliss, especially not for women, as Betty Friedan clearly argued in *The Feminine Mystique* in 1963.[4] Massive urban renewal projects that bulldozed vibrant-if-poor urban neighbourhoods in the name of "slum" clearance were not solving poverty, they were further entrenching race and class segregation. Block by block, the culture of cities was being ripped apart and paved over, and Jacobs was a strident voice crying out that something special was being lost.

However, some people were defying the social, economic, and political pressure to suburbanize by buying up working-class urban houses, moving into empty lofts in areas like New York's SoHo (adjacent to Jacobs' beloved Greenwich Village), and, as Glass described, gradually transforming the social character of all sorts of neighbourhoods. What they were searching for, according to scholars of this phenomenon like Jon Caulfield, David Ley, and Sharon Zukin, was a kind of authenticity that could not be found in cookie-cutter suburbs.

Urban sociologist Jon Caulfield's research on gentrification in Toronto through the 1970s and 1980s describes it as a kind of "critical social practice" in which gentrifiers expressed counter-hegemonic desires for social diversity, relief from the existential numbness of modernism, and a sense of community but without the need for conformity.[5] David Ley, also writing about Canadian cities, labelled gentrifiers as a "new middle class" who constituted their class identity through conspicuous consumption of a set of amenity packages, like trendy restaurants and art galleries.[6] These desires were believed to generate a demand for gentrification based on shifting tastes.

Sociologist Sharon Zukin's examination of the emergence of loft living in New York's SoHo neighbourhood revealed that the availability of lofts was a product of market circumstances such as deindustrialization and chronic undervaluation. However, the "acceptability of lofts as an alternative to more traditional products of the urban housing markets depends on the emergence of a new set of social and cultural values."[7] These new values, though, do not arise out of nowhere and they do not touch down in just any neighbourhood. In fact, the arrival of an authenticity-seeking middle class was usually preceded by groups like artists, musicians, students, and sometimes immigrants whose efforts to build community and a rich cultural life gave urban neighbourhoods a new kind of visibility.

REMAKING PLACE

By the time I went to the University of Toronto in the mid-1990s, the Yorkville neighbourhood, which borders the northeast edge of campus, was the kind of place I only went if my wealthier house-mates were in the mood to pay for drinks. Fashionable restaurants shared space with designer boutiques in narrow converted town-houses, their very tininess screaming exclusivity. If I had arrived just a generation earlier, however, I would not have found what is now known as "Mink Mile." I would have been at the centre of Toronto's music and hippie scene, perhaps bumping into Joni Mitchell or William Gibson on the sidewalk. In fact, the area with some of the world's most expensive real estate per square foot today was then considered by some to be a "festering sore" in the heart of the city.[8]

One might experience a similar culture shock by travelling back in time to New York's SoHo. Today, you'd be surrounded by high-end shopping, fine dining, tourists, and sought-after loft-style residences with stern doormen standing sentry. In the 1960s and 1970s, however, those lofts, left vacant by a shrinking garment industry seeking cheap labour offshore, were filled with artists and musicians. Coveted worldwide today, these spaces were viewed as alternative, marginal places to live. The lack of amenities and services nearby was willingly accepted for floor-to-ceiling windows and most importantly, cheap rent. As artists, musicians, poets, and other bohemians embraced loft living, lofts became less associated with sweatshop labour and more associated with culture and creativity.

The change in values that the presence of artists creates cannot be underestimated as a force in gentrification. Although lacking the financial power to transform space through capital investment, artists and other creative people are a bridge that takes a neighbourhood from industrial, rough, and dangerous to vibrant, interesting, and edgy. Artists are often deemed to be part of a "first wave" of gentrification in a model that sees successive waves bringing more and more financial and cultural power to bear on a neighbourhood. In the first wave, there is little financial might, but there is just enough cultural and tastemaking influence to attract a next wave of attention.

Feminist geographer Damaris Rose coined the term "marginal gentrifiers" to describe the contradictory positioning of first wavers such as artists. In her research in Toronto and Montreal, she found that low-income women like single mothers played a role similar to that of artists in terms of "priming" a neighbourhood for gentrification.[9] Rose argued that for women, a return to the city offered a spatial fix for the demands of juggling paid work, domestic work, child care, and leisure. Seeking affordable areas that could support their paid and unpaid work, but lacking the financial capital to spark a large-scale transformation, these women brought just enough cultural capital to be part of the so-called first wave.

Artists, musicians, students, and single moms do not tend to be multi-million-dollar investors. They are probably not even homeowners. The early gentrifiers who sniffed at the heels of artists to find interesting and cheap neighbourhoods were not part of an investor class, either. Although dubbed the "new middle class" by writers like Ley, this group was defined less by income and more by an adherence to a new set of tastes. Or, perhaps more accurately, a set of tastes that were new for an educated group of white professionals. The question is: How much does taste and preference matter? What does it have to do with class?

CULTURE AND CLASS

When we use the term class in everyday conversation, we are usually referring to income level or wealth, albeit somewhat vaguely, as the vast array of modern occupational categories and lack of firm boundaries between what constitutes "working class" or "middle class" or even "rich" these days means that we are likely to describe both our own and others' class positions in ways that are both unclear and often contradictory.[10] Still, we maintain a sense that it has something to do with money.

At the same time, however, our judgments about class—our own and others—are inflected by less tangible qualities. For example, the status that accrues from the kind of car you drive is not only related to its cost, but to its status or "coolness" at a given moment and within your cultural group. Just as Ruth Glass noted, for early London gentrifiers the size and price of urban homes was not in direct relationship with their desirability and trendiness. Class can be marked not only by price, but by other features that create distinctions between groups of people. These distinctions translate into what sociologist Pierre Bourdieu famously called "cultural capital."[11]

Bourdieu developed this concept to help explain different kinds of assets an individual or group can draw upon. Cultural capital refers to the

> collection of symbolic elements such as skills, tastes, posture, clothing, mannerisms, material belongings, credentials, etc. that one acquires through being part of a particular social class. Sharing similar forms of cultural capital with others—the same taste in movies, for example, or a degree from an Ivy League School—creates a sense of collective identity and group position ("people like us").[12]

Although they might be "symbolic," these assets are very real in that "certain forms of cultural capital are valued over others, and can help or hinder one's social mobility just as much as income or wealth."[13] What this means is that even without a huge amount of wealth or a terribly high income, people who hold the right kind of cultural capital at the right place and time can enact class power. Of course, the possession of cultural capital is related to financial capital in that you are likely to develop these assets by growing up in a middle- or upper-class household or going to school with others from these class groups. Cultural assets are a currency that can be traded or mobilized in exchange for more tangible forms of capital or power, such as a bank loan, a job, or the benefit of the doubt in an interaction with the police.

When it comes to gentrification, this cultural power gets wielded through practices that begin to alter the appearance, function, value, and meaning of urban places. The conversion of factory spaces into lofts, for example, shifted their identity from dangerous and exploitative sweatshops to alternative live-work spaces for artists and countercultural bohemians to modern open-concept homes for an urban elite. Parks that served as gathering spaces for unhoused people can morph into children's play areas as middle-class families arrive and begin to take over these spaces to serve their own needs.

The power to define the meaning of a place is also the power to create symbolic boundaries of inclusion and exclusion. Who feels welcome? Who belongs? And whose presence becomes out of line with the redefined sense of place?

These symbolic boundaries easily morph into more substantial gates and barriers. As neighbourhoods get redefined through symbols, media discourse, and the embodied presence of a new group of inhabitants, they muster some gravitational force. They begin to attract a world of culture, consumption, leisure, work, and politics that mirrors and builds upon the changing brand. Eventually, the places that served the needs of long-time residents or simply felt like home are replaced by different, often more expensive, businesses that speak to a different set of needs and desires. Enter the yoga studio or organic grocery store. Exit the residents who can no longer afford rent, groceries, or a social life in the neighbourhood.

This cultural capital or cultural power helps explain the seemingly counterintuitive moves of early gentrifiers. On the surface, it seemed like they were making choices that ran against their class interests by eschewing mainstream (and white) middle-class markers of taste and distinction in favour of a lifestyle that was rather more rough around the edges and perhaps less certain to translate into wealth and power. However, in finding ways to both define class through taste and redefine spaces through symbolic acts, these gentrifiers were still "doing class" in ways that would, in short order, result in more wealth and material advantage for many.

Of course, not all taste- and placemakers get to stick around to reap the fruits of their cultural labours. In a situation we might call the "paradox of priming for your own displacement," groups like artists, bohemians, single moms, queer folks, and students do the initial work of sparking cultural changes in a neighbourhood. For example, artists move into factory spaces and suddenly the potential to rezone and recapitalize on unused industrial spaces exists.[14] Single moms open a co-op child care centre and organize children's activities in the park every Sunday, generating a family-friendly vibe. Students attract used bookstores and thrift shops and domesticate greasy cafés by studying there all day.

These subtle changes make it possible for professional households to see themselves in the neighbourhood. Over time, the artists and others—groups that typically have little more than cultural capital—are priced out by successive waves of gentrifiers with relatively more capital of all kinds.

The wave narrative is helpful for understanding phases of placemaking and displacement, although it problematically erases what, and who, came before the marginal gentrifiers. It implies that nothing of value or interest was happening in the neighbourhood before students, artists, and others came along. While it may be the case that the process of gentrification does not seem to start in some places until after the cultural changes initiated by artists, it is not as though those artists were working on a blank canvas.

Working-class, racialized, and immigrant communities whose neighbourhoods are being transformed have of course been engaged in community building and social development. This work has often occurred under difficult circumstances. These neighbourhoods have typically experienced a lack of investment in their physical and social infrastructure, including roads, schools, transit, and green spaces. Many are located near polluting industries. Many experience the violence of over-policing. And yet, families are raised, businesses are run, and communities are sustained. Rarely, however, is this work acknowledged or valued.

———

As important as cultural power is, there is a risk to focusing too much on this story about gentrification. If we follow the trends and not the money, we might unwittingly miss the big picture and the financial power behind the changes.

It is easy to fixate on the tastes and aesthetics that have become associated with gentrification. Whether it is a cereal café, a neatly waxed handlebar moustache, or a baby in a onesie with a Judith Butler quote, we can probably all think of looks, sounds, or foods that scream "gentrification." So, if the problem of gentrification is embodied by hipsters, creative-industry workers, freelancers, and anyone else found working on a Mac in a café in the afternoon, then the solution must surely be to keep them out, right?

While these people certainly possess a great deal of cultural capital, even the lucky trust fund-endowed among them are not likely to be billionaire property developers with seats on the boards of powerful municipal planning organizations. Precariously employed twenty- and thirty-somethings like freelance writers and yoga teachers are themselves easily priced out of changing neighbourhoods or one late paycheque away from moving into their parents' basements. Their indie cafés are not financed by the might of transnational corporations and they are not buying up entire city blocks to raze for new luxury housing.

What I am saying is that it is not helpful in a critique of gentrification to get overly stuck on the styles and preferences of a group, when, for many decades now, gentrification has been propelled by much stronger forces than aesthetic trends. Certainly, these gentrifiers may be playing the part of unwitting (or mostly unwitting) foot soldiers of neoliberal real estate capital, doing the on-the-ground, day-to-day work of priming minority and working-class neighbourhoods for large-scale revitalization projects or new housing developments.

However, in the context of massive, state-sponsored, corporate redevelopment schemes, the power of these gentrifiers is questionable. Furthermore, what we have been calling cultural power is now strategically wielded by those who actually have enormous capacity to remake cities and neighbourhoods, like developers and city policymakers. In many places, this has occurred through the implementation of a set of ideas that have come to be known as "the creative city."

THE CREATIVE CITY MACHINE

In 2007 I lived in a bit of a nowhere-area at the boundaries of Toronto's Junction and Bloordale neighbourhoods. I owned a small townhouse in a development, shoehorned between live-work spaces in former factories and warehouses, a thrift store, and a railway line. Occasionally a sweet, chocolatey smell drifted our way from the Nestlé candy factory to the south. Part of the block remained an open construction site for many years while another apartment building went up. In general, it was not the kind of area you expect to find touched by a glitzy urban spectacle like Nuit Blanche, a city- and corporate-sponsored all-night installation art festival.

Nevertheless, one January night my daughter and I wandered up to the corner just past the thrift store to see a filmmaker friend from university, Will Strug, build an ice house within which he projected video onto the glistening walls. Across the street, the House of Lancaster "gentleman's club" was open for a family-friendly capoeira performance. Strollers clogged the entranceway. The servers delivered Sprite to children and tried not to look annoyed at their drastically reduced tip potential for the evening.

Feminist geographer Heather McLean stopped by the same site a few hours later than me, finding "a room of predominately white revellers clapping excitedly to a drum circle on the stage while paper mâché lanterns lit up the ceiling and tables. Especially striking was that the strippers who worked in the club were nowhere to be seen."[15] McLean situates the event as a Nuit Blanche satellite courted by the Bloordale Village Business Improvement Area to "light up" this section of Bloor Street and kick-start its "revitalization." It was official: the creative city machine had arrived in my neighbourhood.

The creative city concept is an enormously influential urban policy agenda that grew out of ideas initially developed by urban scholar Charles Landry in the late 1980s. Landry, with Franco Bianchini, developed a "creative city toolkit," urging cities to focus on twenty-first-century industries that would depend on knowledge, creativity, and innovation. The "old paradigm" centred on manufacturing, the physical environment, and a technical-rational approach to planning had reached its limit, in their view. In order to compete successfully with other cities, places would need to strategically market themselves as hubs for research, culture, and technological advancement.[16]

Economist Richard Florida launched the creative city concept into the mainstream with his 2002 book, *The Rise of the Creative Class*, and its 2008 follow-up, *Who's Your City?*[17] Florida argued that urban economic development tactics, which historically were devoted to attracting major industries and corporations to the city in order to provide employment and a tax base, were deeply out of touch. Maybe this plan worked if you assumed that just about anybody could do the kinds of jobs on offer, such as manual labour or generic office jobs, and that people would happily go wherever the jobs were. In today's knowledge economy, however, a highly specialized workforce is required, and its constituents are unlikely to settle for Pittsburgh or Milwaukee.

So, Florida flipped the script and offered a new formula: attract these workers first, and their industries—desperate for their specialized skills—will follow. In order to lure this so-called "creative class," the city needed to remake its cultural life, its parks, its leisure spaces, and its physical realm in ways that appealed to the aesthetic and lifestyle sensibilities of educated, cosmopolitan "creatives."

According to Florida, this group valued experiences over possessions, community over suburban isolation, authenticity over corporate branding, and diversity over homogeneity. If this is starting to sound a little familiar, as though the creative class identity maps quite well onto the gentrifier desires noted decades ago, you are onto something. The idea of the creative class and the urban interventions being suggested to service it were quickly questioned by scholars and others who saw it as a green light for a gentrification agenda.[18]

Still, the concept took off. Cities all over the world, large and small, embraced a set of cultural and place-based initiatives—including festival events like Nuit Blanche—to brand themselves in ways that would appeal to this seemingly new "class." Florida himself became a highly sought after speaker and consultant, widely seen as the man who had the secret formula to transform cities into twenty-first-century powerhouses.

There is not anything inherently bad about cities investing in public art, cultural events, placemaking, green spaces, or festivals. Indeed, this felt like a welcome change from the usual economic development tactics of giving tax breaks to polluting industries, building football stadiums, and constructing convention centres. Unfortunately, these creative class amenities, alongside the attention and financial investment directed at a fairly well-off group of city dwellers, helped to drive up the cost of living across cities.

Additionally, government support for new housing developments to house the influx of creative professionals bolstered gentrification by rapidly changing the social and demographic characteristics of neighbourhoods. Cultural revitalization put a colourful, seemingly politics-free face on cities' attempts to attract new residents, tourists, businesses, and investors. For critics, this dressed-up version of urban neoliberalism was only going to make life harder for those struggling to make ends meet.

The creative class idea, despite its assertion that diversity was desirable, was notably white and male-centred in its definitions of creativity and its valorization of certain modes of work. Feminist geographer Brenda Parker notes the cities that scored highest on creativity indexes, like San Francisco and Minneapolis, were some of America's most racially segregated in terms of geography, income, and occupation. The occupations listed as part of a "supercreative core," including scientists, engineers, professors, architects, and lawyers, represented white- and/or male-dominated fields.[19]

Moreover, the money that was suddenly released into the arts sector to support creativity was flowing toward white artists and communities. McLean argues that queer- and racialized-women artists, as well as non-binary and trans artists, remained on the margins of the creative city project in Toronto, struggling to survive while multi-million-dollar festivals like Nuit Blanche and Luminato invaded their neighbourhoods.[20] Parker also contends that the emphasis on certain creative jobs reflects an ongoing gendered division of labour in the home and within professions. She notes that Florida's ideal creative worker is a "workhorse," not afraid of long and irregular hours, able to move at the drop of a hat, and unencumbered by domestic responsibilities. For those who still do a disproportionate share of care work inside the home, namely women, burning the creative candle late into the night to deliver the latest video game update is much less feasible. Indeed, many of the lauded creative professions have been shown to be hostile work environments for women.[21] Furthermore, the idealized vision of the creative class did not extend to service workers—who are mostly women—or to the unpaid labour of raising children and taking care of the home.

Some twenty years after the creative city concept took urban policy making by storm, it is clear that cities' efforts to attract a new-new middle class—the creative class—and the industries they work in has been successful, but at a cost. Even Florida himself has reflected on the faults in his own urban prescriptions, acknowledging that cities have not become more equal and integrated despite the surface-level valuing of diversity and cultural difference.[22]

For example, "supercreative" San Francisco is an even more deeply divided city, with untold numbers of unhoused people eking out a life on the streets while tech millionaires catch helicopter rides to Palo Alto. Teachers, nurses, firefighters, and even your average six-figure-earning tech worker cannot afford to live there.[23]

Housing prices have skyrocketed in other major cities and in smaller regional centres as well. We are witnessing yet another counterintuitive trend: the suburbanization of poverty, as families are displaced from central cities into far-flung commuter communities where ironically, housing is cheaper, but little else is.[24] Artists remain among the lowest-income occupations, and the freelance and contract-based nature of much "creative" work has led to great precarity and economic instability for many in the very "class" that has been meant to benefit.

The creative class idea is not the only force to blame for gentrification. However, it illustrates how culture, as a factor in gentrification, operates at a level of power and influence far beyond the individual. Of course, individuals may come to embody these corporate- and state-generated visions of creativity, and developers and cities take careful note of cultural trends on the ground to help them market their projects in ways that will resonate with tastemakers.

Cultural factors cannot be hastily dismissed, not when their power is easily co-opted by capital. Trends in denim and facial hair are not responsible for gentrification. But when large groups of people are redefined as a class based on their tastes, occupations, and aesthetics, they become a market and a justification for urban interventions.

CULTURES OF WHITENESS

Cultural power, like all forms of power, intersects with other systems. We cannot disentangle the thread of culture from sexism, racism, colonialism, and heteronormativity. These systems shape, in overt and covert ways, the things that we value and like as well as what we consider creative, artistic, cultured, and cool. In her 2012 documentary *My Brooklyn*, filmmaker Kelly Anderson captures the work of whiteness in assessing culture and creativity as she explores New York's plan to tear down a vibrant and economically strong Black shopping district, Fulton Mall, and replace it with luxury high-rise housing and corporate chain stores.[25]

Anderson takes her camera to the weekend farmers' market in a nearby Brooklyn neighbourhood and asks patrons how they feel about the proposal to redevelop Fulton. Without any prompting, the nice, liberal white folks buying organic produce are quick to disparage Fulton Mall as "fine if you want a cell phone case," noting that "you can't polish a turd." It is clear that none of them will miss Fulton if it disappears.

The Black shoppers Anderson approaches do not necessarily spend a lot of time at Fulton, but they never speak ill of it. Despite Fulton Mall's important place in American social and cultural history, for hip hop, fashion, and literature, it is not viewed as a place of cultural value under a white gaze. Indeed, as then-Mayor Bloomberg's redevelopment agenda proceeded through policies like up-zoning and development tax breaks, Black- and other minority-owned businesses were shuttered, and today retail space on Fulton Street is among the most expensive in the city.

The kinds of businesses that emerge during gentrification, often displacing previous businesses, can also communicate racial exclusivity. They do not need to hang "whites only" signs, as in the Jim Crow days. Today, a message of exclusion can be communicated through softer cultural tactics, ones that white business owners might even be unaware of.

In their research on retail gentrification in a Black neighbourhood in Portland, Oregon, Daniel Sullivan and Samuel Shaw observed that long-time Black residents felt alienated in new white-owned businesses due to a number of factors, including price, but also less tangible elements like the kinds of products offered, the decor, and the attitudes of workers and other shoppers. While many had difficulty putting their finger on exactly what the problem was, they knew that "the new places are for Yuppies, who are 'people who want to go sit down and drink coffee and eat donuts and eat whatever it is that they eat.'"[26] Sullivan and Shaw identify "creative class" and "bohemian" businesses as particularly unappealing to Black people.

Other research on gentrification has similarly found that it is often different cultural norms around which conflict coalesces. Whether it is about the way spaces like street corners and parks are used,[27] the kinds of food offered in new stores and restaurants,[28] or the sounds and smells coming from homes and businesses, gentrifiers and longer-term residents often have different ideas about what expressions of culture are acceptable. Mexican food? Great.

A weekly parade of low-riders down the central commercial strip? Not so much. Slick global hip hop music? Sure. Black kids playing plastic drums on the street corner? No, thank you.[29]

Whiteness also works through appropriating minority culture, food, music, fashion, and activism while actively displacing actual people of colour. In Pilsen, Chicago, Latinx people are declining as a percentage of the population while whites are increasing, but symbols of Latinx culture continue to decorate the neighbourhood.[30] When I was a researcher there, I stayed in a new apartment complex named for the Aztec goddess Chantico. The building was a deep red colour and adorned with Aztec symbols. The local maintenance hole covers were embossed with Aztec designs. Murals depicting Mexican history and cultural figures enlivened the sides of buildings up and down 18th Street. But actual Mexican and other Latinx people are fighting to stay in their homes as gentrification roars through the community.

In Harlem, a statue of Harriet Tubman rises into the sky over expensive brunch spots, and murals referencing the struggles of Black people look out over shops like American Apparel. A tweet from Kelly Wickham Hurst sums it up: "How do I know that gentrification is happening? They keep replacing Black folks with 'Black Lives Matter' signs in their yard" (@mochamomma, June 29, 2019).

A nasty little feature of whiteness as cultural power is that it operates under a cloak of invisibility and deniability. Because it is both the water we swim in and a largely empty void into which whites can selectively pour whatever cultural norms and tastes they desire, it is hard to see whiteness in action. Rather, it is not hard for non-white people to see, but it is easy for white people to deny that their tastes, norms, and actions have anything to do with whiteness.

A noise complaint is just about noise, right? Noise is not about race. Or so a typical denial of whiteness in action might go. But when those complaints target, for example, particular kinds of music, establishments, events, and groups of people—but not others, who may be making just as much noise but in different forms—whiteness as cultural power is working to redefine what, and who, is acceptable in the neighbourhood.[31]

Resistance to the whitewashing of the urban landscape acknowledges the centrality of cultural expression as a politics of staying put. When white residents of new apartment buildings (which no doubt involved years of very noisy construction) in Washington, D.C., began to complain about the sounds of go-go music coming from Black-owned businesses in historically Black neighbourhoods, the community rallied around go-go as an expression of local Black identity that should not be silenced.

Geographer Brandi Thompson Summers characterizes this movement as Black Washingtonians asserting "their belonging to the city by reclaiming cultural property that had been 'muted' by gentrification."[32] Summers argues that the sounds of gentrification—construction, barking dogs, music from beer gardens and rooftop patios—are heard as the sounds of progress and development, while noise attributed to Black communities is criminalized. The #DontMuteDC movement refused to cede the cultural soundscape to the norms of whiteness, pushing back against a sense of white entitlement that believes it has the right to curate the city in line with its own sensibilities and sensitivities.[33]

The role of whiteness and the more direct actions of white people (calling the police, for example) will come up again when we look at displacement in more detail. Considering the cultural power of whiteness is crucial for starting to understand how the kinds of class distinctions marked by taste and aesthetics are always informed by prevailing systems of power, including, but not limited to, race. Our preferences and desires are never neutral, never fully individual, and never outside of power relations. Most of us prefer to believe that we just like what we like and that our tastes are expressions of our unique identities. This goes for everything from shoes and food to houses and neighbourhoods. Unfortunately, these choices are fully bound up with our conscious and unconscious socialization into cultural norms and values that are deeply informed by gender, race, and other systems of power.

THE CULTURE STORY

It is easy to focus on the world of taste, aesthetics, and cultural values. Maybe it is because these are the realms where individual choice, and therefore the possibility of control, is foregrounded. This certainly is not limited to the ways we think about gentrification. Consider, for example, how feminism is often reduced to a set of personal choices and cultural tastes, or how actions to "save the environment" focus on consumer preferences and lifestyle changes.

It is not that personal choice is irrelevant. Choices and tastes both reflect and harden into powerful sets of cultural norms that have real-world effects. In most cases, however, the impact of individual choices—even multiplied across thousands or millions of people—will not make a substantial difference without the simultaneous action of the much more powerful corporations and governments who tolerate a gendered wage gap, permit terrible environmental degradation, and, coming back to cities, promote policies that prioritize profit-making over people.

The tastes, desires, and feelings of gentrifiers remain a major area of fascination. Some scholars argue that far too much attention has been given to the gentrifier at the expense of those who are displaced and disadvantaged.[34] Conveniently, the white middle class gets to remain the protagonist of this gentrification story. Others suggest that a focus on cultural factors distracts us from the real mechanisms propelling gentrification, namely the workings of capitalism through urban land markets.

The economic story is the next layer to examine as we move through the many ways that gentrification has come to be understood. I am always a fan of "following the money," since within a capitalist society, this usually leads up the ladder of power. However, it is wise to resist the lure of any single story. Even an economic approach can benefit from a critical, intersectional viewpoint.

4

GENTRIFICATION IS ABOUT MONEY

In April 2020, the massive chimney of the Crawford coal-fired generating station was demolished, blanketing Chicago's Little Village neighbourhood with thick, choking dust in the middle of a pandemic.[1] To many, it felt like the latest, and probably not the last, insult added to injury in an area bearing the effects of over a century of air, ground, and water pollution, much of which came from the power plant itself.[2]

I went to Chicago in 2015 to find out more about what might happen in Little Village as its long battle to close the power plant came to an end. In the adjacent Pilsen neighbourhood, the Fisk plant had closed at the same time when the company that owned both refused to perform environmental upgrades.[3] I was curious as to whether the redevelopment of these defunct sites could lead to gentrification as the neighbourhoods became perceived as cleaner. "Oh yes, gentrification is a huge problem in Pilsen," people told me, "but Little Village? No. Gentrification is not going to happen there."

On the surface, Little Village did seem like an unlikely candidate. It was stigmatized not only for pollution, but for crime, gang activity, poverty, and a racialized immigrant population from Mexico. The massive Cook County jail sits right in the centre of Little Village, next to the neighbourhood's only park. Guard towers and barbed wire are not part of the gentrifier aesthetic.

While the culture story does not seem to predict gentrification for Little Village, another story does. An *economic story* is less interested in what attracts the white middle class to an area and more interested in what attracts capital. What conditions make it favourable for investment to flow into a neighbourhood like Little Village? The answer to this question points toward the other important driver of gentrification: profit potential.

In some ways, this story is a simpler one than the culture story. While early examples of gentrification seemed counterintuitive to many observers at the time, others felt the explanation was quite obvious, if you understand what motivates the movement of capital. This was a different version of the "back to the city" narrative, where the protagonist was not the alternative lifestyle-seeking gentrifier, but the money associated with the process. As geographer Neil Smith put it in an article that would become a sacred text for economic theories of gentrification, gentrification is "a back to the city movement by capital, not people."[4]

This story is firmly grounded in urban political economy. Political economy is an approach to understanding the relationship between political systems and institutions, and the economic system. Contemporary political economy, especially that which falls under a Marxian framework, emphasizes the power, actions, and agency of entities like the state and corporations in making decisions about how to distribute resources and regulate the economy.[5] For Marxian economic geographers like Smith, political economy is also a way of describing the value systems and power relations that emerge and interact at both the state level and the individual level. While the focus rests on structural forces and powerful institutions, political economy also appreciates how prevailing economic value systems touch down and shape individual and household motivations and desires.

CAPITAL ON THE MOVE

In his oft-cited 1979 article, Smith argued against the idea that gentrification was driven by disaffected suburban residents going against previous "laws" of outward expansion of the middle class, as the Chicago school had put forth. He contends, instead, that "gentrification is not a chance occurrence or an inexplicable reversal of some inevitable filtering process. On the contrary, it is to be expected."[6] Why is this?

Smith notes that the decline in house and land values of some urban areas over long periods of time—due to everything from redlining to abandonment to physical deterioration—produces a rent gap. The rent gap is the difference between the *potential* value of a property if raised to its "highest and best use," and its value under its current land use.

Imagine, for example, the difference in profit potential between a three-storey, low-income rental building and a twenty-storey condominium on the same lot. Smith explains:

> Gentrification occurs when the gap is wide enough that developers can purchase shells cheaply, can pay the builders' costs and profit for rehabilitation, can pay interest on mortgage and construction loans, and can then sell the end product for a sale price that leaves a satisfactory return to the developer.[7]

What Smith is describing is a key feature of capitalism: the search for ever-expanding profit-making potential. While it might seem like a wise decision for that developer who wants to build a twenty-storey luxury building to purchase land in a popular location with lots of other successful high-end housing projects, the profit potential is actually lower in that scenario. This is because there is not as great a disparity between the current value of the land in a well-capitalized district than there would be in a "riskier" neighbourhood.

The goal is a version of "buy low, sell high," and in order to maximize the difference between the two, the developer ought to seek out a really good low. At a smaller scale, the gentrifier household is making a similar bet: buying a home at a low cost in a less-than-premium neighbourhood on the chance that with home improvements and neighbourhood upscaling, the investment will be worth it.

In case this sounds like another naturalistic explanation for gentrification, Smith is quick to assert that neither decline nor the flow of capital into less-valued areas is inevitable. A wide array of forces, actors, values, and deliberate decisions go into producing the conditions that make this possible in any given place. Capitalism and a lack of regulation of housing and land markets are key culprits. Zoning and land-use decisions—where to put a freeway or a factory or a park—are also critical.

For neighbourhoods like Little Village, this analysis of the causes of gentrification offers an explanation for why it can occur in areas that, on the surface, have few of the qualities that gentrifiers are seeking. The very factors that made Little Village seem unlikely to gentrify were, in fact, quietly generating an attractive disparity between potential and current land use that might encourage capital to flow once the timing was right. Those factors included polluting industries, disinvestment in the urban infrastructure, and social stigma that depressed real estate values. With environmental clean-up on the horizon and neighbouring Pilsen already being gentrified (thus having less disparity between profit potential and current value), Little Village started to look like an enticing option for real estate capital.[8]

Indeed, as early as 2014 conversations about gentrification were circulating in the media as the city approved the Paseo, a green walking and cycling trail along laneways and disused rail tracks through Little Village into Pilsen and toward the central business district (the Loop). This raised fears that property values and taxes would rise along the route, as has happened with green path projects like Atlanta's Beltline and New York's High Line.[9] A local alderman boasted that "local businesses will flourish with new customers and add value to the existing homes and centers of Little Village . . . bringing Little Village to the center of Chicago's booming neighborhood improvements."[10]

However, a housing-assistance worker noted that "families are stressed as more investors from outside Little Village are buying property there than in recent memory."[11] In the summer of 2016, a real estate investment firm bought an apartment building and evicted the seven families living there; in the spring of 2017, other residents posted letters on social media from developers offering to buy their properties, and commercial real estate publications began to note the "opportunities" offered by the conversion of former industrial (brownfield) sites in Little Village.[12] In 2020, a developer bought the Discount Mall, a place where over one hundred vendors sell Mexican goods and where many local entrepreneurs started their businesses. Concerned residents protested on Mexican Independence Day, declaring, "We're not gonna let things get taken away from us anymore."[13]

As capital moves to fill the vacuum created by decades of environmental racism and neglect by the city, residents gear up to push back against displacement, an all-too-common occurrence for Mexican communities in Chicago.[14] In many ways, what residents face are almost invisible market forces that are suddenly being redirected to a place shunned for almost a century. The representatives of these forces are developers, landlords, planners, and investors who follow the pull of increased profit potential (the rent gap). Will this pull, though, be enough to attract wealthier homeowners to an area adjacent to a ninety-six-acre jail? A polluted canal? Ongoing industrial land uses? In other words, does economics trump culture in the push to gentrify Little Village and places like it?

We have to dig deeper into the economics story to get a better sense of the variety of forces, trends, and changes that generate the conditions for capital to move. The rent gap thesis, powerful as it is, is not the entire story. The unevenness of the urban landscape in terms of investment and disinvestment is shaped by even bigger national and global processes. Underlying all of these changes are the foundations of imperialism, settler colonialism, and racial segregation.

GLOBAL FORCES

Take a look at the label of just about any piece of clothing in your closet: was it made in the United States? Western Europe? I bet you the price of this book it was not. There is a much better chance you will find place names like Vietnam, Bangladesh, and Indonesia. The outsourcing of clothing manufacturing to the global south left garment districts in cities like New York, Toronto, and London with little more than a historic moniker to revive as part of neighbourhood branding initiatives decades later. In the meantime, garment workers were unemployed and the multi-storey factories where they had once worked awaited a new purpose.

It is no secret that most of the manufacturing activities that supported the economies of global north nations have moved offshore, meaning, in most cases, to the global south. Starting in the 1960s, cities in the "great manufacturing regions" of Canada, the US, UK, and Europe started to see a shrinking percentage of the workforce engaged in blue-collar labour. The opening of borders and advances in communications and transportation technologies associated with the acceleration of globalization meant that manufacturing work could suddenly be done wherever the costs were lowest.

We are familiar with the stories of unemployment and hardship that landed on the backs of workers in industries like auto making and electronics while their parent companies raked in profits. Michael Moore's award-winning documentary *Roger and Me* clearly exposes this injustice in his hometown of Flint, Michigan. The closure of General Motors plants in the 1980s sent Flint into a downward spiral, which eventually led to the cost-cutting measures that resulted in the contamination of Flint's water supply with lead in 2014.[15] What many of us have paid less attention to is how deindustrialization in the global north reshaped not only the economy, but the cities that are its focal points.

Hulking factories sat idle and abandoned as pollution continued to seep into the ground beneath. Communities that had housed generations of workers fell into disrepair and disrepute as job losses, poverty, and evictions set in. Those who were able to escape—often white people—left, consolidating yet another layer of racialized class inequality. The supporting industries and businesses struggled with dwindling customers, while city infrastructure, including roads, schools, and public services, suffered from a shrinking tax base. In many places, the only growth industry to be found was in prison construction.[16]

The US's "rust belt" cities, such as Detroit, Cleveland, Buffalo, and Pittsburgh, became emblematic of this decline. Filmed in the mid-1980s, *Roger and Me* shows Flint, once a prosperous small city that seemed to embody all the promise of American industry, wracked by crime, homelessness, and despair. Residents scramble to make ends meet by donating plasma, breeding rabbits and selling them for "pets or meat," recruiting neighbours into multi-level marketing schemes, and trying to get hired at Taco Bell, where the managers do not think former auto workers are a good fit for the service industry. The busiest man in Flint seems to be Sheriff's Deputy Fred Ross, who oversees evictions day in and day out.

Like nearby Detroit, Flint was infamous as a site of industrial abandonment. Images that some came to call "ruin porn" circulated of the crumbling factories, schools, homes, parks, and libraries that were once the foundations of vibrant manufacturing towns all over the country.[17] However, even in the midst of profound economic crisis, cities like Flint were attempting, some much more successfully than others, to create a post-industrial economy and the urban infrastructure to support it.

This new economy was based on the service industry and knowledge professions—fields and industries requiring a degree and/or technical training. As part of the transition, cities tried to both attract knowledge workers and reconfigure the built environment to successfully launch themselves into this new era. In *Roger and Me*, we glimpse how the optimistic- and entrepreneurial-minded imagined a rebirth for Flint. Some tried to boost the tourism industry with modern hotels and family-friendly urban amenities. Others tried to cater to a small, but powerful, group of wealthy residents by promoting Flint's yacht club and golf course. The mayor brought in televangelist Robert Schuller to deliver an inspirational sermon for the unemployed.

As you might guess, Flint has not yet emerged as a post-industrial urban success story. Other cities, however, have been much more adept at capitalizing on new vectors of wealth accumulation and transforming themselves into post-industrial powerhouses.

POST-INDUSTRIAL DREAMS

In the 1996 movie *Trainspotting*, protagonist Renton and his friends languish in the crumbling council estates of suburban Edinburgh, struggling with poverty, joblessness, and heroin addiction.[18] The bleak landscape of abandoned spaces and empty futures provides a stark contrast to the scene when Renton, trying to stay clean, moves to London to work as a real estate agent (a job that perfectly symbolizes the post-industrial city). A rapid montage of shiny London landmarks, vibrant streets, enthusiastic tourists, and busy workers conveys the city's wealth and optimism about the future. Indeed, London can be considered a pinnacle of post-industrial global power. It is a fitting place for Renton, having stolen the money he and his former friends make in one last drug deal, to finally "choose life."

The cities we call global cities today are all post-industrial cities. This means that rather than relying on manufacturing and providing employment in blue-collar sectors, the urban economy runs on service- and knowledge-based industries and occupations. The so-called FIRE industries—finance, insurance, and real estate—dominate in terms of financial clout. But tourism, media, technology, research, education, arts and culture, entertainment, and law are also key sectors. This white-collar workforce requires postsecondary degrees or specialized and professional training; in other words, knowledge.

The growth of this highly skilled and mostly well-paid workforce has been matched by the service sector that supports—often invisibly—its enterprises. Who dry cleans those white collars? Prepares coffee and lunch? Walks designer dogs? Cleans the office overnight? The retail service sector is the crucial support network that allows those with the right amount of education, knowledge, and, usually, privilege, to dedicate their work lives to intellectual and creative pursuits. For retail workers in what have been dubbed "McJobs," minimum-wage, non-unionized, part-time, informal, and precarious work is the norm. The post-industrial city is thus two cities: the gleaming city of knowledge work and the shadow city of service work.

Physically, the built environment of the post-industrial city reflects these economic priorities. Office towers rise over the central business district; tech firms build sprawling campuses in nearby suburbs; tourist attractions form familiar landmarks on the skyline; and a dizzying array of consumption sites—shops, cafés, restaurants, bars, salons, and more—are available 24/7 along every major road.

If you are a Millennial or Gen Z reader in a global north city, you might never have known a time when your city's port, railway tracks, or major avenues were buzzing manufacturing hubs. Even for Gen Xers like myself, the industrial landscapes of our cities were already being transformed throughout our childhoods. So what has happened to these spaces?

Although cities like London, New York, and Toronto have always had important financial sectors, they were also sites of manufacturing and industry, especially along their waterfronts. It is worth noting that even in these high-functioning post-industrial cities, some manufacturing is still present.[19] However, much of the industrial built environment no longer needs to function as it once did. In fact, former factories, stockyards, and distribution centres sit on some very valuable urban real estate, which is no longer working to generate income. Thus, cities have used a range of tactics to repurpose, rezone, and reintegrate industrial sites for uses that support, and capitalize on, the post-industrial economy.

Lofts are a good example. While some lofts are entirely new construction, many residential loft buildings are converted from factory spaces. As early as the 1970s, contends sociologist Sharon Zukin, loft conversion was seen as "part of a general urban resurgence" as the lost spaces "changed from sites where production took place to items of cultural consumption."[20]

In Toronto's Liberty Village area, the massive Massey-Ferguson tractor and farm equipment site was transformed when the city rezoned the land from "industrial" to "residential/commercial" in the 1990s. This permitted developers to swoop in and buy up undervalued land and buildings just a stone's throw from the central business district and a revitalized entertainment district. Capitalizing on the historic value of the area, developers, where possible, converted factories into residential lofts, office spaces, and commercial sites for restaurants, bars, and shops. This process brought the rebranded Liberty Village into the twenty-first-century post-industrial economy and, critically, allowed capital to flow and grow through an underused space.[21]

In this way, the post-industrial city can take advantage of geographer Neil Smith's rent gap. Deindustrialization has created a glut of spaces with the potential for a new "highest and best use." The growth of the post-industrial economy, and its work-force, generates a demand for different kinds of spaces for work, leisure, consumption, and home. Cities, eager to recover lost tax bases from the closure of factories, suburbanization, and the flight of the wealthy, are happy to encourage the remaking of urban space by developers, foreign investors, and corporations. They do this through rezoning, providing tax incentives for developers, and generating urban plans and legislation that encourage some spaces and forms of development over others.

The post-industrial urban era promotes the right mix of

spatial, economic, professional, and cultural change to spur gentrification forward. And cities are not content to simply wait and see whether the process unfolds in the way that they desire. The post-industrial city is often an entrepreneurial city, one that actively seeks to generate growth and profit, rather than to simply manage growth and distribute services.[22]

Like all entrepreneurs, cities have to brand and market themselves in order to stand out from the competition—in this case, other cities. City branding has been around for a long time, as have urban rivalries (Chicago-New York, anyone?). In the post-industrial era, however, competition has taken on new urgency. As the physical location-dependent factory economy shifts to the global south (becoming less fixed itself), cities have to compete for investors, businesses, tourists, and residents who are looking for something special. In order to succeed in a post-industrial economy, cities seek to distinguish themselves in a variety of ways, from the banal (a city motto) to the spectacular (the world's tallest skyscraper).

When the historically working-class port city of Bilbao, Spain, took a chance on a Frank Gehry-designed, titanium-clad outpost of the Guggenheim Museum in 1997, it was a bold gambit on the chess board of urban competition. The undulating titanium hull resembles a ship, evoking the city's past while steaming right into the future. The once-crumbling industrial port area now boasts a site that represents the foundations of the post-industrial economy: tourism, culture, urban spectacle, and a place on the map. Almost immediately, the museum attracted millions of tourists, generating a huge bump in revenues for the local economy.

The "Bilbao effect" became a sought-after strategy, with other cities chasing this dream through eye-popping architecture and once-in-a-lifetime events. It has proved hard to duplicate, however, as it is rare for one building to make this kind of aesthetic and economic impact. Critics have also noted that these projects create footholds for further urban transformations, including gentrification and other forms of redevelopment that displace people and remake place in the image of a fantasy global city.

The rise of the entrepreneurial city cannot be understood without paying attention to another global economic trend: neoliberalism. Neoliberal theory demands that the state "roll back" its role in regulating the economy, providing social services, and even maintaining infrastructure. Simultaneously, the state "rolls out" measures designed to open global markets, reduce trade barriers, and enable the privatization of government services.[23] Citizens are expected to provide their own safety nets, for, as neoliberal UK Prime Minister Margaret Thatcher famously proclaimed in 1987, "there is no such thing as society."

At the urban level, neoliberalism looks like your water and waste services being contracted out to private employers who pay low wages and prevent unionization. It looks like fees for the use of city-run recreational spaces and programs. It looks like the sell-off or demolition of public housing. It looks like the removal of informal settlements and the forced movement of residents to new housing projects controlled by private developers. It looks like public spaces that are actually owned by corporations and patrolled by private security. It looks like anti-homeless architecture. It looks like your familiar streetscapes transformed by modernist behemoths and corporate box stores.

Marxist geographer David Harvey uses the concept of "accumulation by dispossession" to describe the work of neoliberal urbanism.[24] This phrase captures the idea that the wealth accruing to developers, financiers, speculators, and so on is the result of the forceful, and even violent, exploitation of people, nature, and resources as well as the dispossession of people from their homes and neighbourhoods, a process that strips them of their means of survival.

This can be seen in both global north and south cities, although the particular mechanisms of displacement, exploitation, and dispossession may be different, and some have critiqued Harvey for not clearly articulating the ongoing role of imperialism in the global south.[25] Under this framework, we can start to understand gentrification not just as a form of privilege for some, but as an act of theft: of place, and of social, economic, and cultural resources.

New, ultra-profit-driven forms of gentrification have emerged under neoliberalism. Scholars have coined terms like "super-gentrification," "condoization," "financialization," and "new-build gentrification" to distinguish these sweeping corporate- and city-backed transformations from slower, smaller-scale gentrification. For example, super-gentrification refers to a layer of highly extractive gentrification on top of already-gentrified neighbourhoods in areas of global cities like London and New York that have "become the focus of intense investment and conspicuous consumption by a new generation of super-rich 'financifiers' fed by fortunes from the global finance and corporate service industries."[26]

Condoization is a shorthand that gestures to the complex mix of agents, knowledges, logistics, legalities, and processes that have arisen to make possible the "condominium conquest" of cities like Toronto, Vancouver, New York, and others.[27] Real estate speculation driven by gentrification has also led to an increase in housing deliberately left vacant while investors simply hold on to units as part of their asset portfolios. This contributes to the supply problems in cities to such a degree that some, like Vancouver, have introduced additional taxes for owners who do not occupy or rent out their properties.[28] The rise of these accelerated forms of gentrification under the intentional direction of powerful financial agents is part of a package of neoliberal urban strategies to open the city to greater flows of investment and profit-making.

AIRBNBIFICATION

In the late 2000s, another opportunity emerged from the hive mind of Silicon Valley. This one cloaked itself in the warm and fuzzy language of kindergarten lessons: the sharing economy. The logic behind the sharing economy is that people who have certain resources, like cars, homes, pools, skills, or equipment, can "share" them with those who do not by charging a fee for their temporary use. All of this is facilitated by information technology in the form of apps that connect the sharer with the sharee. In reality, this model is less about sharing and more about finding ways to monetize one's resources in new, fast, and under-regulated ways. The term "platform capitalism" is an alternative phrasing that more closely captures the profit-driven motivations of "sharing."

In cities, ride-hailing apps like Uber and Lyft are ubiquitous examples of the impact of platform capitalism. Look up at the new apartment buildings you pass by in your Lyft and you are likely looking at the other major example of platform capitalism in cities, Airbnb. The short-term rental app has made it possible for millions of people to "share" their spare bedrooms, couches, or whole homes at rates that are usually lower than a hotel stay, but certainly higher than what the owner might fetch in a long-term rental arrangement. While this trend was initially feared to have a significant impact on the hotel industry, cities are now realizing that the massive rise of short-term rentals of whole homes is affecting overall long-term resident vacancy rates, affordability, safety, and the spread of gentrification more generally.[29]

Research over the last few years has found that short-term rentals of whole houses and apartments are siphoning off the supply of long-term rentals that could serve residents rather than visitors. A Canadian study claimed that short-term rentals pull over 30,000 possible rental units out of the market each year.[30] This is a significant number when many cities already have historically low vacancy rates and unaffordable rent. In Paris, the city estimates that Airbnb "deprives the city's residents of about 30,000 homes used exclusively for short-term tourist lets, including up to 25% of apartments in the four central arrondissements."[31]

The significant turnover of visitors also has effects on the fabric of community. While there are certainly abundant horror stories about "party houses" that fill with rowdy, inebriated strangers every weekend, there are also more subtle frustrations that come from not knowing your neighbours and worrying about issues like safety, community decision-making, and property damage.[32]

In popular tourist cities like New Orleans, short-term rentals are taking over communities still struggling to recover from the destruction and displacement that followed Hurricane Katrina.[33] Historic neighbourhoods like Treme, Marigny, and Bywater have the highest concentrations of short-term rentals in the city, effectively turning whole blocks into hotels that sit empty for half the week, then explode with young, largely white tourists and partiers on the weekends.[34] As a consequence, these areas have seen remarkable jumps in house prices over the last several years. Meanwhile, landlords are also evicting long-term tenants in order to make space for more profitable short-term units.

Housing advocate Breonne DeDecker calls short-term rentals "jet-fuel on the fire" of gentrification and a lack of affordable housing. The situation is pitting "the needs of low- and middle-income residents in the majority Black city against the financial interest of mostly white investors." On my last visit to New Orleans in 2017, "Neighbors, not Airbnb" signs and stickers were everywhere, as many in the city are fed up with the takeover. In 2019, New Orleans moved to strictly regulate Airbnb-style rentals in response to these complaints.[35]

It is important to acknowledge that while many landlords and property-owning corporations are using short-term rentals as a quick profit mechanism with little care for the wider effects, for other homeowners home sharing is a strategy that allows them to cope with their own housing or labour market precarity. Geographer Kiley Goyette points out that for women, older people, and lower-income owners, renting out a spare room to make ends meet is not new.[36] In fact, these groups have historically used their homes to make up for lower wages, cover the cost of child care, or supplement a fixed income. Research from the National Women's Law Center in the US found that Black women, Latinas, and non-Hispanic women were more likely to be behind on mortgage payments than their white counterparts, and more likely to be facing an imminent loss of employment income.[37] These factors may push women to take on Airbnb "hosting" as an additional source of income.

In order to address Airbnbification, then, we need a much broader response to the housing crisis that Airbnb capitalizes on and inflames, one that addresses a dangerously inflated housing market, gendered and racialized wage gaps, declining earning power, the need for child care, cutbacks to social assistance, and workplace insecurity.

DISASTER CAPITALISM

When Hurricane Katrina began to make landfall on August 29, 2005, I was sitting in the airport in Bermuda, waiting for a flight home after a trip to visit my father. The tiny television screen showed Anderson Cooper reporting from the Gulf Coast, barely remaining upright as the wind and rain lashed him relentlessly. Over the next several days, I, like millions of others, was glued to the news as the levees broke and thousands crowded into the Superdome and Convention Center.

To this day, certain moments stick with me from those broadcasts: FEMA director Michael Brown telling the incredulous reporter Soledad O'Brien that they were not aware of people in the Convention Center, to which she shot back: "We've been showing the footage for three days!" Kanye West staring straight into the camera to say to the world, "George Bush doesn't care about Black people." Former First Lady Barbara Bush telling a reporter at a shelter that "this [being forced to relocate] might actually be the best thing to happen to some of these people."

This last comment was one of a string of reactions that positioned before-Katrina New Orleans and its residents as in need of saving. Like something straight out of the Old Testament, a flood had washed the urban slate clean. New Orleans' reputation for corruption, crime, and racialized poverty was contrasted with what seemed like a God-given opportunity. Then-Governor

Kathleen Blanco said: "It took the storm of a lifetime to create the opportunity of a lifetime. We must not let it pass us by."[38] The streets were not even dry before commentators, right-wing think tanks, and politicians suggested that New Orleans be rebuilt in ways that would finally align it with flows of fresh capital investment. Conservative columnist David Brooks did not equivocate:

> If we just put up new buildings and the allow the same people to move back into their old neighbourhoods, then urban New Orleans will become just as run-down and dysfunctional as before [. . .]. The key will be luring middle-class families into the rebuilt city.[39]

Brooks simultaneously blames poor and Black people for New Orleans' problems while positioning the middle class as its saviour. Gentrification in a nutshell.

Critics quickly framed this response as a form of "disaster capitalism." Author and climate activist Naomi Klein describes this in her book *The Shock Doctrine* as the ways that capital (in the form of powerful financial actors) takes advantage of the chaos, instability, and damage caused by a disaster to put in place free-market-friendly reforms while a beleaguered public has little capacity to respond.[40] The disaster creates an opening for gentrification to proceed with few barriers to slow its progress.

Geographer Jamie Peck characterizes this as a "first-world" version of structural adjustment policies, where the disaster and its aftermath seem to necessitate the privatization and marketization of city spaces and services, since, according to other commentators, New Orleans was clearly helpless to save itself even on a good day.[41]

Since the storm, not only has New Orleans experienced the explosion of short-term rentals, it has lost an estimated one hundred thousand Black residents who never returned. Housing prices have increased rapidly, retail spaces targeted to white, affluent consumers are proliferating, and high-end market-rate housing is replacing thousands of units of public housing.[42]

While New Orleans has been the poster child for post-disaster gentrification, it is certainly not alone. Researchers have traced similar patterns in post-Superstorm Sandy Lower Manhattan; post-earthquake (1985 and 2017) Mexico City; and post-IRA bombing central Manchester.[43] As the Covid-19 pandemic decimated local retail and restaurants, and job loss led to evictions of many from their homes in cities all over the world, urbanists have wondered whether the post-pandemic economic "recovery" will be yet another vehicle for gentrification.

The economic story of gentrification lends credence to these fears, given that in this account, gentrification is encouraged by uneven urban land markets and the devaluing of urban space through processes like abandonment. While other potential changes, such as those in the world of work, will assuredly have an impact on what any urban recovery looks like, capital does love the increased profit potential generated by a sudden decline.

GLOBAL GENTRIFICATION

It is a sign of gentrification's power that an online search for "gentrification in Nanjing" or "gentrification in Moscow" will generate results.[44] Places that were not even, and are still not entirely, capitalist when Ruth Glass coined the term are experiencing their own versions of gentrification, many of which do not look much like the kind noticed in north London in the 1960s. By the early 2000s, argues Neil Smith, gentrification had become a "global urban strategy" for capitalist expansion into new markets.[45] Given its global reach, the story about white middle-class tastes seemed to have less explanatory power than ever. Instead, actors like the state, corporations, banks, private finance, foreign investors, real estate agents, developers, and tech companies are now seen as the right class—the capital class—to focus on.[46]

Gentrification's transformation into a global juggernaut is not natural, at least not in the sense that it happened on its own or that it is inevitable. It does make sense, however, within the context of globalization, global urbanization, and the spread of neoliberalism. The economic story, writ at a global scale, certainly seems to predict and explain, to a large extent, how gentrification fulfills the need of capital to accumulate profits at expanding rates and to extract maximum value from urban space.

This focus on the impacts of major global shifts like deindustrialization and neoliberalism seems quite disconnected from the cultural story of the desires and fantasies of the middle-class homeowner or the urban hipster. Still, gentrification as an economic process is never divorced from culture. Even in milieux where the particular desires of western gentrifiers make little sense, cities and developers have to draw on (and sometimes invent) locally relevant narratives that reflect the aspirations, values, and tastes of those they hope to attract. It is always a question of *how* economic factors interact with the cultural rather than whether they do at all.

Nonetheless, as gentrification has matured, it has largely been lifted out of the hands of city dwellers themselves. Decisions made in the chambers of city hall and the boardrooms of banks are shaping the on-the-ground realities of gentrification in ways that make it hard to pinpoint a villain, unless that villain is capitalism itself.

Capitalism obviously has a lot to answer for when it comes to gentrification. However, capitalism can all-too-easily become an overly deterministic framework for understanding the social and economic world, one that ignores the presence and possibility of alternatives. As my colleague Heather McLean and I suggest, the political-economic story about gentrification, with its focus on neoliberal urbanism, has become the dominant story.[47] There does not appear to be an "outside" to neoliberalism.

As powerful and important as this mode of understanding urban transformations has been, it tends to reinscribe a story about the city for which we already know the ending. With neoliberal outcomes as a foregone conclusion, "abstract, detached, colonial, and masculinist modes of urban knowledge production look for similar patterns that will confirm that which they already know and foreclose the possibility of studying or working with radical world-making projects."[48] In this way, the economic story mimics "the totalizing ambitions of global capital."[49]

It is also a story that has a bad habit of making other, arguably no-less-global forces into secondary characters there mainly to support the central figure: capitalism itself. These forces include colonialism, imperialism, racism, heteronormativity, and patriarchy. Feminist, queer, post-colonial, and anti-racist critiques of the economic story remain sidelined. The result is that we are stuck with not only single-minded theorizing, but a limited set of possibilities for imagining alternatives to our current urban trajectories.

5

GENTRIFICATION IS ABOUT CLASS

The statement "gentrification is a class-based process" has been repeated so often it might as well be dogma. As important as class is, this declaration promotes a tunnel vision that leaves other significant forces in the shadowy periphery.

My own introduction to the world of gentrification came via a set of gender-related questions about the condominium boom shaking Toronto's real estate market in the 2000s. This form of owner-occupied high-density apartment housing was actively marketed to a young, educated, and often female demographic. Enthusiastic real estate columnists touted condominiums as no less than a great stride for women's liberation.[1] Being a rather prickly feminist, I had to raise an eyebrow and wonder, what exactly was going on here?

Conveniently, I had just started my PhD and it seemed as though a viable topic had landed in my lap. So, I set out to talk to developers, planners, and most importantly, women condominium owners themselves, to figure out how ideas about gender were embedded in this larger urban revitalization project. On the surface, the condominium boom seemed to be about a middle-class consolidation of the central city. In line with neoliberal urban policies, it was a way to help capital circulate anew through the well-established city core.

I was curious about a different sort of story about neoliberalism, however, one that understood gendered norms, ideas, and roles as part of the very fabric of neoliberalism itself. Gender, it seemed to me, was not only a category for thinking about the *effects* of something like gentrification under the guise of revitalization. Rather, it was a foundational element of the process.[2]

What I found was that gender was informing every part of condominium building. Traditional notions about women's need for safety and security as well as freedom from household maintenance were there. Feminist ideas about women's need for financial independence were co-opted into the mix. Cultural phenomena such as *Sex and the City* influenced a narrative about women's professional, sexual, and psychological freedom in the city. Condominiums seemed to offer a path toward equalizing women's footing in the home ownership world, where patriarchal housing policies that had excluded women from home ownership or subsumed their needs under the husband and family had long left women at a disadvantage.

The story that I told about the condominium boom resisted the closures of the truism that "gentrification is a class-based process." It certainly is that, but it is not only that. In many cases, class is not the central driver; it needs to be understood alongside careful attention to factors like gender, race, heteronormativity, age, and colonialism. In other words, it requires an intersectional analysis.[3]

When gentrification researchers insist on foregrounding class at the expense of other power relations, we are not just missing something. We are potentially misunderstanding the process itself. And, as feminist geographer Winifred Curran argues, this will not actually help us move toward the end goal of all this research: resisting gentrification.

A more intersectional story about gentrification offers greater clarity on how and why specific groups are targeted for displacement and the discourses and practices that are used to accomplish this. It assists us in seeing the connections between different forms of violence and oppression used to seize control of the city. And critically, it enables us to imagine solidarities and alliances among different groups of city dwellers based on shared struggles, without reducing those struggles to a single issue.

GENDERING GENTRIFICATION

The condominium boom brought me into feminist research on gentrification in the 2000s, but, in fact, research on gender and gentrification began decades earlier. Initial studies suggested that women's increased participation in the paid workforce, their higher educational attainment, and the growth in dual-income families were causes of gentrification.[4] Feminists pointed out that suburban life was not set up to support a family with two working adults. City life, in contrast, could allow women to better integrate paid work outside the home with their still-disproportionate share of domestic duties.[5] Optimistic accounts in the 1980s proposed that gentrification could be emancipatory for women, allowing them to break out of the strictures of the patriarchal family that the suburbs supported so well.[6]

Researchers like Damaris Rose noted that for women-headed households, the access to services, schools, employment, and different housing forms in the city was essential to their survival. Unfortunately, as Curran notes, gentrification did not result in an upending of gender roles or restructuring of care work. In fact, while a small number of very privileged women have undoubtedly benefited from gentrification, the effects for the majority of women have been less than emancipatory.

Despite this early wave of research on gender and gentrification, gender became a footnote as the scholarly focus on gentrification and neoliberalism narrowed. There did not seem to be much appetite for considering how sexism might be important to understanding neoliberalism. Still, feminist urban scholars continued to resist a one-note account of gentrification as they investigated issues like displacement, violence, care work, poverty, and activism through a gendered lens.

In her study of the emergence of a neoliberal urban agenda in Milwaukee, feminist geographer Brenda Parker draws attention to the fact that men, and masculinist ways of "doing" politics and city-building, were at the centre of Milwaukee's revitalization attempts.[7] She shows that patriarchal work, household, and institutional relationships were fortified at women's expense as a wave of gentrification, privatization, and creative city initiatives was unleashed. These changes disproportionately affected Black women and women of colour. At the same time, men consolidated more wealth and power as new opportunities for capital accumulation were opened up.

Given the long-standing gender inequalities in political power, as well as the significant overrepresentation of men as the owners and leaders of the kinds of companies that play a major role in gentrification today (banking, construction, development, insurance, and so on), power and money flow to men via gentrification. Yet, the patriarchal hoarding of resources is rarely mentioned in gentrification research. Why is this?

My guess is that even when gendered inequalities are noticed, they are seen only as by-products of class inequality, rather than part of the very roots of the systems that allow gentrification to exist. However, there is no real reason for class to trump gender here. After all, patriarchy was around long before capitalism and the particular configurations of class and wealth extraction that it produces.

Gender and class do not have to compete for first place in the analytical Olympics, though. We can try to work intersectionally, in a way that does not separate class and gender dynamics. We can open up the class-based story to think about gentrification as a kind of sexist capitalism in which these systems of power reinforce each other.

These systems are strengthened through the flow of money and power, but also through violence against women. Globally, the World Health Organization (WHO) estimates that almost one in three women have experienced physical and/or sexual violence from an intimate partner, and as many as 38 percent of all murders of women are committed by intimate partners.[8] The WHO notes, "Gender inequality and norms on the acceptability of violence against women are a root cause of violence against women."[9] Changing these norms is critical to ending domestic violence, but violence against women is not only an ideological problem: it is a structural one, reinforced by systems and policies in many spheres, including housing.

One of the major barriers preventing women from leaving abusive relationships is the lack of affordable, safe, and long-term housing. Indeed, domestic violence is a leading cause of both short- and long-term homelessness for women. As gentrification raises the costs of housing, women attempting to flee violence see their options narrowing. Emergency shelters are often full and have to turn women away; in the best-case scenario, they can offer about six weeks of shelter and referrals to public housing waiting lists.[10] Second-stage, or transitional housing in between the shelter system and the regular rental system, is in short supply.

The question posed to so many victims—"Why don't you leave?"—is absurd when no one can offer an answer to the retort, "Where should I go?" During the Covid-19 pandemic, stay-at-home orders led to a spike in calls to domestic violence hotlines, as leaving, even temporarily, became almost impossible.[11] In the first months of the pandemic, countries around the world noted increases in reports of domestic violence, in some cases double or triple the annual average.[12]

Domestic violence can also result in women being evicted by landlords who see family violence as a threat to their property values. Curran notes that in some cities, landlords are fined for calls to 911 that are deemed nuisances.[13] Reflecting long-standing problems with the policing of partner abuse, domestic violence-related calls often get downgraded to nuisances. Landlords find it easier to evict women and their families than to deal with the fallout from these calls. Because a history of evictions makes it difficult to obtain housing in the future, women become reluctant to call the police, leaving them at the mercy of their abusers.

Housing precarity caused in part by gentrification also puts women in danger of sexual harassment and violence from landlords. Landlords use the threat of eviction and the knowledge that affordable housing is scarce to prey on women, demanding sexual favours in return for delayed evictions, lower rents, or late-payment leniency. During the pandemic, when people's options to move were even more constrained by public health restrictions, job loss, and overall economic uncertainty, the National Fair Housing Association in the US found that tenant organizations were reporting a rise in calls about sexual harassment from landlords.[14] One woman's landlord suggested she spend the night with him when she asked to delay rent until her government stimulus cheque arrived. She told reporters, "He knows I don't have a job. He knows I don't have anywhere to go—he's preying on me."[15]

Outside of the home, gentrification propels violence against sex workers through a suite of policies and practices that push this activity into more dangerous spaces. Red light districts may be targeted for "cleanup" and removal in order to make way for more family-friendly tourist attractions, middle-class housing, and high-end consumption sites. Increased policing in gentrifying areas leads to more harassment of sex workers and clients. Trans women and trans and cis women of colour report very high levels of police harassment tied to assumptions that they are sex workers when they occupy public space.

Sex workers may find themselves working in more isolated spots with less access to transportation, warm spaces like coffee shops, and the safety of other people. They can be driven off the streets altogether, which is not necessarily safer depending on the particular laws that govern where sex work can and cannot happen.[16] This may push women into more exploitative arrangements with pimps and brothels when they lose the ability to work independently.

Gentrification also operates through practices that directly and indirectly target women. Having children is the best predictor of the likelihood of being evicted in the US, reports the *New Republic* in a piece titled "Why Landlords Target Mothers for Eviction."[17] Single mothers struggle to make enough income to support a family, especially given the gendered and racialized wage gap, and are typically employed in more precarious occupations that do not offer a steady, predictable income.

In this context, "Landlords—eager for an excuse to rid themselves of tenants whose children might cause noise complaints or property damage, or for whom lead hazards have to be abated or child services called—are often all too happy to begin eviction proceedings." The potential to raise rents to take advantage of gentrification fuels the temptation to find ways to evict tenants paying lower rates. The fact that mothers are easy targets is not just incidental; it is part of the mesh of power relations that make gentrification possible.

A less direct but no less hostile method of targeting women comes via the removal of public housing. In cities all over the world, public housing projects are being converted to private housing or mixed social and market housing. Many projects have been demolished altogether to clear valuable central-city land for more profitable forms of development. A part of the story that is often missing is that women-headed households make up the greatest share of public housing tenants.

In the US, this number is as high as 75 percent overall, with higher numbers in cities like Chicago and New York.[18] Curran points out that the gender-equity implications of public housing conversion or demolition are rarely remarked upon, even though it is clear that women—especially women of colour—and their children will be the group most severely affected.

Again, it is not sufficient to dismiss this as a coincidence. Curran brings home this point: "Structural inequalities have accomplished the gendered segregation of social housing. The gentrification of social housing is therefore by definition gendered, as a specific population is targeted for displacement, with no viable means to access affordable housing at the urban core."[19] In New York, the Citizens Housing and Planning Council developed a Feminist Housing Plan in 2021 to bring attention to this issue within the New York City Housing Authority.[20]

Even if public housing tenants are rehoused, they may find themselves far from the services and connections of the downtown area. Centrality and proximity are critical to the survival of women-headed households in the city. Early research from the 1970s and 1980s illustrated that women make more intensive use of urban services, including public transportation, parks, social services, health care, and other resources that, by their proximity, make juggling family and paid work, especially for low-income women, possible.[21] Women also rely heavily on the informal, place-based networks that they develop in order to help with child care, elder care, transportation, and more.[22]

Displacement is, therefore, not just an issue of having access to housing, but of having access to those networks and services. When women lose their housing, they also lose babysitters, carpool buddies, and all sorts of other informal helpers who make up the patchwork of care necessary to survive in places with inadequate social services. We can connect this back to neoliberalism, which rolls back these public services and relies heavily on women figuring out how to pick up the slack.[23]

This is far from an exhaustive accounting of the patriarchal roots and impacts of gentrification. Given its ability to both exploit and exacerbate gender inequalities, gentrification is a process that reinforces women's subordinate position in the home and shores up heteronormativity. With constrained options in the housing market for single women and women-headed households, women are structurally compelled to form traditional domestic partnerships, despite the violence and exploitation of domestic labour that typically accompanies these relationships. Gentrification can thus be seen as a prop for what feminist scholar and poet Adrienne Rich called "compulsory heterosexuality," a system that leaves women few choices but to rely on the nuclear family.[24]

This lens on gentrification complicates the class-centred

story in ways that allow us to understand how gentrification works through multiple systems of power. As Curran contends, "Failure to recognize the gendered nature of displacement is not simply an oversight; it is an obfuscation of the process of gentrification and what it is actually accomplishing on the ground."[25]

THE SEXUAL POLITICS OF GENTRIFICATION

The last time I was at a Pride parade in a major city, the hundreds of thousands of other spectators and I found ourselves waving rainbow flags printed with the name of a major retailer, wearing rainbow stickers with bank logos, and holding colourful balloons with corporate slogans as massive floats sponsored by Canada's biggest companies inched past. You do not need to be especially cynical to observe that Pride in cities like Toronto is a corporatized, money-making spectacle. One might say it has been gentrified, a claim one could also make about the neighbourhood surrounded by the parade route, the Church Street Gay Village.

Early observations about the relationship between gay communities and gentrification date back to the 1980s.[26] Since then, the gentrification of "gaybourhoods" dominated by white, cis, gay men has been documented in cities across the global north. Scholars note that some members of the queer community have benefited from gentrification, while many others have been displaced or faced continued exclusion. In recent years, some have seen gay communities as active proponents of gentrification as their claiming of space has extended into nearby communities that are home to marginalized groups.[27]

It is tempting to draw a line from ghettoization to acceptance to gentrification. However, this simplified story glosses over the limitations of a perspective on gay gentrification that focuses only on long-standing, identifiable neighbourhoods.[28] It also downplays the ongoing role of gentrification in bolstering heteronormativity and marginalizing sexual and gender expression that is less amenable to commodification.

While it is important to critique the gentrification of gay neighbourhoods, queer feminist geographer Jen Jack Gieseking writes that "the long-term fixation on the lgbtq, lesbian, and/or queer neighbourhood [is] tied to the white heteropatriarchal promise of territory and the project of ownership," a project that has always been exclusionary.[29] Instead, we ought to keep the focus on what gentrification means for the most vulnerable members of the queer community, those who already had the least access or acceptance in gay villages. This framing highlights how gentrification preys on and reinforces existing divisions and hierarchies of sexual and gender acceptance.

The over-policing of particular queer bodies in and around gentrifying gay neighbourhoods and former red light districts has meant increased systemic violence against trans women and especially trans women of colour, as well as queer and trans youth of colour.[30] Arrests of trans women on suspicion of engaging in sex work have accelerated in gentrifying areas, leading to incarceration in men's prisons under dangerous circumstances.[31] Queer youth, who are more likely to be living in poverty or experiencing homelessness, are targeted for ticketing or arrest by police enforcing anti-panhandling laws and nuisance complaints. Queer people of colour face racial profiling that manifests in stop-and-frisk tactics or carding, and of course the greater likelihood of police violence.

All of these groups deal with this violence in a context where they know they have little support from the mainstream queer community, who may be actively encouraging over-policing of undesirable, unruly queers that threaten their property values and acceptance from the wider society. When big Pride parades started to welcome police officers marching in uniform, the message about who would be "safe" under the umbrella of the "rainbow" community was loud and clear.

Gentrification has also been particularly hard for lesbians and other queer and trans women who face the compounded effects of sexism, homophobia, and transphobia. Those who have studied (and often lived) the history of queer women's spaces in cities note that rarely have queer women occupied and claimed space in the same way as gay white men; namely, they have rarely had defined neighbourhoods of their own.[32]

Instead, they have relied on what Gieseking, based on their research in New York, calls a "constellation" of sites that are more spatially dispersed but linked by shared political commitments. Unfortunately, such spaces (like bookstores, bars, and cafés) have perhaps been more vulnerable to displacement from gentrification as they are more isolated than similar institutions serving gay men in identifiable gay neighbourhoods. In many major cities, including Toronto, San Francisco, and Montreal, there are no more exclusively lesbian or queer spaces oriented to women.

Queer women themselves are also more vulnerable to displacement, as are many women-headed households. Lower-than-average incomes, less wealth, the effects of divorce, raising children: women are more likely to bear the brunt of these disadvantages, which affect their ability to find and stay in adequate housing. The gentrification of gay neighbourhoods has not resulted in wealth accumulation or the consolidation of spatial power for women as it has for others in the queer community. Rather, women have been further excluded from the territorial power of the "gaybourhood." Gieseking notes that the neoliberal transformation of these spaces in line with a narrow vision of acceptable queerness has proven hostile to many who no longer feel as though spaces like New York's Greenwich Village are "safe."

Gentrification has both taken advantage of and intensified long-standing divisions and inequalities within the queer community. Here, it relies not only on the class inequalities among, for example, women and men, cis and trans people, white and racialized queer people, but also on the boundaries of social tolerance for gender and sexual difference. In other words, gentrification firms up and depends on homonormativity: a version of queer life that largely conforms to the institutional, political, familial, and sexual norms of heterosexuality, for example, monogamy, marriage, parenthood, property ownership, and nationalism.

Queer life that does not fit into, or in fact deliberately exceeds, these norms is being gentrified, sometimes literally, to death. In this way, gentrification supports a liberal agenda of gender and sexual tolerance that accepts and even celebrates a thin slice of the queer community at the expense of others. It also benefits from these social and political dynamics in that it capitalizes on the desire for acceptance by some by offering pathways to normativity through property ownership, consumption, and lifestyle choices.

In a particularly pernicious example of gentrification preying upon queer life, scholar and activist Sarah Schulman describes the way that New York's East Village apartments, made vacant by the deaths of people with AIDS in the 1980s and 1990s, went back on the market at inflated rates. She recalls: "The appearance and rapid spread of AIDS and consequential death rates coincidentally enhanced the gentrification process that was already underway."[33] As tenants passed away, rent-controlled apartments could be pulled back into the market-rate pool.

Schulman remembers that the rent on her neighbour's apartment almost quadrupled after he died of AIDS. This process accelerated the transformation of the neighbourhood from "an interracial enclave of immigrants, artists, and long-time residents to a destination location for wealthy diners and a drinking spot for Midtown and Wall Street businessmen."[34] As AIDS devastated a generation, property owners and developers took advantage of death and disease to widen the opportunity for profit.

Inequalities across gender, sexuality, and gender identity help to set up the structures within which gentrification operates. Without these pre-existing differences, urban neoliberalism would have to create them in order to accomplish the privatization and marketization of urban space that it relentlessly pursues.

RACE, WEALTH, AND GENTRIFICATION

In 2021, Evanston, Illinois, a suburb of Chicago, announced a program to distribute ten million dollars to Black residents "who can show that they or their ancestors were victims of redlining and other discriminatory 20th-century housing practices in the city that limited the neighborhoods where Black people could live."[35] Taking the form of housing grants to assist with home repairs, mortgage payments, and down payments, the plan is part of a (slow) growing trend in cities to recognize the ongoing repercussions of slavery and a century and a half of housing discrimination through some form of reparations.

Although there is debate as to whether measures like this really fulfill the mandate of reparations, they do seem to represent an acknowledgement that monetary efforts to redress the harm of racist housing policy are long overdue. Indeed, it is hard to overestimate the significance of housing to ongoing racial stratification in the both the US and many other countries.

The home is the major vehicle of wealth creation for average people. It is the single largest purchase most people will ever make and the biggest asset most will ever own. People look to home ownership as a saving strategy for carrying them through retirement and old age. The expectation is that you pay off the mortgage while the home increases in value over time, leaving you mortgage-free and sitting on a robust asset that can be sold or otherwise leveraged to cover living expenses after retirement. In countries with high percentages of homeowners, homeowners are much better off in retirement than life-long renters.[36] This is especially true in places where social safety nets like pensions and old age security have been eroded over time (thanks, neoliberalism).

Gentrification accelerates this process of wealth accumulation through home ownership by capitalizing on that rent gap and ensuring high levels of return on the initial investment. After all, if you buy a cheaper home, you will have a lower mortgage to pay off; and as the neighbourhood gentrifies, your home will increase in value at a higher rate than a home in a more stable or already wealthy area. Your profit margin is a healthy one. Even if you are just looking to buy the kind of house you can afford (rather than greedily rubbing your hands together at the thought of future profit), you will still likely benefit, at least financially, from gentrification.

Unfortunately, under capitalism we cannot all be winners in the property market, as anyone who has ever played a game of Monopoly well knows. In fact, gentrification exacerbates already existing wealth divides and actively capitalizes on long-standing histories of racial discrimination in the housing market. This dynamic is particularly stark in the US context. Understanding the racial economics of gentrification today requires knowing something about the history of redlining and other forms of racist housing policy throughout the twentieth century. The uneven geographies of home ownership, racial segregation, and neighbourhood investment produced by these policies have shaped the flows of capital that enable gentrification.

Redlining was a policy originating in the 1930s whereby the US Federal Housing Authority (FHA) determined levels of lending risk based on the racial composition of a neighbourhood. They used colour-coded maps to indicate green and blue areas that were seen as low-risk areas for lending. Yellow and orange areas carried more risk, but the red areas—those "redlined"—were effectively barred from accessing mortgages, loans, and other financial services. The FHA did not guarantee bank loans made to homeowners in those areas. Redlined areas were those with noticeable Black populations. Areas could be swiftly downgraded from green or blue by the addition of just one or two Black households.[37]

Over time, whole neighbourhoods were shut off from sources of financial support. Black residents were unable to sell their homes, few people were able to move in, and residents were trapped in districts where no new forms of investment were available. Redlining denied Black homeowners the chance to see their real estate increase in value; in fact, homes in redlined areas could only decline in value over time. Many neighbourhoods endured neglect from cities with cuts in services like garbage pickup, water treatment, and infrastructure maintenance. In the US, redlined inner-city areas became symbols of racialized poverty, crime, and abandonment.[38]

Redlining was part of a suite of racist housing practices. These included racial covenants that restricted the sale of homes to Black and other racial minority buyers; predatory lending at high interest rates with punitive terms; contract buying, which was a risky version of rent-to-own but one of the only avenues to ownership available to Black families under redlining; whites-only suburban housing developments; an inability to take advantage of housing opportunities via the G.I. Bill because of banks' refusal to lend in redlined areas;[39] the New Deal's Fair Labor Standards Act, which excluded domestic, agricultural, and service occupations;[40] and blockbusting, whereby real estate agents whipped up racist fear in white homeowners and convinced them to sell their homes at low rates, which could then be resold on contract or at inflated prices with high-interest rates to Black buyers.[41]

Black neighbourhoods have also been targeted for destruction through processes like urban renewal and freeway development. After redlining pushed these areas into poverty, cities could conveniently declare them "slums" and justify urban renewal projects that razed entire neighbourhoods in the name of modernization. Freeway construction, usually designed to connect whiter, wealthier suburbs to the downtown core, also has a long history of destroying Black communities. In 1964, New York's infamous Cross-Bronx Expressway accelerated such a period of decline for the South Bronx that by the 1970s, huge swaths of the area were abandoned, burned, and crumbling.

In Canada, Vancouver's Georgia Viaduct displaced the Black neighbourhood known as Hogan's Alley; and in Halifax, the desire to build the MacKay Bridge was part of a host of reasons that led to demolition of the historic Africville Black community. Not only have homes and businesses been destroyed to make room for freeways, but the value of the remaining properties has plunged due to their proximity to one of the city's least-amenable land uses, in yet another instance of the theft of Black wealth.

In his pivotal essay, "The Case for Reparations," author Ta-Nehisi Coates connects the more recent theft of Black wealth through discriminatory housing policy to the historical theft of Black wealth under slavery and Jim Crow laws.[42] He argues that the effects of centuries of robbery do not disappear through things like civil rights legislation. Even if civil rights guaranteed that no more theft happened, the law does not return what has been lost.

For Coates, the case for reparations is not only made on the grounds of the horrors of enslavement, but on the injustice of the ongoing practices that have denied Black people that most cherished vehicle for financial security and intergenerational wealth, the home. One of the points that Coates makes clear is that when someone is robbed, someone else gets richer. In other words, the theft of Black labour, property, and wealth is the foundation upon which the wealth of white people is built. I appreciate his insistence on this. It is too easy to focus on the harm of slavery without acknowledging the other side of the coin, which is that it made white wealth and power possible, and still does.

When we look at housing, we also need to acknowledge that the harm of redlining and other practices contributed to the wealth of white homeowners, and still does. According to the Brookings Institution, in 2016 a typical white household held ten times the amount of wealth as a Black household: "In fact, the ratio of white family wealth to Black family wealth is higher today than at the start of the century."[43] Differences in the value of inheritances, for which the home is likely a significant proportion of assets for most families, account for most of this ongoing gap.[44]

It is important that we do not take these racial disparities as add-ons or side effects of the capitalist logic that drives processes like gentrification. The framework of racial capitalism, a term coined by political theorist Cedric Robinson, insists that capitalism is not incidentally racist; rather, racial differentiation is essential to the functioning of capitalism as we know it and was indeed fundamental to the development of capitalism.[45] Historian Robin D. G. Kelley explains that capitalism developed in a context already saturated with racism: "Capitalism and racism, in other words, did not break from the old order but rather evolved from it to produce a modern world system of 'racial capitalism' dependent on slavery, violence, imperialism, and genocide."[46]

Professor of English and Africana Studies Jodi Melamed argues that "capital can only be capital when it is accumulating, and it can only accumulate by producing and moving through relations of severe inequality among human groups."[47] In other words, capitalism is reliant on white supremacy.

We noted earlier that the economic story of gentrification argues that gentrification is propelled by a gap between the current and potential values of urban land. The production of that gap depends in large part on the racist policies and practices that forced some areas into prolonged periods of decline. This gap is also widened by the racist stigma attached to minority neighbourhoods. Narratives that emphasize crime, drug use, gangs, violence, poverty, and dysfunction work to further lower the cultural and economic value of such places.[48] Within these conditions, those who profit from and encourage gentrification (today, largely a concerted effort of city and corporate actors) are also capitalizing on white supremacy.

Some have argued that gentrification might bring benefits to Black and other racialized communities, especially for those who are homeowners.[49] However, research shows that there are limited economic benefits for Black and Latinx homeowners, and that ultimately, most of the surplus value produced through gentrification does not trickle down to these groups.[50] In fact, the theft of wealth continues for racialized homeowners in myriad ways.

Environmental racism—the siting of hazardous and polluting land uses near communities of colour—diminishes home values over time, while simultaneously exposing people to illness and shortened life expectancy.[51] Notably, white communities actively benefit from cleaner air and water while their home values increase. In Flint, Michigan, for example, the use of a lead-tainted water supply as part of cost-cutting measures by the city has not only poisoned thousands of children, but further stripped away what little value Flint homeowners might have retained.[52]

Recent news stories have also exposed racial bias in home appraisals. In one article, homes that were known or appeared to be owned by Black and South Asian families were assigned lower values than comparable homes in the same area owned by whites.[53] Likewise, homes in majority-Black and Latinx neighbourhoods are regularly appraised at lower values than those in white neighbourhoods, in part because they are compared to sale prices of similar homes in the same area. This "basically grandfathers in racist home pricing" from the era of redlining and overtly racist valuations.[54]

The Rice Kinder Institute for Urban Research reports that in the United States, "racial inequality in home values is greater today than it was 40 years ago, with homes in white neighborhoods appreciating $200,000 more since 1980 than comparable homes in similar communities of color."[55] Under these conditions, even gentrification is not going to allow households of colour to realize the full value of their investments.

Movements for housing-related reparations recognize that the theft of wealth and opportunity from racialized communities laid the groundwork for the accumulation of wealth and opportunity for white people. These movements are not only calling for financial compensation for individuals, but for ways to put entire areas under the control of racialized communities who were displaced or otherwise harmed by urban development.

In Vancouver, where the Black community known as Hogan's Alley was destroyed to build two viaducts in the early 1970s, the current plan to tear down the viaducts and "revitalize" the area has been met with calls to let the Black community form a Community Land Trust to determine the future of the space, as a form of redress for the earlier displacement. Lama Mugabo of the Hogan's Alley Society says: "Our request is rooted in justice. We have been wrongfully displaced, we have been dispossessed, we've lost our core, our sense of belonging, a place we once called home."[56] Still, people fear that tearing down the viaducts will allow Vancouver to revitalize and gentrify yet another swath of its already wildly expensive waterfront.

However, it is not only the destruction of and disinvestment in Black neighbourhoods that have made them (or their former sites) targets for gentrification. It is also the fact that in many places, Black communities—despite the terrible circumstances they faced—kept urban neighbourhoods alive and protected from total abandonment.[57]

The contributions of Black people and other racialized groups to cities has been all-too-easily erased by narratives of danger and disorder that accompany discussions (both academic and mainstream) about the "inner city." Geographer Katherine McKittrick argues that spaces of Blackness are represented in these ways to deny the care, connection, and community labour that form a Black sense of place. This erasure eases the spread of gentrification by perpetuating the narrative that there is nothing of value in such neighbourhoods.

Toronto's Little Jamaica has long served as both a reception place for Jamaican immigrants and a hub for the wider Caribbean community in the Greater Toronto Area. However, the construction of a light rail mass transit project on Eglinton Avenue has been taking a toll on this diverse, low-income neighbourhood for over a decade. Student journalist Karel Peters remembers the significance of the area to his family:

> On weekends, Eglinton was the place to be. The streets were always busy and filled with people from the Caribbean diaspora walking to the various Black immigrant-owned shops and restaurants. The community was filled with not only those from Toronto but with people like my dad, who lived outside of the GTA and yearned for a sense of belonging.

Journalist Amanda Parris has similar memories: "Growing up I recall the crowds that would flood the streets of Eglinton West for Kiddies Carnival. I remember standing in front of Randy's Patties with friends after school or meeting up with a crush at Trea-Jah-Isle record shop."[58]

Filmmaker Sharine Taylor explores the effects of a project

that is ostensibly meant to bring great benefits to the city: "Years of noisy construction, constant road closures and hijacked sidewalks have led to a plunge in revenue for the local businesses that once populated the area." Taylor tells Parris, "There were people that I spoke to who were just like, 'I've given up. I'm not even trying to fight anymore. They've taken so much from me.'"

Little Jamaica is more than a place where people come to buy authentic groceries, get their hair and nails done, and hear music from their island homes. It has also been a place where Black people—having faced historic and ongoing housing discrimination—have created "their own spaces of refuge and belonging where communities, institutions, and culture were built."[59] While boosters of the transit project tout the eventual benefits to business owners, history suggests that it is unlikely the immigrant-run, Caribbean-culture-based businesses that have made Little Jamaica will survive long enough to enjoy them.

The displacement or closure of local businesses in Little Jamaica diminishes the already small number of places that Black people can call home in Toronto and evokes traumatic displacements of Black communities there and in other Canadian cities. The disruption of Little Jamaica is not an unfortunate yet isolated event related to one particular transit project. Rather, it is a continuation of long-standing historical processes of dispossessing Black communities of their homes and businesses to make way for projects that are likely to serve another, better off, community.

In New York City, areas of Queens and Brooklyn are being explicitly targeted by revitalization and gentrification initiatives driven by an investor class. In Flushing, Queens, urban studies scholar Tarry Hum notes that a long history of racist urban planning has, over and over again, put places with significant historical, cultural, and economic value to Black communities at risk of redevelopment. The repeated battles to save the site of the Macedonia AME Church—a likely stop on the Underground Railroad and a historic burial site—illustrate the constant devaluation of Black spaces in the face of potential investment and commodification: "Once a racially and [culturally] diverse, working-class neighborhood, Flushing is now an epicenter of luxury residential and commercial condominium development."[60]

In Brooklyn, urban scholar Amanda Boston notes that the building of the Barclays Center adjacent to Fulton Street—"one of the largest contiguous Black communities in the United States"—symbolizes, for some, the "new" global, revitalized, Brooklyn. Meanwhile, for others, "the arena represents the death rattle of Brooklyn's homegrown authenticity. By their and many others' accounts, the arrival of a billion-dollar arena has portended the triumph of global capital over local communities and culture."[61]

Boston argues that these processes cannot be explained by class alone. She places the development of the Barclays Center in the context of what she calls the "serial forced displacement" of Black Brooklynites over many decades. She notes that redlining and segregation created the conditions wherein Black households were especially vulnerable to foreclosure (more equity theft) in the 2008 housing crisis, since they had been pushed into the dangerous sub-prime housing market.

Structural racism thus creates the conditions where redevelopment seems natural, necessary, and desirable in Black neighbourhoods. Thus, racial-spatial processes "have valorized and protected spaces racialized as white while designating non-white spaces for neglect, exploitation, and destruction."[62] Out of these ashes, Boston notes, "racialized hyperinvestment" rises as the saviour that will "fix" the problems of racialized disinvestment.

Hyperinvestment in the form of luxury development, condominiums, and sports stadiums does not further disadvantage racialized communities by coincidence. Rather, Boston argues, deepening racial inequality is "a defining feature of neoliberal urbanism." Urban sociologist Christopher Mele contends that a "color-blind racial ideology" interacts with and reinforces neoliberal urban policies and practices: "With respect to urban development, [colour-blind racial discourses] ultimately deflect responsibility for problems of structural inequality from society to the individual and ignore the persistence of structural and systemic racism."[63]

State- and corporate-led gentrification is positioned as beneficial to all social groups. Indeed, Boston notes that Shawn "Jay-Z" Carter's vocal support of the Barclays Center project was rooted in the idea that Brooklyn (his hometown) should benefit from both his, and the stadium's, entrepreneurial success. His celebrity status overshadowed local activism against the stadium and furthered the narrative that neoliberal urban redevelopment ought to be welcomed in Black communities.

The colour-blind ideology of neoliberal urbanism has been mirrored by a colour-blindness in the class-focused literature on gentrification. There is no reason why, in many contexts, gentrification could not be called a "race-based process." No one would deny the role of class; however, the consistent centring of class has the effect of always making race and other systems incidental or secondary to class. This is not helpful when we are trying to understand the specific dynamics of gentrification in different places, especially as the process has affected neighbourhoods that, forty years ago, were seen as very unlikely to gentrify, for example, areas with large pockets of public housing or predominantly Black neighbourhoods.

Class might have seemed adequate to the task of telling the story of gentrification through the 1960s and 1970s, but today it is less viable as a central explanation. As activists, community organizers, and scholars have been arguing for some time now, race is foundational to gentrification because it is foundational to class differentiation and capitalism itself.

COLONIAL PROPERTY LOGICS

As gentrification perpetuates the theft of wealth from racialized communities, so too does it continue long processes of settler colonial dispossession of Indigenous peoples from their land. One of the ways this happens is through gentrification's expansion of home ownership and private property regimes in cities.

Historically, the division of urban land into neat little parcels through the imposition of the grid layout for streets was a method of facilitating the conversion of land into property.[64] Those tidy parcels were "just the size to attract settlers," notes historian Nadia Rhook, writing about Melbourne. Of course, these divisions and sales were done without the consent of the local Indigenous groups. Rhook argues, "land sales literally firmed the grid foundation upon which settlers would assert their sovereignty to build and maintain gross racial inequalities." Today, most of us take both the grid layout of many cities and the sanctity of (and desire for) private property for granted. Even anti-gentrification movements do not always question these foundational elements of settler cities. Yet, gentrification undoubtedly depends on the continuing colonial domination of urban space.

The rise of urban neoliberalism with its emphasis on privatization has deepened our economic and cultural commitment to private property. However, as legal geographer Nick Blomley suggests, "We tend not to reflect on the ways in which the first world city is a propertied space."[65] Furthermore, we often—very adamantly—refuse to reflect on the connections between how we understand property today, the commodification of people as property under slavery, and the roots of taken-for-granted parts of urban life like police forces in slave-catching and the suppression of Indigenous peoples.[66] The logics of possession codified under slavery and colonialism, asserts Black diaspora cultural studies professor Rinaldo Walcott, continue to shape our cities today.[67]

Gentrification can be contested not only in terms of the inequalities in who owns property and how it is valued, but on the very basis of ownership itself. This requires connecting anti-gentrification work with decolonization efforts, rather than seeing these as separate struggles. What might it look like to go even further in our denaturalization of capitalism to question the colonial foundations of the city itself?

I do not have simple answers to these difficult questions, but contemporary Land Back movements are pushing those of us who are settlers, settler descendants, and recent arrivals to settler colonial countries to take concrete action toward facilitating

Indigenous control and sovereignty. Nickita Longman, Emily Riddle, Alex Wilson, and Saima Desai explain:

> "Land Back" is the demand to rightfully return colonized land—like that in so-called Canada—to Indigenous Peoples. But when we say "Land Back" we aren't asking for just the ground, or for a piece of paper that allows us to tear up and pollute the earth. We want the system that is land to be alive so that it can perpetuate itself, and perpetuate us as an extension of itself.[68]

The propertied city undoubtedly makes this challenging, but that does not mean we can place decolonization on the back burner while we contest gentrification. Generating a different urban vision demands that we imagine both.

CITY OF YOUTH AND HEALTH

In the 2009 documentary *Vanishing City*,[69] filmmakers follow elderly residents of a small Manhattan apartment building as they are evicted from the homes some of them have lived in for almost four decades. As eviction day approaches, some still do not know where they will end up. Despite their long tenure, these vulnerable residents fell victim to landlords taking advantage of tenant-legislation loopholes that permit evictions if the owner claims to be turning the building into a single-family home. The seniors find themselves with few options for affordable housing and few resources with which to fight back.

Scenes like those in *Vanishing City* are almost a staple of films about gentrification, yet the specific impact of gentrification on senior citizens is rarely discussed. Gentrification's effects on disabled people and people with mental health issues have similarly been under-studied. Considering how age, disability, and mental health intersect with gentrification helps to again expand the story about gentrification to include the ways that vulnerable groups are deliberately targeted and disproportionately harmed.

In Ottawa's Sandy Hill neighbourhood, a group of tenants who are elderly, in poor health, and on social assistance are fighting eviction from rooming houses that have fallen into such a state of disrepair the city has deemed them too dangerous to live in.[70] Tenants claim that the new landlord's "repairs" are partly to blame for the situation, as key infrastructure was removed from the buildings. Although several tenants have successfully outstayed their eviction orders so far, it is unclear how long this situation can last, and more importantly, whether they will be allowed to return after the renovations. Tenant William Weaver has lived there since 1978. He told reporters, "It would be very difficult [to move] because everything I require [is nearby . . .] Any other place, I wouldn't have all that."

Seniors, disabled people, and people with mental health concerns are all more likely to be living on fixed incomes, to rely on government assistance, and to need supportive, affordable housing in areas that are close to health and social service providers. Those who may have been living in their apartments for decades are especially vulnerable because necessary upgrades to property can end up coupled with high-end renovations or conversions to non-residential or single-household properties, meaning that residents may not be able to return.

Regardless of explicit intentions, it seems clear that property owners are able to take advantage of the systemic vulnerabilities imposed on older tenants and disabled tenants. Both the effects of gentrification and the methods by which it proceeds are shaped by age and ability in ways that the class-focused story of gentrification misses.

While images of seniors being evicted offer shocking reminders of the cruelties of gentrification, the slow violence of neighbourhood transformation also has insidious effects. Even if elderly people are able to stay in their homes, they may find their lives disrupted by other local changes. Indeed, the relatively small amount of research on aging and gentrification emphasizes the importance of the physical and social characteristics of place for older residents, especially those who are racialized.

In their research with older Latinx residents of gentrifying Chicago neighbourhoods like Logan Square, Humboldt Park, and West Town, Ivis García and Mérida Rúa point out, "Proximity to various resources, such as stores, transportation, and other services are vital to older adults' quality of life and their engagement in community."[71] Their interviewees were frustrated and saddened by the loss of affordable, friendly spaces to get coffee, do their grocery shopping, or socialize with friends and neighbours.

For example, in a neighbourhood teeming with trendy cafés, resident Manolo said he would like to have a place to go for a cup of coffee, illustrating the notion that gentrifier spaces are not seen as welcoming or "homey." Instead, Manolo takes two buses to a McDonald's in Humboldt Park where he can sit and chat with friends for hours. Places like fast food restaurants, coffee shops, diners, local shops, and parks are critical infrastructure for seniors and others who do not work, as these are the sites where social connections and community care happen.

In her research with older adults in a gentrifying area of Manhattan, sociologist Stacy Torres found that "place magnifies in significance for urban elders as spatial proximity to socializing spaces also grows in importance."[72] However, retail gentrification meant that older shops and cafés were being priced out of their locations, and seniors, even if not displaced themselves, felt trapped in their homes with few local spaces to go and decreased physical ability to go outside the neighbourhood.

Critical health scholar Shellae Versey's research in Harlem also illustrated that elderly residents were eager for spaces to socialize and concerned with the changing character of the neighbourhood as it became whiter: "The shifting demographic, and the creation of new, exclusive 'third' social spaces (e.g., coffee shops, wine bars, sidewalk cafés) coupled with the closing of several neighborhood establishments left seniors feeling 'forgotten' despite living in the heart of the neighborhood."[73]

These feelings have material effects on the well-being of seniors. For the many older adults who live alone, frequent social contact with others in the neighbourhood functions as a routine check on physical and mental health. In Torres's study community, a resident who went into hospital was supported by other regulars from his local bakery: "At least 20 people he knew from the bakery visited him in the hospital and brought him food, newspapers, cards, balloons, and well wishes for a quick recovery."[74] When elderly people lose access to local supports and lack the ability to travel further afield, they lose independence and become more reliant on family and social services.[75]

Older residents also experience a sense of injustice as their contributions to the neighbourhood are erased, their neighbours are pushed out, and they themselves are pressured to leave. Elderly people may view themselves as the ones who built, improved, and stabilized their neighbourhoods and communities. However, an influx of new residents who do not seem to respect that past or the people themselves leaves seniors feeling invisible.

In Harlem, seniors told Versey:

I'm telling you, people walk past me and look down on me. Listen to me, I was born in Harlem. I'm where I belong, what are you doing here? And they walk through here like they own the place! And when you go to certain stores, you don't see them in there. You don't.

I will not give up on this place, because it was here before we were and as far as I'm concerned, I'm going to fight to keep the Old Harlem and bring it back that way. I'll do whatever I have to do to make that happen.

Seniors also fear their community's intergenerational ties to the neighbourhood are being broken, as younger family members cannot afford to live in the area.[76]

Elderly residents also recount active pressure to push them out from landlords, public housing corporations, eager buyers, developers, or real estate agents. In Center City West, Philadelphia, resident Alda Ballard told reporters that she feels "besieged by strangers who view her home as a valuable commodity and her presence as a nuisance. 'They are always knocking on my door telling me they want to buy my house,' she said. 'Well, I am not selling.'"[77] In Harlem, one senior recalled:

> They would come around and offer residents $30,000 dollars to give up their apartment so they could redo it. And people took this money. People took this money and then realized that they can't find anywhere else to live and wind up in the shelter system with me.[78]

If these direct tactics do not work, the eventual rising costs of living in gentrifying areas may do the trick. Even homeowners are affected, as tax bills skyrocket when home value assessments double or triple over the span of a few years.[79]

Displacement may be deadly. The Centers for Disease Control (CDC) states that seniors are at increased risk of negative consequences from gentrification, included shortened life expectancy, higher cancer rates, diabetes, and cardiovascular disease. Health disparities widen as marginalized residents are pushed out of healthier neighbourhoods and away from the conditions that allow them to flourish.[80]

In her summary of work on gentrification and aging, social work scholar Sandra Edmonds Crewe notes that sudden homelessness for older people is most likely to be a result of a change in their housing situation, like their home being sold or expensive renovations. Lower-income and racialized elders are especially vulnerable in this case.[81]

The health impacts of gentrification are not only experienced by the elderly. In fact, many organizations consider gentrification a threat to public health more generally.[82] The CDC's summary of available research suggests:

> Vulnerable populations typically have shorter life expectancy; higher cancer rates; more birth defects; greater infant mortality; and higher incidence of asthma, diabetes, and cardiovascular disease. In addition, increasing evidence shows that these

populations have an unequal share of residential exposure to hazardous substances such as lead paint.[83]

A study of gentrifying New York neighbourhoods found that "displaced residents who moved to non-gentrifying, poor neighborhoods had significantly higher rates of emergency department visits, hospitalizations, and mental health related visits for about five years after displacement" compared to non-displaced residents.[84] The loss of social networks and social spaces that comes from displacement or neighbourhood change also has an impact on mental well-being.

As some groups of people are pushed into or trapped in neighbourhoods that are bad for their health, others benefit from the health services available in wealthier and gentrified communities. This has been apparent in access to Covid-19 vaccination sites in cities like Toronto, where, ironically but perhaps not unexpectedly, the gentrified inner city areas with the least Covid-19 cases initially had the most vaccination sites available and the highest rates of vaccination.[85] Conversely, the city's "inner suburbs" where the majority of low-income and racialized residents live had the highest rates of Covid-19 infections and fewer vaccination sites. Gentrification contributes to class- and race-based health inequities by shaping access to health care and exposure to risk of disease and harm.

This is all quite ironic in a context where gentrification is often characterized as creating health and wellness in communities. Indeed, you might notice early signs of gentrification in the form of yoga studios, organic grocers, or juice bars. Industrial, immigrant, and working-class neighbourhoods are often "rehabilitated" through image-makeovers that focus on health, environmentally friendly products and services, and the wellness industry.

Political scientist Jessica Parish documented the transformation of an area of west Toronto through the presence and gradual upscaling of wellness services, especially holistic and alternative services like acupuncture, osteopathy, and massage.[86] What she calls the "healthification" of Parkdale was a critical part of its rebranding. Parkdale was long associated with mental illness, poverty, and disability due to the presence of large numbers of psychiatric patients living in the community in rooming houses near the Centre for Addiction and Mental Health, Toronto's oldest and biggest psychiatric hospital and treatment centre. Gentrification and "healthification" went hand in hand as those rooming houses were converted back to single-family homes and Parkdale could become linked to wellness in ways that were attractive to a health-minded middle class.

The gentrification of what have been called "psychiatric ghettos" or "service-dependent ghettos" like Parkdale has been observed in many places where the trend toward deinstitutionalization of people with mental health issues, cognitive disabilities, and physical disabilities produced neighbourhoods with high concentrations of people requiring a localized system of social, medical, and economic support. People struggling with addictions, sex workers, low-income seniors, and formerly incarcerated people also became concentrated in these areas. As geographers Michael Dear and Jennifer Wolch documented, deinstitutionalization was rarely coupled with adequate support for "care in the community," pushing people into poverty, precarious housing arrangements, dependence, and homelessness.[87]

Although such neighbourhoods, like Vancouver's Downtown Eastside and San Francisco's Tenderloin district, and the people who live there, are deeply stigmatized, the real estate they occupy has increased in potential value as gentrification pressure builds throughout the city. Once functioning as "containment zones" for a host of social problems that cities could not or did not want to address directly, these areas are being aggressively "cleaned up."[88] In San Francisco, Mayor London Breed has gone so far as to force some individuals in the Tenderloin district into state conservatorship in order to remove them from the street permanently. She has been known to undertake "unannounced inspections of neighborhoods, sometimes carrying a broom."[89]

The heterogeneous group of people who rely on the proximity of critical services to affordable housing share a high vulnerability to displacement. Rates of social assistance have utterly failed to keep up with the costs of rent and food. Landlords can easily evict people who have few social networks or diminished capabilities to challenge evictions. Irregular or illegal tenancy arrangements offer few protections. Moreover, these neighbourhoods are playgrounds for delinquent landlords, who let their properties fall into deplorable conditions with the knowledge that their poor, old, and vulnerable tenants have no other options.

These conditions also make it easy for landlords to evict people for necessary major renovations, processes that often result in permanent displacement when rents go up. Many of the gentrifiers who move in are not particularly tolerant of neighbours who exhibit signs of mental illness or other "undesirable" behaviours. During a time when folks in the Junction neighbourhood of Toronto were debating the imminent arrival of a Starbucks, online commenters were clear in their views:

> Starbucks in the Junction—YES BRING IT ON! [. . .] I'm sick and tired of the bums, vagrants, prostitutes, mentally ill freakshow people who maraud the Junction Streets and expose themselves indecently in front of children [. . .]. They can't afford Starbucks.[90]

It is not hard to see gentrification here as a process designed to weed out those deemed unhealthy, weak, old, and ill. In 1999, as the city of Toronto was acting to close rooming houses in Parkdale, activists decried "social cleansing in Parkdale."[91] The impulse to "other" and expel that which is considered dirty, impure, and polluting to the "health" of the community is a deep one, albeit one that few would admit to, given our desire to distance ourselves from appalling histories of social cleansing and genocide.[92]

However abhorrent we claim to find ideas like social cleansing, they are remarkably close to the surface of the discourse on gentrification from those who support or facilitate it. Furthermore, it is clear that gentrification and gentrifiers capitalize on the stigmatization and vulnerability of older, disabled, and struggling residents. In many ways, it is more palatable to talk about and even critique gentrification as a class-based process than it is to acknowledge it as one that also borrows from the playbook of social cleansing.

The declaration that "gentrification is a class-based process" is inadequate for understanding the multiple axes of power that gentrification manipulates and works through. Class is always relevant, but it is not always the most salient or effective lens for getting at what is really going on. Picking up different lenses, or, even better, an intersectional lens, gives us a clearer picture of the how and why of gentrification. By considering both the differential effects that gentrification has across factors such as gender, race, sexuality, age, and health, as well as the various processes, practices, and discourses that gentrification makes use of, we can move beyond the limitations of a class-centred story.

GENTRIFICATION IS ABOUT PHYSICAL DISPLACEMENT

Ruth Glass was certainly prescient when she predicted the complete social transformation of neighbourhoods in her 1964 definition of gentrification. Displacement, she suggested, was at the heart of gentrification. Since then, displacement has remained central, yet confounding, as there are many different definitions, causes, and ways of measuring displacement. What does displacement really look and feel like? What are the everyday experiences that lead to a lost sense of place or belonging? For qualitative researchers like me, people's personal accounts are compelling data. For quantitative analysts, measuring changes in household type and income, housing tenure, and rates of eviction based on census, planning, and other survey data is usually preferred. Whatever approach you take, any study of gentrification must confront displacement in all its forms and reckon with the deep and lasting impacts on people's lives.

The standard story of gentrification has tended to focus on

one form of displacement: the out-migration of working-class and/or racialized residents from gentrifying areas. A picture gets painted of a neighbourhood undergoing a total turnover in the class and identity of inhabitants, businesses, and services over a period of time. This story implies that few, if any, "original" residents remain. Here, gentrification has a distinct before and after. This story compels us to look for quantitative evidence of the physical departure of certain people from the community. Without proof of this particular trajectory and kind of displacement, some observers do not believe gentrification has occurred at all.

Unfortunately for those who like to have neat graphs and uncomplicated narratives, gentrification is often messy, drawn out, and without a clear endpoint. The desire to tell a straight-forward story means researchers and writers might be pulled toward studying places where displacement has "happened" in some kind of eventful way, rather than considering the ordinary neighbourhoods where displacement and gentrification are affecting people slowly, emotionally, and often quietly. Sometimes we have to eschew clean notions of a measurable before and after in order to understand displacement as a multi-layered, multi-temporal, and relational process that defies simple packaging.

We need to shake up the displacement story. It is more productive to work with multiple understandings of displacement at the same time rather than privileging one version over another. This approach lets us look at displacement from many angles, including how it happens, what its effects are, and what kinds of power relations are operating. Most importantly, it opens our hearts and minds to the heartbreak and violence of displacement, which manifest in ways both banal and spectacular, spatial and temporal, old and new.

DISPLACEMENT IS NOTHING NEW

Displacement is happening every minute of the day, all around the world. Refugees fleeing war, conflict, and natural disasters number in the millions every year, a figure that has grown steadily since the 1990s.[1] Climate change is pushing people off their lands and out of their homes through flooding, drought, pestilence, and storm activity. Farmers and rural people are displaced to cities in search of sustainable livelihoods as agriculture is transformed into a global industrial complex. Policies of apartheid (systems of racial discrimination and/or segregation) and ongoing colonization force groups of people into reserves, missions, and camps. Criminal punishment systems rip people from their communities to incarcerate them far from home for decades.

Displacement is nothing new and not especially rare. Even within cities, physical displacement has a long and infamous history. From the forced removal of Indigenous people from the lands that became the central administrative, military, and trade centres of European empires, to the slum clearance and urban renewal projects of the nineteenth and twentieth centuries, cities have not hesitated to actively displace people by the thousands.

The justifications take many forms: Olympic stadiums, suburban commuter freeways, urban green spaces like Central Park, subway tunnels, bridges, and more.[2] The scale can be small and slow—a few households here and there—or massive and rapid—thousands of informal settlement dwellers evicted as bulldozers start their engines on the outskirts of the area. Sometimes, the same communities are displaced again and again in a process urban policy and health scholar Mindy Fullilove calls "serial displacement."[3]

With this long history, it is important to remember that physical displacement has not been, and will not be, limited to gentrification. Nonetheless, gentrification is one of the processes behind displacement today, physical and otherwise.

DISPLACEMENT AS UNWILLING MOVEMENT

The history of people's forced removal from their homes and neighbourhoods, even from the city itself, nudges us toward an initial definition of displacement as physical; that is, as a literal movement through space. We see this understanding in narratives about gentrification pushing people, such as long-time residents and precarious newcomers like artists, out of the neighbourhood as others move in.

There are various mechanisms of physical displacement, some of which are more direct and immediate than others.[4] Direct displacement happens through processes like evictions, tearing down homes and apartments, or selling a home and moving to a different area. Indirect displacement, also called displacement pressure, is a slower process, where gradual changes in the neighbourhood make it less affordable, less familiar, or less suitable for residents. Research on displacement via gentrification has been inclined to search for evidence of direct physical displacement, and to a lesser extent, displacement pressure.

This search has not been an easy one. After all, a fair amount of movement is normal and expected within, between, and out of cities. People's reasons for moving are likely linked to several simultaneous life circumstances, not to mention intertwined with psychological, emotional, and financial conditions. So how can we distinguish displacement induced by gentrification from other kinds of movement? And if we do find such displacement, is it necessarily "bad"; for example, were those who moved worse off because of it?[5]

These questions have spawned numerous research methodologies, debates about terminology, and even some rather heated exchanges amongst gentrification researchers, as we have failed to agree on either what we are looking for or how to empirically show what happened. After all, how do you even find the people who have left a neighbourhood? As urban geographer Rowland Atkinson noted decades ago, social surveys are typically administered at residences; displaced households are already gone from the places we might go looking for them.[6]

And if you manage to find other evidence of out-migration, how do you uncover the reasons for those movements? Furthermore, given the wide range of issues affecting any given city at once—work opportunities, air quality, transportation, school quality, to name a few—how can you pin down gentrification as the culprit pushing people away?

I may sound as though I am playing devil's advocate to my own book. Despite these methodological challenges, there is ample evidence of involuntary movement due to pressures that include those related to gentrification.[7] The problem is that amidst the squabbles over physical displacement, we may have sidelined other possible ways of understanding and measuring displacement. In fact, many have argued that the emphasis on direct physical displacement, as the only valid reason for a critique of gentrification, is misleading or distracting.[8] Do people have to be immediately pushed out of their homes for gentrification to have a negative effect on them as individuals or on their community more widely?

The emphasis on physical displacement relies on a narrow understanding of how places come to matter to human beings. As urban geographer Mark Davidson notes, focusing on the loss of or removal from physical space ignores the fact that the connection between people and their neighbourhoods is not created and strengthened by physical presence alone.[9] Relationships, memories, shared histories, emotions, events, and more constitute a *sense of place* that is deeper than location.[10] That connection can be disrupted even if people do not move away. Thus, studies of displacement need to be more attuned to place than to space.

Similarly, attending only to physical displacement misses the ways that gentrification extends beyond particular moments in time that correspond to removal. People's actual experiences of changes to their sense of place are not necessarily bound to such specific moments. Change might be slow and gradual; slow and then fast; fast and then slow. Time itself is experienced subjectively. Moreover, histories of displacement live on across generations, especially within those communities that have experienced serial displacement.[11] As such, displacement might be felt across the past, present, and future in ways that do not neatly correspond to spaces on a map or dates on a calendar.

Physical displacement and quantitative methods for capturing it are important and will always have a place in gentrification research. However, contemporary researchers and commenters also take a more humanistic approach to displacement, one that includes the affective, everyday, banal, and interpersonal experiences that accumulate over days, months, and years. Although less attention-grabbing than immediate moments of expulsion and dispossession, these experiences matter and they also generate a tremendous wealth of knowledge about displacement and gentrification. Moreover, they constitute potential sites of political action and resistance.[12]

DISPLACEMENT AS LOSS OF HOME

Humanistic approaches to displacement start with how it is felt and lived, what it does to the heart and the body, what it creates and what it takes away. What matters is the effect that gentrification has on people, regardless of whether they are literally or metaphorically excluded from their neighbourhoods.

A variety of terms have been deployed to capture this wider sense of displacement: symbolic displacement, cultural displacement, un-homing, rupture, severance, placelessness, slow violence, root shock, urban wounding, and topocide, urbicide, and domicide.[13] The words that everyday people use to describe their experiences are also powerful: not for us, exploitation, uncomfortable, hollow, dying, disappearing, stealing, loss, disconnection, loneliness. For example, a Harlem elder says: "That new building going over there on 125th Street, it's not for us, come on, please. They're getting the new people up in here, it's for them. That's why they're trying to move us out."[14]

This way of knowing displacement comes from the ground up. It does not rely on state-centred sources of data, like censuses, eviction records, or development applications. It arises out of lived experience and is captured qualitatively, sometimes by researchers but also by journalists, essayists, memoirists, filmmakers, social media posts, oral histories, storytelling, music, and even fiction.

Unabashedly subjective, the data generated from these accounts—whether shared in a peer-reviewed article or a rap battle—nonetheless offers compelling evidence for a widely shared set of experiences of displacement. These range from the radically life-altering to the everyday mundane, but they all suggest that disruptions to our sense of place, especially those that come from outside forces, are deeply troubling to human beings.

Exploring this requires interdisciplinary approaches that are attentive to the emotional, psychological, embodied, material, relational, and even intergenerational elements of displacement. Such approaches recognize that displacement is likely to be a cumulative and multi-faceted process. A variety of experiences across time and space build up and gradually condense in a feeling of being cut off from "home," broadly defined. Impacts on the body and mind may also be slow to manifest: the accumulation of stress, fear, insecurity, and grief makes itself felt and known over years. Urban geographer Rachel Pain calls this "chronic urban trauma" in her work on housing dispossession in a former coal-mining town in the north of England:

> The trauma created by slow violence not only oscillates over time, but becomes magnified where the source of violence continues and proliferates; trauma becomes, in turn, a powerful force sustaining the effects of violence. [. . .] Chronic urban trauma has a material embodiment, held in place even when people who witness earlier harmful events have moved on.[15]

This wider story about displacement recognizes the fundamental importance of place and home in people's lives. Even when people who have been physically displaced find themselves in higher-quality accommodations, they often report negative outcomes in terms of their health and happiness.[16]

This speaks to the fact that where we live is much more than a location. It is a set of networks and relationships. It is family and friendship. It is identity and belonging. It is support and stability. It is strength in numbers and a political future for marginalized communities. It is attachment to the past and hope for the future. When we are "un-homed," as geographers Adam Elliott-Cooper, Phil Hubbard, and Loretta Lees put it, we experience "a form of violence that removes [our] sense of belonging to a particular community or home-space."[17]

Although I have suggested that the pain of loss of place is a near-universal feeling, we have to recognize that the actual occurrence of un-homing is unevenly distributed. We are not all equally vulnerable to displacement, and indeed some groups have been experiencing different forms of forced displacement for hundreds of years. For many, gentrification is just the latest affront to their ability to establish and maintain community.

Displacement will also have different effects on people across factors such as age, ability, gender, race, and class. For a working single mother who relies on a nearby network of friends and family to help her get the kids to school and then watch them until she gets home, for example, any move is likely to have ripple effects that fray the already-thin fabric of her life. For elderly people, changes to the social spaces and services in the neighbourhood accelerate the isolation and vulnerability of aging, as seniors are less likely to make use of new spaces.[18]

The "right to stay put" is a common rallying cry in response to the dangers of displacement. Drawing inspiration from the broader notion of the "right to the city," the right to stay put insists that communities are entitled to remain in the places they have contributed to. Furthermore, "the right to dwell extends beyond simply having a home in an area, encompassing the right to continue using commercial, community and public spaces and institutions, as well as the dignity of defending such rights."[19]

Importantly, it recognizes that agency is a critical factor. People do not want to be forced to move, nor do they want to be forced to stay in place. Rather, people value choice, the ability to participate in decisions that affect their communities, and the right to resist when they need to. As such, it is also important not to cast those experiencing or struggling against displacement as passive victims, especially given the long histories of resistance to displacement.

The attachments that we have to place are not merely sentimental or mired in nostalgia. They reflect the importance of home, neighbourhood, and city in enabling us to grow, develop relationships, build financial and psychological security, and to survive in places and situations that are increasingly insistent on our need to get by with as little support as possible from the state. A nuanced view of displacement allows us to see how various systems of power shape experiences of loss and un-homing in different ways. We can look at a wide range of processes, practices, and even time scales that include the structural and institutional as well as the micro and everyday and begin to understand that these are mutually reinforcing in the context of loss of place.

DISPLACEMENT IN EVERYDAY LIFE

Everyday life includes all of the habitual, mundane, day-to-day activities and interactions forming the routines that carry us through our days and nights. For most of us, everyday life is heavily place-centric. That is, our habits and routines are grounded in specific spatial contexts, including the home, neighbourhood, workplace, and city. For a long time, everyday life was not of much interest to social scientists, including geographers. It was seen as outside of, or mere background to, seemingly more important questions of power, production, capitalism, technology, migration, and globalization.

Feminists have been instrumental in recapturing the significance and history of everyday life, in part because it has typically been women's lives, interests, and activities that were relegated to the realm of the everyday. Marxist philosopher Henri Lefebvre's text *Critique of Everyday Life* also argued that everyday life required greater attention, because capitalism was colonizing everyday life in ways that would reduce the possibilities of human freedom and self-expression.[20] In the context of gentrification, everyday life gets reshaped in many ways, big and small, and these have a significant impact on how people understand their place in the neighbourhood.

Everyday interactions are an important site where even subtle shifts in social norms can communicate powerful messages about belonging and exclusion. In Harlem, researcher Shellae Versey's older Black interviewees noted experiences such as this: "When I step outside this building here, you understand, people pass me and look at me like I'm in the wrong place."[21]

These day-to-day micro-aggressions affect people's sense of trust and reciprocity. Seniors recalled a time when there was a sense that the community was looking out for itself: "And if anything was seen that was wrong, the elders in the community were on you—even the ones who were out there hustling." Another noted: "I used to work on 125th Street. I used to walk to work and everybody would speak to one another. It was beautiful. People said good morning, they stopped and chatted and music was in the air." Overall, these long-time residents felt that a unique aspect of the character of Harlem had shifted, leaving them feeling out of place in their own neighbourhood.

In Cáceres, Spain, where tourism-related gentrification is rapidly changing the character of neighbourhoods, sociologist Lidia Domínguez-Parraga found that long-time residents experienced loneliness and isolation as local apartments became "home" to tourists and short-term renters and local businesses became more tourist-oriented: "No, I do not have any neighbors. So I am telling you, there are times when I miss them, I mean the neighbors . . . who help you out . . . I tell you, I'm there all alone."[22]

Similarly, in Chorlton, Manchester, sociologists Tine Buffel and Chris Phillipson found older residents felt a loss of social cohesion: "I see a lot of changes. When I came here first, you had good shops . . . and there was a sense you might meet somebody . . . Now that's gone. There doesn't seem to be any cohesiveness."[23]

These changes to the norms of everyday social interaction are also related to disruptions in social networks. Social networks are more than friends and acquaintances with whom to have a chat; they are the contacts and contacts of contacts who help us find work, babysitters, doctors, social services, carpool rides, housing, and so much more.[24] Sociologists call this "social capital" because it has material value in our lives. Social networks are not solely place-based, especially in the Internet age, but proximity and familiarity matter when you are looking for child care, a health care provider, or schools.

Although some gentrification research, notably Lance Freeman's work in Harlem,[25] argues that gentrification enhanced social capital for long-time residents, other researchers, like Versey, suggest the opposite: that residents had greater social capital *before* their networks were disrupted by physical displacement, changes to the social spaces in the neighbourhood, and a lack of neighbourliness from newcomers. Writer Princess McDowell reflects on the changes to her community of Vickery Meadows in Dallas: "we didn't ask for an upgrade or a Starbucks or a goddamn R.E.I., never needed one. only needed each other and a bus pass and a familiar street. always had everything we needed within walking distance."[26]

Changes to the social environment lead to disconnection, since it is the everyday activities we engage in that connect us most profoundly to place: the neighbour we wave to every day, the pub we have lunch in on Sundays, the chit-chat we make on the sidewalk at school drop-off. They may be mundane activities, but when they are lost or fundamentally altered, so is the very fabric of our lives.

SENSORY DISPLACEMENT

The sensory neighbourhood includes all of the tangible and intangible elements—sights, sounds, smells, tastes, and feelings—that convey the character, culture, heritage, history, and identity of an area. It is tempting to call this "neighbourhood character," but that is a slippery term typically wielded by conservative or wealthy communities to serve NIMBY (not in my backyard) agendas.[27]

The sensory environment, however, is part of what makes any community special to the people who live there. It is also the context in which we often notice the first signs of gentrification. An old mural is painted over. The kind of music emanating from patios and bars changes. The scents of food change or disappear altogether. A Harlem resident opines:

> These other people that are moving to Harlem, they knew what Harlem was before. They knew the culture of Harlem. They knew we sat on the stoop. They knew we make music. They stopped them from playing the drums that have been playing for years in Marcus Garvey Park.[28]

These changes are experienced by many as a break in their sense of belonging: a sensory displacement, if you will. Unfortunately, because the sensory world of Black, working-class, or immigrant areas is rarely seen as valuable or worth preserving, appeals to slow gentrification down based on neighbourhood character have little impact.

In Sarah Schulman's work on the gentrification of queer spaces in New York, she argues that alongside evictions, rising rents, and the physical displacement of many queer people, artists, and immigrants from the East Village came an eviction of the imagination from urban spaces; a homogeneity that stifles creativity, diversity of thought, and progressive movements.[29] There is something potent about the mix of classes, lifestyles, histories, occupations, desires, and identities in urban neighbourhoods that helps us create art, ideas, and social change. When that mix is lost, the context for creative expression is stamped out.

Homogenization of cities happens, in many cases, through the whitening of neighbourhoods. As discussed earlier, the power of whiteness as a force constitutes the tastes and aesthetics of gentrification. It is important to revisit this in the context of displacement to understand how white gentrifier takeovers produce un-homing for racialized residents. "They are gentrifying my neighborhood in silence," writes Princess McDowell:

Strip malls fenced for being too "crime-ridden." (read: commercial properties torn down because they are afraid, in the day time, of black folks sitting in front of property like it's their own. like they live there. like they're comfortable with the shadows.)[30]

This "silent gentrification" tiptoes in via the sensory norms of whiteness: where to sit, what kinds of shops to have, how property should look.

In his research on gentrification in Los Angeles's greater Eastside, communications scholar Jaime Guzmán calls gentrification a "whiteness project."[31] Exploring Boyle Heights' struggle against gentrification, Guzmán argues that so-called neighbourhood beautification projects do not benefit working-class Latinx communities because they are not meant to; rather, they are designed to cleanse the city of people of colour. While some elements of culture like food and music may be retained, overall the goal is to prepare urban space for white, wealthy inhabitants.

Guzmán specifically draws attention to what community members called "artwashing" in Boyle Heights, in which city-facilitated artist-led gentrification puts a creative and colourful veneer over violent displacement processes. The designation of an Arts District and the arrival of new, high-end art galleries and white artists were viewed as destructive forces by the community. As one local resident put it: "These galleries are coming in and trying to replace the current culture that is already in Boyle Heights. They are not looking to attract members of communities."[32]

It is hard to argue against art and beautification, a fact that makes it difficult to point out the power imbalances and harmful practices that are covered up by pretty murals, sculptures, and fresh coats of paint. In Boyle Heights, activists recognized that this seemingly innocuous change to the aesthetic environment of their neighbourhood signified, to outside forces, that the area was investment-ready.

Displacement is almost always happening on many levels at once. While rising rents and building conversions are physically displacing some, those who remain (for however long) are experiencing cultural displacement as the look, feel, sound, and smell of the neighbourhood changes and becomes unfamiliar. Some might try to console themselves and others with the idea that gentrification via the sensory environment is a softer, less-violent form of displacement. Unfortunately, that is far from the truth, as these "harmless" changes are often enforced through overtly violent practices.

MOBILIZING STATE VIOLENCE

Gentrifiers are able to weaponize the changes they want to see in "their" neighbourhoods by using the police to address issues such as noise, loitering, games, or other activities they interpret as unpleasant or disorderly. An unhoused person in Toronto's Parkdale neighbourhood told researchers:

> When the Gladstone and the Drake [boutique hotels] finished, that's when everything started happening bad. If I walk this area from nine o'clock in the morning until nine o'clock at night, I can guarantee you, guarantee you without a doubt, I will be stopped at least five times a day. I'm talking handcuffed, searched, put up against the car. Sometimes put under phony arrest, just so that they can throw me in the back of the cop car.[33]

This kind of harassment represents an implicit accord between the police and gentrifiers: by needlessly interfering with people experiencing homelessness, police perform their role as protectors of white middle-classness.

Research has shown that as neighbourhoods gentrify, particularly with white newcomers, calls to 311 (a non-emergency municipal services line) about issues like noise increase substantially. For local bar and restaurant owners, this is more than a nuisance: it often results in fines, harassment of patrons, and threats that they might lose their licences. In New York, the NYPD's "MARCH" project—multi-agency response to community hot spots—is viewed by many as a way of targeting less-desirable businesses and activities in gentrifying neighbourhoods.[34]

Long-time residents are suddenly policed for everything from playing board games on the block to listening to their car stereos. Harlem resident Ramon Hernandez told a Buzzfeed reporter his neighbourly sidewalk domino games were being watched by the police: "It makes me feel bad. I've been living here for more than forty years."[35] Communities targeted by over-policing have long known what gentrification scholars are now beginning to name: that the police act as "shock troops" of gentrification and displacement, enforcing city- and corporate-led development strategies through tactics that lead to the removal of working-class and racialized residents.[36]

In their *People's History of Detroit*, Mark Jay and Philip Conklin argue that the plan to "recapitalize" Detroit uses an explicit law-and-order agenda involving both city police and private security to reassure potential employers that the city is safe.[37] Quicken Loans, the largest mortgage lender in the US, has been at the forefront of this strategy, partnering with police and private security to ensure constant surveillance of the city. This facilitates the further criminalization of poor people and people of colour. Mass incarceration is one way to continue to hollow out inner-city neighbourhoods and prime them for gentrification.

As we well know, calling the police for minor concerns can lead to lethal consequences, especially for people of colour, those with mental illness or disabilities, people experiencing homelessness, and queer and trans people. The murder of Alejandro (Alex) Nieto in March 2014 by police in San Francisco after white newcomers to his Latinx neighbourhood called police while he ate a burrito in a park is just one heartbreaking case of the fatal violence of gentrification. Reporting on the story, Rebecca Solnit noted that the young, white tech workers who considered Nieto suspicious and called 911 mistook his 49ers jacket for gang colours.[38] When the 911 caller's dog went after Nieto's burrito, Nieto reached for his work-issued Taser. Despite being the victim of aggression from the dog, Nieto was killed by police less than five minutes later.

Solnit describes the sentiment of the community that came together to support Nieto's family as the officers eventually went on trial: "Nieto stood for victims of police brutality and for a Latino community that felt imperilled by gentrification, by the wave of evictions and the people who regarded them as menaces and intruders in their own neighbourhood."

In March 2020, Breonna Taylor was murdered by police while sleeping in her home in Louisville, Kentucky, as police implemented a no-knock warrant. In the wake of this egregious killing, lawyers for Taylor's family allege that the raid was part of a "Louisville police department operation to clear out a block in western Louisville that was part of a major gentrification make-over."[39] Their filing argues that the city has been trying to clear certain "hold-out" residents from a particular block, including a former boyfriend of Taylor's: "The origin of Breonna's home being raided by police starts with a political need to clear out a street for a large real estate development project."[40]

Urban studies scholar Henry-Louis Taylor Jr. calls killings like Breonna Taylor's part of a "distinct genre of racially motivated police aggression, harassment and violence that has emerged over the past two decades" in areas targeted for gentrification.[41] He notes:

> Many of the high-profile killings of Black men in America have two things in common. Rayshard Brooks, George Floyd, Freddie Gray, Elijah McClain and Alton Sterling were all killed in gentrification pressure zones for low-level crimes—sleeping in a car, passing a $20 counterfeit bill, running away from police, walking erratically and selling CDs.

The scholar claims that in this context, it is clear that white property values matter more than Black lives.

Policing and military actions are also deployed in cities in the global south, where raids of poor and informal settlements are often connected to efforts to "clean up" the city in advance of spectacular global events, such as the Olympics, the FIFA World Cup, or a World's Fair. In Brazil, military action in the favelas around Rio leading up to the Olympics and World Cup was widely reported.[42] Although authorities claim to be cracking down on criminal activity, these actions endanger the lives, homes, and livelihoods of residents and may be precursors to larger-scale clearance efforts.

Some refer to these efforts as "mass evictions" or "mega-displacement" events designed to clear city space for urban renewal or mega-projects that are not meant to serve the poor.[43] These evictions are deeply disruptive in contexts where there may be little in the way of resettlement rights and a lack of essential services available outside the city.

COLONIZATION AND ONGOING DISPLACEMENT

These forms of state violence have a deep history, one that we can trace to the violent displacement of Indigenous and colonized peoples from their lands through the centuries-long processes of European colonization. While it is tempting to de-link these forms of displacement, Indigenous and colonized or formerly colonized[44] people do not experience colonial conquest and gentrification as separate events.[45] As observed earlier, Indigenous people push back against the ideas that gentrification is a "new" form of colonization and that colonization is a good metaphor for gentrification, given that so many continue to live under and within "old" forms of colonialism that have never disappeared.

In Vancouver's Downtown Eastside, where many Indigenous people struggle with homelessness, poverty, addiction, mental health issues, and the ongoing trauma of colonialism, Indigenous women identify gentrification as a threat to the little stability the service-rich neighbourhood provides. In the collaboratively written "Red Women Rising" report from the Downtown Eastside Women's Centre, Indigenous women recount the challenge of finding safe and suitable housing in a context where "the rich are moving in and we're getting pushed out."[46] On top of this, discrimination against Indigenous women is common:

> There is so much discrimination against Indigenous women looking for housing. I get asked questions like if I have a criminal record or if I drink. I see so much housing being built down here that's condos, but what about social housing for us? It's getting cold and people get sick and die on the streets.[47]

Given that ongoing colonialism has created the violent conditions under which so many Indigenous women are pulled into and kept in spaces like the Downtown Eastside, it is not hard to understand gentrification-induced displacement as yet another manifestation of colonial conquest. For many Indigenous women, however, the violence of displacement goes further than un-homing. Indeed, settler colonialism is much more than a process of displacement; it is also a process of replacement designed to destroy Indigenous people—physically, culturally, spiritually, politically.[48]

Canada's National Inquiry on Missing and Murdered Indigenous Women and Girls called the rates of death and disappearance of women a genocide.[49] Gentrification is one pathway through which this state violence proceeds. Already a highly over-policed zone, gentrification surrounding and infiltrating the Downtown Eastside gives police added opportunities for street checks, fines, arrests, use of force, and detention: "I don't like the cops. I got beat up for nothing. They should do what they have to do instead of being crooked ass."[50]

This activity drags Indigenous women into a criminal justice system that is egregiously stacked against them and is also a source of violence and psychological trauma. Thus, it is important to connect displacement to the forceful erasure of Indigenous presence, power, and sovereignty in settler colonial states, as it continues, in its own particular guise, the destruction of Indigenous communities.

In Sydney, Australia, the historic Redfern Aboriginal community, known locally as The Block, serves as a site of resistance to colonization and ongoing struggles for space and self-determination.[51] As gentrification proceeded in neighbouring areas, geographer Wendy Shaw argued that the racialized "othering" of The Block accelerated through media discourse, positioning the area and its residents as criminal, failed, doomed, and sick. This narrative drew on centuries of racist colonial representations of Aboriginal people in order to facilitate the displacement of the community to allow gentrification to spread.

Discursive tactics of displacement are layered on a much deeper, structural foundation of private property and capitalism that continues settler domination and control of urban space. Urban scholar Liza Kim Jackson argues that gentrification in settler colonial cities like Toronto is an extension of colonial logics. She observes that "an individualized sense of spatial and moral entitlement" among gentrifiers extends beyond their own property lines to include streets, parks, and other urban areas. This entitlement gives gentrifiers, and the city more broadly, the impetus to securitize through "neighbourhood watch-style sociality, the denigration of and infringement on low-income public and private spaces, and demands for surveillance and heavy policing that contribute to the vulnerability and further marginalization of poor, racialized, Indigenous, and disabled inhabitants of the city."[52]

The accumulation of wealth and property through gentrification and the displacement it entails is very much taken for granted as a norm, and even as something good, in western capitalist society. Although numerous scholars have challenged this from a Marxist perspective, we also have to challenge it from an anti-colonial perspective that sees gentrification as incompatible with decolonization.

PROPERTY RULES

While colonial property norms extend and facilitate displacement through long-standing ownership practices and regimes of private property, there is a wide array of what we might call "techniques of property" that are used to produce displacement. Some are not new, while others have evolved in line with digital technologies and platforms. And some are merely modern manifestations of old practices of property theft from marginalized communities. What connects these techniques is their reliance on capitalist, colonial notions of property, as well as their effects: they all produce a traumatic un-homing for those displaced.

Scholarship on eviction has been grappling with the complexity of both the techniques of eviction and its effects on people, neighbourhoods, and cities. As geographer Alexander Baker contends, "the moment of being physically removed is just one in a long set of processes that constitute eviction."[53] Furthermore, eviction has effects that extend far beyond this moment. It is also more complicated than the relationship between a landlord and a renter, as a variety of local and global actors, individuals and state forces, governments and corporations, participate in and influence eviction processes.

Eviction is clearly facilitated by the inequality in property rights between owners and renters, the balance of which has, in neoliberal times, tipped even further in favour of owners. This power is further consolidated as those who control property draw on a constantly evolving set of techniques to accomplish eviction.

Popular discourse has us thinking about eviction as a last-resort tactic used by landlords to get rid of problem tenants, including those who do not or cannot pay rent, who destroy property, or who use the property for illegal activities. However, the profit potential generated by gentrification has created another set of reasons for eviction that have nothing to do with the tenants themselves and everything to do with taking advantage of red-hot property markets to either drive up rents or sell property at a profit.

Without tenant-related reasons to evict, property owners turn to a set of loopholes in tenancy laws. These vary from jurisdiction to jurisdiction, but some of the more widely cited examples include legislation that allows eviction for renovations (known as "reno-viction"), converting the property to single-family occupancy, or renting to a family member.

Owners also make use of subjective and shifting understandings of tenant problems, include nuisance laws, in order to come up with creative reasons to start eviction proceedings. These are particularly effective in targeting families with young children, who cannot help causing noise and occasional damage and disturbances—for example, pulling a fire alarm.[54]

As noted earlier, women who call 911 for domestic abuse can be labelled nuisances. Owners might also draw on zoning laws that prohibit certain property uses to evict people by claiming they are running unauthorized home businesses if, for instance, they are doing family members' hair and nails in their kitchens. In particularly deplorable cases, landlords have called or threatened to call immigration enforcement officials about tenants they suspect are undocumented.[55]

What eviction produces for those affected by it is a hard-to-break cycle of un-homing, as eviction makes it more and more difficult to secure housing. Homelessness is one outcome; hopelessness, depression, and trauma are others.[56] Tyler Marks, evicted with his family in North Carolina, recalled the despair of losing his home: "Four years of memories had to be left behind [. . .] It's like someone having their thumb on your life [. . .] and they can destroy it in a second."[57]

Of course, eviction is more likely to affect some groups than others: women are more likely to face eviction than men, especially Black and Latinx women; people of colour are more likely to face eviction than white people.[58] For many, it is one more link in a chain of historical processes of displacement and dispossession that have affected their families or communities for decades and beyond.

Landlords are not the only property villains out there. Deed theft is a rising crime, in which fraudsters deceive or coerce home-owners "into signing forms that transfer ownership of a property. In many cases, a homeowner is made to believe the documents involve some type of financial assistance, but in fact turn out to be the property deed."[59] These con artists often target Black and/or senior homeowners in rapidly gentrifying neighbourhoods, as the *New York Times* suggested in a report on this crime in Brooklyn—where about 45 percent of all deed fraud complaints in New York originate. Christie Peale, executive director of the Center for N.Y.C. Neighborhoods, notes: "By the time a homeowner realizes what has happened, the home may have already been sold or mort-gaged multiple times."

Fraudsters look for homeowners who, despite having good equity in their homes, are cash-strapped due to rising property taxes and maintenance bills. They also choose neighbourhoods where homes can be quickly flipped for a good profit. Homeowners, once they realize what has happened, can have a difficult time proving they were defrauded, rather than simply being regretful over a "bad deal." This can lead to years of legal battles.

As one victim, waiting over five years for her property to be returned, told the *Times*, "We were living the American dream [. . .] This is a house that your ancestors worked for. They came from nothing." It seems that even the supposed security of home ownership is not enough to protect some from underhanded displacement processes.

ENVIRONMENTAL DISPLACEMENT

As a reminder, my research in Chicago's Little Village was interested in the aftermath of decades-long environmental justice struggles that had seen some forward progress. Activists were successful in their campaigns to create a new park on a Superfund site, to establish a community garden on a vacant lot that had been used for illegal dumping, and in shutting down the Crawford coal-fired power plant.

However, the potential greening of Little Village might be a harbinger of gentrification and displacement for the low-income, Latinx community. I wanted to know whether the community was worried about what has been called environmental gentrification: gentrification that occurs as areas that have been heavily industrial, polluted, and lacking in green space get cleaned up and greened through a variety of environmental initiatives.[60] Research into what happens after sites like the power plant are shut down has rarely shown that local communities benefit from a "greenwave," despite their ardent efforts to combat environmental racism and improve the environmental quality of their neighbourhoods.

Environmental clean-up can unfortunately lead to decreased housing affordability in nearby neighbourhoods.[61] For example, adjacent to the widely acclaimed High Line Park in New York City—an ecological redevelopment initiative to create a park on a defunct elevated railroad track—property values have increased by over 100 percent and new property development has taken off.[62] Communities should not have to choose between pollution, poverty, and disinvestment on the one hand, and opening up to capital, redevelopment, and gentrification on the other.[63]

Without attention to the potential for environmental gentrification and displacement, however, much-needed ecological improvements can end up benefiting the hearts, lungs, and bank accounts of gentrifiers and developers. Those who suffered the effects of diesel fumes, contaminated water, and a lack of green space might be displaced into equally or more polluted areas in search of affordability. Even if some people are not physically displaced, questions remain around who gets to enjoy these green amenities and for what uses.

If new white neighbours are going to report a Black family's barbecue on the Nextdoor app or call the police on Mexican youth playing soccer in the park, these racialized residents could find themselves effectively displaced from green space. Admittedly, environmental gentrification is hard to push back against. While protesting a new luxury high-rise seems reasonable, no one fights against environmental improvements. It is the knock-on effects that need to be carefully considered.

In an age of accelerating climate change, impacts on the natural environment are shaping urban land uses and processes more overtly. A 2021 poll of Americans by Redfin, a real estate brokerage, found that a majority of those considering moving were factoring climate risk into their housing decisions, especially people living near coastal areas.[64] This points to the likelihood that housing prices in areas least impacted by climate change will skyrocket, creating a climate-induced gentrification.

For example, in Miami, lower-income, inland neighbourhoods are seeing gentrification as people want to move farther from coastlines with rising sea levels. Those who cannot afford property or rents in lower-risk areas are faced with displacement as their previously undesirable neighbourhoods (lacking coveted sea views and beach access) are suddenly in hot demand. They will have to choose between affordability and relative climate safety, at least until insurance rates make even lower-cost housing out of reach as the risks of flood, fire, and storm damage multiply.

Elements of nature itself, including specific flora and fauna as well as larger ecosystems, are displaced by gentrification. Recognizing this is not meant to detract from the focus on human-centred effects of gentrification by making a cute squirrel into the new face of displacement. Rather, it is in acknowledgement that human and non-human beings and places exist in relationship with one another and are implicated and affected by processes such as gentrification in intertwining ways.

Geographers Phil Hubbard and Andrew Brooks consider "how urbanisation impacts on non-human animals, how city dwellers react to animals in their midst and how animals are objectified in urban planning processes."[65] They note that particular animal and bird species are more likely to be viewed as pests and targeted in gentrifying areas, including rats, rabbits, racoons, pigeons, crows, seagulls, and stray or uncollared dogs and cats. Gentrifiers and local councils or BIAs may outfit the urban environment with anti-pest architecture such as spikes to prevent birds roosting, even in trees, as happened in Bristol in 2017. Intensified efforts to catch or kill other "pests" are rolled out. These creatures are viewed as "obstacles to clean and 'green' gentrification."[66]

In contrast, other species are cultivated and cared for as part of symbolic upscaling practices aligned with current trends and causes. For example, urban honeybees are "increasingly depicted as charismatic microfauna" in need of protection, and who also contribute to a culture of artisanal food and personal care products made with honey.[67] As writer Fahim Amir notes, roof-top beehives are a way for trendy cultural institutions to heighten their appeal, while also providing new products for sale in the gift shop.[68] The ways that we differentially value certain kinds of flora and fauna shape what kinds of non-human displacements will be tolerated or even promoted.

Back in Little Village, the community's efforts to ensure that the former site of the power plant would be redeveloped in a way that did not contribute to pollution or to gentrification have not, so far, been successful. Hilco Redevelopment Partners, a private company that, notably, botched the demolition of the smokestack and coated the whole neighbourhood in heavy dust, is redeveloping the site into a massive redistribution centre for companies like Target.[69] Although the warehouse work will provide jobs above minimum wage, environmental justice activists are concerned that the centre will bring even more diesel truck traffic to the area, contributing to air pollution yet again.

Environmental gentrification is perhaps not an imminent threat to Little Village. However, pollution can also be seen as a vector of displacement itself. Some residents may be compelled to move to protect their health; others will stay and face the un-homing effects of having their communities rendered less inhabitable, less human, through processes that expose them to disproportionate harm and premature death.

CRISIS DISPLACEMENT: COVID-19

The systemic inequalities in exposure to environmental harms and benefits are mirrored in the systemic inequalities in health and economic risks that have played out so viciously during the Covid-19 pandemic. Geographers and others have noted that where you live and work is a good predictor of several inequities: whether you are an essential worker who has to go to a workplace daily; whether you need to ride crowded public transportation; whether you live in high-density housing; whether you have access to testing sites; and whether you have access to vaccinations, to name a few. As a major contributor to urban inequalities, gentrification is implicated in these issues. Gentrification has also been able to draw on the destabilization caused by the pandemic to accelerate certain kinds of displacement.

What some are calling "Covid capitalism" is generating a set of pressures and processes that, while not entirely new, are indicative of the priorities of the (eventual) post-Covid city.[70] Urban scholar David Madden highlights the protection of property owners at the expense of tenants and workers. Although early initiatives to freeze rent and evictions seemed poised to help those who lost their jobs or faced precarious housing situations, these programs were mostly short-lived and inadequate. In the US, Missouri Representative Cori Bush had to camp out on the steps of the Capitol with housing activists for several days in order to compel the Biden Administration to extend the eviction moratorium in August 2021.[71] Meanwhile, programs to assist property owners continued.

The tenets of disaster capitalism are also operating, whereby "investment firms are looking to gorge on distressed assets and real estate debt."[72] In places with high numbers of fatalities, one might wonder whether a process similar to that described by scholar and activist Sarah Schulman in the wake of AIDS-related deaths is happening: as tenants pass away, are landlords taking advantage of untimely death to increase rents and sell off property?[73]

There have also been startling racial disparities in the

distribution of pandemic aid programs, to the extent that they have been referred to as "modern redlining."[74] In Los Angeles, for example, the multi-billion-dollar Paycheck Protection Program (PPP), designed to help small businesses stay afloat, has loaned money to businesses in majority-white areas at twice the rate of majority-Latinx areas, one and a half times the rate of businesses in majority-Black areas, and over one times the rate in Asian areas.

The investigation by journalists at *Reveal* also found racial disparities in New York, Dallas, San Francisco, San Diego, Las Vegas, and Phoenix.[75] Despite applying, minority-owned businesses had less success getting approved for loans. For others, the onerous process and need to have a relationship with a particular bank were major barriers. Just as redlining denied loans to Black and racialized neighbourhoods decades ago, the PPP is reproducing inequalities in access to credit that will ultimately displace many minority-owned businesses for good, while white-owned businesses receive a boost.

The shift to virtual communication tools for eviction hearings is also proving detrimental to tenants' rights. In both Canada and the United States, housing advocates have found that remote hearings systematically disadvantage renters, who are already fighting an uphill battle as property owners have much more power in these situations. Judges mute tenants; hearings can last as little as thirty seconds; tenants in difficult economic circumstances lack access to stable Internet, laptops, and webcams; only lawyers can file documents online; and multiple tenants may be on the same call, leading to confusion.[76]

Legal aid clinics in Canada report that the hearings are rushed and lawyers for tenants are given little time to prepare. Hearings are also scheduled simultaneously on multiple calls, meaning lawyers cannot be present at all of their clients' hearings. It is ironic, note advocates, that the alleged health-related reasons for holding hearings remotely are not considered enough justification for not evicting people.

Crises like the pandemic form a context where displacement can be accelerated, accomplished through new practices, or simply allowed to happen as factors like job loss, death, and income precarity take their toll. Given the alacrity with which disaster capitalism takes advantage of moments of disruption to enhance privatization and commodification, it would be naive to think that gentrification will not, at least in some places, move forward quite efficiently. The pandemic may also diminish resources and opportunities for resistance, a fact that will no doubt also be taken advantage of. At the time of writing, the outcomes of the pandemic in terms of displacement are not fully known; however, it is quite possible that we are in the midst of a mass displacement event.

WHY CAN'T WE HAVE NICE THINGS?

Displacement and its effects are clearly complicated, especially when we broaden the story of displacement beyond physical displacement to include many forms of un-homing. Moreover, multiple forms of displacement are likely tangled up together across both time and space. Despite the challenges of this complexity, it is necessary to take this perspective in order to better comprehend how gentrification affects people.

The Harlem senior who stays in her apartment but is no longer greeted by friendly faces on the streets, and who knows that her children and grandchildren will not be able to afford to live nearby, is experiencing everyday social displacement and an intergenerational temporal displacement. The effects of this can only really be understood by listening to people and taking their experiences of loss seriously.

The insidious nature of everyday, sensory, and social forms of displacement is a major reason to be wary of the "nice things" that gentrification tempts us with: a cute café, a craft brewery, a green river walkway. Who is against craft beer and clean waterways? Proponents of gentrification argue that working-class and racialized communities are entitled to have nice places to shop, eat, rest, and stroll, especially when they have been denied those things for so long by processes like disinvestment and redlining.

No one is arguing that point. What we have to recognize is that none of these changes happen in a vacuum and that they are always imbued with meanings shaped by ideas about race, class, gender, age, and sexuality. Something as simple as the seating design of that café can communicate strong messages about who is welcome and who is not, as can the decor, the menu, and of course, the prices.[77] As one Manchester senior told researchers: "Quite frankly all the little eateries around Chorlton are quite expensive. But I might not want a panini. I might not even know how to say panini."[78]

Not every change to a neighbourhood is an inevitable engine of displacement. Most people do not expect their communities or cities to stagnate. But, to paraphrase philosopher of power Michel Foucault, not everything is bad, but everything is dangerous. Thus, we have to ask hard questions about "nice things."

Who was consulted? Who are the intended patrons or users? What concrete actions are being taken to ensure that long-time residents are welcome? That craft brewery could, for example, include multilingual signs and staff, have a range of price options, be physically accessible, and offer its space for free or at low cost to community groups for monthly meetings or events. While these actions, and indeed one business alone, cannot stop gentrification in its tracks, they might mitigate some of the more subtle forms of displacement that deprive even those residents who stay of a feeling of belonging.

7

GENTRIFICATION IS A METAPHOR

In anticipation of her return to headliner status at the Coachella festival in 2018, music superstar Beyoncé announced she was going vegan to prepare for what would become the iconic "Homecoming" performances.[1] Although her veganism was temporary as part of her efforts to get into the physical condition necessary to perform after giving birth to twins in 2017, she joined other high-profile celebrities who have publicly embraced a plant-based diet. Names include Benedict Cumberbatch, Bill Clinton, Natalie Portman, Madonna, Ariana Grande, Venus Williams, and James Cameron.[2] It seems that veganism has well and truly left behind its stereotypical association with pale, protein-starved college students.

The transformation of veganism's image is an example of how something—a practice, a style, a cultural item—can go from obscure and ridiculed to mainstream and desirable. Some might even say that veganism has been gentrified. Gentrification has come to be used as a metaphor for processes of mainstreaming, commodification, appropriation, and upscaling that are not necessarily or directly connected to cities. In this story about gentrification, gentrification stands in for any sort of change that pulls a thing or a practice out of its original context and increases its popularity, priciness, and profit-making potential.

Even though this book is about the primarily urban transformations that we call gentrification, it is important to explore this wider use of the term. It shows that the story of gentrification has been useful in ways that stretch beyond the original definition. The concept of gentrification provides a critical framing for social and cultural processes that some might dismiss as neutral or natural hybridizations.

Gentrification encapsulates an understanding of power that belies the idea that all cultural metamorphoses, like mainstreaming or commodification, are inevitable and benevolent. Moreover, as the examples illustrate, there is good reason to believe that these changes in the cultural realm *are* linked to actual on-the-ground gentrification processes. As we have seen throughout this book, the social and cultural world is intertwined with the economic forces that propel gentrification and displacement.

MAINSTREAMING: MAKING POPULAR

When I got my first tattoo in 1995, I was careful to ensure it would be easily hidden from my parents. By the early 2000s, however, my mom was sporting a freshly inked blackbird on her lower back. Today, no one even blinks at the multiple, prominent tattoos that I and countless others proudly wear, unless it is to ask who the artist is and how to find them.

The "gentrification of tattoos" expresses the idea that tattoos have gone from counterculture to mainstream. While tattoos have ancient and revered histories in many cultures, modern western culture linked them with biker gangs, prison inmates, circus performers, and punk rockers for many decades. Sociologists Karen Halnon and Saundra Cohen note that tattoos started to morph into artful adornments rather than rebellious statements around the early 1990s.[3] In the 2000s, tattoo-centred reality television shows like *LA Ink* and its multiple spin-offs spawned tattoo artist celebrities like Kat Von D, who started a global makeup company and has a burgeoning music career. Tattoos are visible on celebrities, politicians, athletes, and professionals in all fields.

With this cultural shift came a professionalization of the industry in order to make the presence of tattoo parlours palatable in urban neighbourhoods.[4] Training, hygiene, safety, artistry, comfort, and professional reputation were emphasized as part of the process of gentrifying this once-derided trend. Today, it is not hard to find boutique-like tattoo studios in trendy neighbourhoods.

Describing tattooing as gentrified highlights what people mean when they use the term outside of the urban context. For one, gentrification in the cultural realm often involves taking something that is associated with a marginalized group or lifestyle and repackaging it, thus reframing its meaning. Halnon and Cohen describe this as a "middle-class invasion" of cultural terrain that was once forbidden.[5] Moreover, tattoos, symbols that used to detract from one's cultural capital in most aspects of "normal" life in western culture (such as getting a job), have become a positive form of cultural capital used to signal a variety of aesthetic, political, and interpersonal commitments.

The mainstreaming of subversive symbols and practices is all around us. Having immersed myself in multiple seasons of *RuPaul's Drag Race* in order to stay entertained during the pandemic, it is easy to see why some describe drag as gentrified.[6] The global success of the show, which has multiple spin-offs, live shows, a DragCon convention, merchandise, and a record-setting number of Emmy awards, has nudged drag closer to the mainstream. As the seasons of the reality competition show have progressed over more than a decade, the contestants' clothes, wigs, and makeup have become more expensive; it is now standard for the drag queens to wear custom looks created by professional fashion designers.

Just as actual gentrification made living in inner-city areas mainstream again for the white middle class, gentrification in the cultural realm often refers to bringing the subversive, unusual, and underground into popular culture. The link between these two phenomena is more than metaphorical, though. The cultural symbols and practices that become gentrified can feed into and off of urban gentrification.

As both tattoos and drag, for example, have become more mainstream, they have been professionalized, upscaled, and have generated a host of associated spaces and industries that touch down in cities. Both tattoos and drag now have multi-day conventions in big cities. The popularity of live drag performances and the celebrity status of *Drag Race* contestants is part of the mainstreaming and gentrification of queer spaces in cities. Drag shows draw bigger, higher-paying, and straight audiences to gay bars that once served a lower-income queer community. Tattoo parlours are no longer hidden away in the "bad" part of town. Now they are prominent sites on gentrified retail strips.

As discussed previously, certain kinds of businesses, aesthetics, and even people themselves serve as signs of gentrification. These signs tell some people that they are less welcome. They inform others (and capital) that this space is now ready for them. Of course, tattoos and drag are not responsible for gentrification. However, it is useful to notice how the mainstreaming of certain parts of culture is reflected in urban landscapes that are being gentrified. In this way, using gentrification as a metaphor for mainstreaming is effective in drawing our attention to these connections.

COMMODIFICATION: MAKING MONEY

What do you need in order to practise yoga? According to the ancient Yoga Sutra, nothing more than a patch of earth to sit on. Today, however, the list of spaces, equipment, clothing, and educational materials that you "need" is both extensive and expensive. My current home practice involves the following: a mat, travel mat, yoga towel, two blocks, yoga strap, leggings (yes, those leggings), sports bras, and a monthly subscription to a fitness app with everything from classes in Spanish to a Justin Bieber-themed yoga flow. I have easily spent thousands of dollars over the years to move through a set of poses never even mentioned in those ancient texts.

Yoga can be considered gentrified because it has been highly commodified—turned into a set of goods and services that can be bought and sold—as it has been westernized. The ubiquity of yoga and its associated products and spaces is relatively new. Cultural historians suggest that interest in yoga in Europe and North America did not begin until well into the twentieth century, at which time yoga did not resemble the practices and aesthetics that we are familiar with today. Originally a meditative practice without movement, the development of the physical "asana" (yoga poses) came later and was itself heavily influenced by eastern European physical health practices such as calisthenics and gymnastics.[7]

From the 1960s through the 1980s, yoga in the west was an alternative practice, associated with West Coast, new-age spirituality. It was not until the 1990s that yoga began to go mainstream, experiencing a massive upsurge in popularity, especially in North America. It is estimated that Americans spend upwards of five billion dollars a year on yoga.[8] Yoga's transformation from a niche spiritual practice that cost next to nothing into a massive industry has been accompanied by an explosion of consumer products that range from basic plastic mats to luxury yoga retreats. Classes, clothing, gear, apps, books, videos, magazines, diets, travel, celebrity teachers, and teacher training are just some of the things a yoga practitioner can drop their hard-earned cash on.

Gentrification works as a metaphor for the commodification of yoga because it alludes to a process where something that is seen as having little monetary value gets pulled into the consumer marketplace and starts generating a lot of money, for some. Commodification is happening constantly in capitalist economies, where companies are always looking for ways to generate income from things that were previously un- or under-commodified.

The so-called "gentrification of parenting" is another example.[9] The growth in industries selling specialized products for babies, kids, and parents is incredible. Boomer parents would not even recognize half the products on a typical baby registry today. From devices to warm up your baby wipes to a "genie" for diaper disposal, the list of "essentials" that new parents are expected to have has gotten longer and more expensive. Parents are encouraged to not only have the right products, but to have the right brands (preferably Swedish), too.

The commodification of yoga and parenting also have urban effects. They can both be read as signs of gentrification. A boutique baby store and a yoga studio are likely to signal gentrification as readily as a Starbucks. The arrival of these kinds of businesses is a response to the presence—or hoped-for presence—of white, middle-class households who engage in commodified cultural practices as part of the act of distinguishing their classed and raced identities. These particular practices—yoga and intensive parenting—shore up a modern, aspirational white femininity that is tied to having a certain kind of body and fulfilling the white, liberal feminist maxim of "doing it all" in parenting, personal care, and work.[10]

In my past work on embodiment and gentrification, I suggested that gentrification involves the condensation of a set of socio-spatial practices that mark and situate bodies within a web of relations around gender, race, class, (post)coloniality, ability, and sexuality.[11] Practices like yoga and gentrified parenting are marked on the bodies of those who practise them, and in turn those bodies send messages about the spaces in which they belong.

Businesses and spaces that reproduce the commodification of different kinds of practices, whether those are yoga, parenting, or any number of others, may be part of neighbourhood gentrification processes as they raise the overall cost of participating in community life and perhaps displace other, more affordable, spaces. Often, commodified practices become so through a process of westernization that tends to detach culture from its original context in order to make it palatable and desirable to white, middle-class people. As we discussed in previous chapters, working-class and racialized communities often experience this as a form of theft. Yoga is a clear example of what is often called cultural appropriation. Gentrification has close ties, both metaphorical and literal, with this concept as well.

APPROPRIATION: MAKING MINE

Step into just about any yoga class in North America and the next hour of your life will be filled with sights, smells, and sounds that are meant to evoke yoga's Hindu origins: incense, Sanskrit, lotus flowers, mandalas, concepts from the Yoga Sutra, chanting, kirtan music, and of course, the ever-popular invocation of "namaste" at the end of class. Step out of that yoga class and chances are you will be no more familiar with the cultural origins and context of yoga than you were before, but you might feel very entitled to believe that you are. This is how appropriation works, and why some use the term gentrification as a metaphor: it involves claiming and assimilating the cultural property or space of another group and making it yours.

Cultural appropriation refers to the use of symbols, food, clothing, practices, music, art, and any other aspect of culture by a member of another culture without permission, attribution, or understanding. Of course, cultures have long been shared and hybridized. It is practically impossible to assert cultural purity. Nonetheless, we can certainly recognize that not all pieces of our cultures, religions, and languages are as available for open use by others.

Métis legal scholar Chelsea Vowel notes that all cultures have features that exist along a continuum from unrestricted to restricted.[12] In most cases things like food are fairly unrestricted. Clothing styles and music might be somewhere in the middle. At the restricted end, however, lie those components of culture that are more sacred, honorific, or related to specific rituals and rites of passage. All cultures have items and practices that are more significant than others, more core to the identity, history, and particular struggles of a group. Yet, people routinely disregard or remain ignorant of the different meanings and values of, or protocols and responsibilities around, cultural objects and practices, considering them free for their own use. In the case of restricted, sacred, or deeply meaningful aspects of culture, their (mis)use by outsiders can be perceived as insulting, colonizing, and as a form of theft.

Appropriation is not limited to the intercultural sphere. Ultimately, it is an exercise in power where one group is able to take over something important to another. In 2019, the term "mentrification" was coined by Tumblr user @thelilithnoir to describe what happens when "the history of female achievement and participation" is written over by men.[13] The original Tumblr conversation was about the lack of acknowledgement of the role of women in cementing the popularity of the original *Star Trek* series: women were the show's first significant fan base. Similarly, the Beatles were made global superstars by the devoted girls and women who first recognized their greatness. How did these two cultural phenomena go from fluffy, girly, silly, and frivolous to the domain of serious nerds and fandoms? The answer is, of course, when men started liking them.

Can men not join the fun? Well, instead of just joining the fun, they come to dominate every conversation and substitute their expertise and opinions for women's. All too often, women's original contribution to a fandom is completely erased. Their ongoing attempts to engage are ridiculed. New female fans are met with condescension, if not hostility and derision. Women become trespassers in an area they once belonged.

As *Guardian* writer Van Badham points out, mentrification is not limited to the realms of television and music. She cites women's scientific contributions to fields like computing and aerospace as areas where women's innovations have either been forgotten or claimed by men. Rosalind Franklin's discovery of the structure of DNA, only for it to be claimed by Nobel-winners James Watson and Francis Crick, is a particularly well-known example. Mentrification stands in contrast to feminization, where jobs, areas of culture, and practices once the domain of men—like teaching and clerical work, for example—become undervalued and stigmatized once they are associated with women and femininity.

Gentrification and appropriation are linked in material ways, so it is not surprising that gentrification can, linguistically, stand in for appropriation. In cities, the contributions of marginalized groups to sustaining neighbourhoods, creating vibrant cultures, and developing the economy are often erased as the neighbourhood is primed for white, middle-class newcomers.

In my research on condominium development in Toronto, I found it was common for developers to describe their projects as "building community," "creating a neighbourhood," or "bringing life" into an area.[14] They would rename neighbourhoods, branding them as if they were being created out of thin air. For example, the condominiums built as part of the "revitalization" of the stigmatized Regent Park public housing project were not named after Regent Park. They were named after nearby streets and landmarks that did not conjure up any of the stereotypes so often applied to this decades-old community. While some new residential projects are built outside of pre-existing residential areas, most are located in or adjacent to long-standing communities. So, what exactly is being created, and what is being forgotten?

As a kind of appropriation, gentrification is all about a more powerful group taking over and remaking something in ways that reflect its values, identities, and norms. Whether it is through the appropriation of spaces, community buildings, or aesthetics and culture, gentrification is built on finding ways to take what others have created while simultaneously wiping away their presence, contributions, and history.

Typically, appropriation also involves the commodification of what has been taken through engineering profit-making opportunities. This is particularly egregious when what is being commodified is a sacred symbol or spiritual practice. Even less precious aspects of culture, like food, which is already commodified, can undergo gentrification when they are "upscaled" in order to make them more expensive and exclusive.

UPSCALING: MAKING EXPENSIVE

When Pittsburgh restaurant owner Adam Kucenic, who is white, decided to open a "90s hip hop-themed fried chicken restaurant" in 2017, cries of cultural appropriation and gentrification rang out from the city's Black community. Reporter Brentin Mock describes his own struggle to pinpoint what felt so wrong about this enterprise:

> As an African-American connoisseur of fried chicken and hip hop, I gotta say—I was not personally offended when I first read about this fast-casual food concept. I did have some slight feels, though, that something might be wrong with this, but I had a hard time coming to terms with what exactly that wrong was.[15]

Mock dug deeper into the issue to explore the history of fried chicken as a food once cooked by enslaved people for their masters, before eventually becoming a staple of "soul food," one that, despite its widespread popularity beyond Black communities, is still used as a trope for racist jokes.[16] In other words, fried chicken is not just fried chicken: it is food with a complicated, fraught history. When white people ignore that history and attempt to capitalize from Black culture by appropriating it and upscaling it, it leaves a bad taste in the mouth.

Attempts to gentrify foods like fried chicken typically involve preparing and serving them in ways that raise their prices. I call this "upscaling." Because price is so closely tied to our perceptions of the real value or desirability of an item within a capitalist system, raising prices is also a way of changing the image of an item to make it appeal to different audiences. As price and perceived value rise, items become attractive to more affluent, and often whiter, consumers.

Examples of the upscaling of food are easy to find. Street and bodega goods, typically made with low-cost, fatty, salty, and leftover ingredients, offer quick, convenient, and cheap meals to people in working-class, immigrant, and racialized communities. However, these foods are regularly "discovered" (in a process nicknamed "Columbus syndrome") by white restaurateurs and celebrity chefs who recreate these dishes with expensive and rare versions of the usual ingredients, or serve them in creative and unusual styles.

An example is the New York bodega favourite "chopped cheese" sandwich: chopped-up hamburger patties are fried with onions, coated in American cheese slices, and served on a sandwich bun with various toppings and condiments. In the documentary *Hometown Hero: The Legend of New York's Chopped Cheese*, locals note that after this rather under-the-radar lunch item was featured on an episode of Anthony Bourdain's show *Parts Unknown*, upscale restaurateurs were eager to debut their own versions, only at four times the usual price.[17]

Countless humble, working-class, and cultural foods have experienced upscaling in recent times. Donuts, ice cream, poutine, and of course, cereal are all examples of simple foods that people have found ways to sell at ridiculous prices. Using "artisanal" processes, organic ingredients, or simply creating fancy concoctions like cereal-themed desserts and cocktails can take these items into a whole new realm of exclusivity. People will line up to buy specialty donuts and ice cream, eager for the chance to fork over four or five times the amount of cash for this treat than what they might pay at Dairy Queen or Dunkin' Donuts.

Back in Pittsburgh, the residents of the East Liberty neighbourhood where the white restaurateur was proposing to locate his chicken shop have good reason to be wary of change. The area was a victim of one of the nation's largest urban renewal programs in the 1960s, where neighbourhoods were demolished and replaced by a ring road that disrupted business and led to an era of economic and social decline.[18] In the 2000s, new developments sparked gentrification and fear that displacement would happen all over again in the mostly Black neighbourhood. While one white-owned fried-chicken restaurant would not be either the primary culprit or the nail in the coffin, residents interpreted the move as a signal that as their food was being upscaled and gentrified, so was their community.

The connections among food and gentrification are plentiful. Eating establishments, grocery stores, and food markets have all been considered markers of gentrification when they contribute to the relative upscaling of a neighbourhood in terms of price and aesthetics.[19]

In contrast, a lack of access to affordable, nutritious, or culturally appropriate food is typically a sign of sustained disinvestment in an area, resulting in what the food studies literature has termed "food deserts."[20] There is a strong correlation between food deserts and racialized neighbourhoods, meaning that communities of colour have fewer options and often rely on bodegas, street food vendors, and fast food joints for daily meals. Although this is not ideal from a nutrition standpoint, when these places are pushed out by gentrification, they are not replaced by equally affordable, healthier options. Rather, the combination of high prices, culturally unfamiliar foods, and white gentrifier aesthetics leaves people feeling like their choices have actually narrowed.

One of the ostensibly healthy food trends that is connected to gentrification is veganism. Beyoncé's temporary veganism is part of a larger trend that has seen the plant-based diet elevated and upscaled into a desirable lifestyle. A growing industry of vegan food and personal care products produced by large corporations has replaced the niche and DIY-nature of the stereotypical hippie vegan lifestyle.

"Veganuary" is a new version of the January detox (Drynuary) that encourages people to go vegan for one month. Even fast food restaurants, diners, corner shops, and big chains are offering vegan options. The image of veganism is shifting away from a highly restrictive, ascetic, politicized diet to one that everyday people can enjoy, one that has its own share of our favourite ingredients: fat, sugar, and salt.

Although veganism still accounts for a small percentage of diets worldwide (somewhere between 1 and 4 percent), it does seem to be rising in popularity.[21] The US and UK have apparently seen rates of self-reported veganism increase from four to six times over the last several years. According to the *Economist*, 2019 was "the year of the vegan."[22] A rising awareness of the environmental implications of meat and dairy production has driven much of this shift, but as the image of veganism itself changes, the trend takes on a life of its own, one that may be quite distant from the environmental and ethical concerns that originally propelled it.

Like other food trends, the enhanced social status of veganism has a more direct connection to actual gentrification processes. In Toronto's Parkdale neighbourhood, vegan culture has been at the forefront of a rapacious neighbourhood makeover. "Vegandale" is assertively claiming space in this low-income, immigrant corridor without, it seems, much respect or consultation with the community.

When I first heard the moniker Vegandale, I assumed it was a term of derision being used by those who are pushing back against gentrification in Parkdale. I googled it, and the first hit was for the slick website vegandale.com. The front page copy read: "Vegandale is a mecca for the ethically minded, with the best of vegan food, goods, and services coexisting on one city block." The About page continued:

> This premiere destination for the vegan and vegan curious is the only one of it's [sic] kind, promoting a world where animal exploitation is a thing of the past. With our roots in abolitionism, our unapologetic messaging is the connection between each project we touch.[23]

Given Vegandale's location, I wonder if veganism is not the only thing they have decided to be unapologetic about.

It seems that the arrival of Los Angeles-based vegan chain restaurant Doomie's was a pivotal moment. In a report titled "My Parkdale Is Gone," *Guardian* journalist Murray Whyte calls Doomie's "a particularly aggressive corporate newcomer that saw the opportunity to craft a new identity for Parkdale entirely."[24] While careful to expose the primary role of global investment firms in leading gentrification in Parkdale, Whyte notes that the corporate owners of a host of vegan businesses were strategically rebranding the neighbourhood in ways that felt like a "brutal invasion." Resident Nerupa Somasale tells Whyte:

> It was an erasure of history, and an intentional one [. . .]. They wanted to change a chunk of the neighbourhood in a way that didn't benefit anybody that had lived here for years. It had that feeling: "There's nothing here, so let's just make it into whatever we want."

One would think that invasion and erasure are antithetical to the values of veganism as caring, ethical, and kind. As I continued to scroll through the Vegandale website, I was taken aback by the strong language used to describe their achievements and goals, including "4 cities taken over" and "Zero meat, dairy, bullshit." The list ends with the spurious claim of millions of non-vegans converted. The self-described "mecca for the ethically-minded and hungry"[25] appears to have a narrow conception of to whom their ethical obligations extend.

Although "cruelty-free" is their branding, their "unapologetic" moral stance on veganism seems to offer them a perverse permission to trample over other ethical concerns. Veganism here has been weaponized to justify the spatial takeover of a marginalized community in the name of the "greater good" of saving animals and the planet.

GENTRIFICATION IS ABOUT POWER

In all the examples in this chapter, gentrification works as a metaphor precisely because it keeps a critique of power relations at its centre. Whether we are looking at tattoos, yoga, or bodega foods, the processes by which they get drawn into mainstream culture in ways that make them more expensive, exclusive, white, or all of the above, are power-laden. In the case of appropriation, dominant groups holding more social and economic power claim aspects of the cultures of less-powerful groups and often find ways to profit from this theft. In mainstreaming, the significance of cultural practices and symbols gets diluted or stripped away from the people that made them meaningful to begin with.

Commodification and upscaling invite us to follow the money: who is benefiting financially when low-cost or everyday items and practices are transformed into money-making enterprises? All of these processes work to consolidate existing power relations across colonialism, race, gender, sexuality, and class.

We all know that what is cool today is not likely to remain so for long. Designers, advertisers, artists, influencers, and other tastemakers are always on the hunt for the next trend, wanting to stay on the leading edge of cool. As historian Thomas Frank noted in *The Conquest of Cool*, counterculture is the place from which the next hip sounds and styles are mined, in a process that eventually dims a counterculture's edgy spark and triggers a search for the newest source.[26] Gentrification operates on a similar logic, whether you privilege the cultural or economic side of the story. Developers and property investors are always looking for the next neighbourhood before it becomes cool, in order to maximize their potential gains.

Gentrification's connection to the concept of displacement also links it to appropriation and commodification. Again, displacement occurs across many registers: emotional, interpersonal, intergenerational, and cultural, as well as spatial. When social and cultural practices are lifted out of their original contexts and communities to be altered and commodified by others, a kind of displacement is happening.

Insofar as our cultures are made up of all the tangible and intangible elements that we identify as special and meaningful, the theft, erasure, or perversion of these elements is a form of un-homing. As our ties to those things that make us unique are weakened, we are unmoored and disconnected from our cultural homes. In this way, the story of "gentrification as a metaphor" is a powerful one for allowing communities to speak back to and resist a set of processes that some feel are innocuous and immaterial to people's well-being.

Mainstreaming, appropriation, commodification, and upscaling are part of the actual neighbourhood gentrification happening in so many places. Author Céline Chuang writes about the grief she feels observing the changes in Vancouver's Chinatown in the Downtown Eastside:

> First, it was the hipster coffee shop which had opened directly across from a long-standing single residence occupancy hotel [. . .]. Next, it was the boutique grocery store, complete with a security guard, then, a vegan pie store, a poke restaurant. Meanwhile, the Chinatown I knew was being methodically erased, a shrinking circumference of cheap produce, convenience stores, herbs, and traditional medicine.[27]

Chuang notes that some of the gentrifier businesses have added Chinese characters to their signs; however, their prices remain out of reach to most of the people who live in one of "Canada's poorest postal codes."

As the spaces, foods, sounds, symbols, and practices of people are gentrified, the effect, as Chuang describes it, is an erasure of shared memory. After all, what are cultures if not repositories of memory kept alive through the items, places, and practices that we pass along through the generations? When gentrification and all of the displacement associated with it comes along, it threatens to erode memory by evacuating meaning and history tied to culture and place. Chuang maintains, however, that fierce practices of memory keeping are part of the long-standing resistance strategies of Indigenous people, racialized groups, and immigrant communities who fight to keep history alive and insist on their right to stay put.

Gentrification, metaphorical and otherwise, can seem frustratingly ubiquitous. As hard as it is to find urban areas untouched by gentrification, it is even harder to find elements of culture that have not been affected by commodification or appropriation. But the search for some idea of pure places or pure cultures is less important than turning our focus to tactics of resistance, perseverance, and survival. Power never operates in only one direction. Wherever powerful forces are acting, people are pushing back.

8

GENTRIFICATION IS INEVITABLE

In November 2019, a small group of women in Oakland, California, entered an empty house with the intention to stay until *someone* did *something* to address the acute Bay Area housing crisis. Oakland Moms 4 Housing called attention to rapid gentrification, a problem exacerbated by speculator-owned properties sitting vacant amidst a major housing shortage. As women experiencing, or who had previously experienced, homelessness, the activists were primarily women of colour whose aim was "to reclaim housing for the Oakland community from the big banks and real estate speculators."[1]

In this case, the home was owned by Wedgewood Properties, an investment company that specializes in "distressed residential real estate." Their business practice is, essentially, flipping homes: they buy cheap foreclosed properties, fix them up, and resell them for a large profit. According to an analysis by *NBC Bay Area*, the company is a prolific flipper in the Bay Area and beyond.[2] Wedgewood's initial take on the protest action was that the un-homed women had "stolen" the house.

Supporters of Moms 4 Housing mobilized as notice came that the sheriff's office would be enforcing an eviction order on January 14, 2020. Activists formed a human chain around the house and provided volunteer security. Nonetheless, sheriff's deputies entered the home and removed the protesters, put their furniture out on the curb, and arrested two. Outside, the crowd took cell phone video of the eviction, which quickly circulated on social media.

This relatively small protest attracted wide attention, including from city councillors, some of whom expressed support for the women's claim that housing is a right and that people should not be homeless while properties sit vacant.[3] The combination of media attention, political support, and perhaps a healthy dose of bad public relations for Wedgewood Properties led to a dramatic and unexpected victory: in late January, Wedgewood agreed to give Oakland's Community Land Trust (CLT) the chance to purchase the home at market rate and rehabilitate it themselves. The group of women would then be able to stay permanently.

More recent updates indicate that in consultation with the mayor of Oakland, Wedgewood has pledged, at least verbally, to give the CLT right of first refusal to bid on some fifty homes they currently own and on future properties they acquire. While this represents a success, at least tentatively, the women who occupied the home wonder why they were forced to endure eviction and arrest—not to mention months of antagonism and negative press reports labelling them criminals and trespassers—to pave the way for this deal.

Nonetheless, it has bolstered city- and even state-wide movements to find innovative ways to combat homelessness, displacement, and property speculation in a city where some four thousand people are unhoused and the Black population has declined by 50 percent over the last forty years. The horror of thirty-six deaths in a fire at the Ghost Ship artist collective, an industrial space in the Fruitvale neighbourhood of Oakland that was being used as a live-work space by artists, is still a vivid memory. It serves as a stark reminder that housing for low-income people like artists is increasingly rare, leading many to live in precarious and even life-threatening situations.

At the beginning of this book, I wrote about the problematic idea that gentrification is part of the natural evolution of cities. Even if you do not subscribe to this idea, it is easy to believe the story that gentrification is inevitable. It has been such a juggernaut and so widespread that it seems assured. We hear few stories of resistance and even fewer where communities have prevented, halted, or slowed gentrification. These cases do exist, but they are rarely known outside of their local contexts. Moreover, despite the vast academic literature on gentrification, resistance remains under-studied and under-theorized.[4]

Just as displacement generates debate about how to define and what to measure, so too does resistance. Can it be quantified? Which factors matter when deciding whether gentrification has been slowed: displacement, housing prices, stalled developments, income levels, people's reported satisfaction or dissatisfaction? Certainly not everyone will agree on whether gentrification was successfully halted in any given place, since the degree to which certain changes are welcome or unwelcome is subjective and depends on one's social and economic location. Resistance also comprises a wide range of practices and responses, ranging from symbolic, to direct action, to policy interventions, to actively building new housing alternatives.[5]

There is often a disconnect between experts, like academics, and activists and community organizers who are doing the work as well as producing strategies and recommendations.[6] Their work does not make it into the "legitimate" scholarly literature on gentrification unless a researcher happens to stumble upon it or is already involved in the community. Because of the way we differentially value knowledge produced in formal (institutional) and informal (activist) contexts, the wisdom created by organizers is deemed anecdotal or unverified. Unfortunately, this means that there is likely deep knowledge of how to combat gentrification that simply never makes it into official stories about the process.

Academics also have a tendency to behave as "coroners" who are all-too-ready to declare the end of communities, especially Black communities, as Black geographies scholar Clyde Woods argued. "Reports of the death of African American community life are truly premature," writes Woods, challenging scholars to reflect on the purpose of their work:

> Have the tools of theory, method, instruction, and social responsibility become so rusted that they can only be used for autopsies? Does our research in any way reflect the experiences, viewpoints, and needs of the residents of these dying communities? On the other hand, is the patient really dead? What role are scholars playing in this social triage?[7]

When scholars, planners, developers, policymakers, or the media fall into the habit of allowing gentrification to seem completely unstoppable, it allows us to assume there is no hope for the neighbourhood or its residents. As Woods suggests, some academics seem to find it strangely satisfying to pronounce the death of entire communities or ways of life, as if the end of these was always foreseen. This is a fantasy that no doubt underlies much of the logic of white-supremacist, capitalist thought. In other words, seeing gentrification as inescapable plays nicely into the hands of those who have always wanted those communities dead or gone.

The language used to describe neighbourhoods that are primed for or experiencing the start of gentrification tends to reinforce these "coroner's reports." Geographer Katherine McKittrick offers a pointed analysis of the vocabulary applied to Black spaces, which, she argues, undermines Black claims to place. These claims to place are central to fighting off gentrification and articulating a right to stay put. When they are dismantled, brick by brick and word by word, gentrification and other forces of displacement and dispossession are easily naturalized. McKittrick lays out this problematic vocabulary that, in her description, "damns" the geographies of the Other by rendering them "uninhabitable." The places available for Black life become "geographies described as battlegrounds or as burned, horrific, occupied, sieged, unhealthy, incarcerated, extinct, starved, torn, endangered."[8]

These adjectives begin to render a place "inhuman." When human presence is elided or erased, gentrification and development can proceed via a modern version of *"terra nullius." Terra nullius* refers to the doctrine that allowed colonizers to claim ownership over newly "discovered" territory if the land was "empty" of inhabitants. It was twisted and defined in such a way as to render the clear existence on and use of the land by Indigenous peoples illegitimate.[9]

As we noted earlier, gentrification writing often employs metaphors for colonization to describe what is happening. It is no coincidence that developers and city planners will describe gentrification projects as "creating a community" in an "undeveloped" space, or that adjectives like abandoned, unused, derelict, and deteriorating will be used to describe neighbourhoods "in need" of revitalization.[10]

What this language does is effectively erase the communities that are already there and deny their connections to place. This is readily accomplished with communities whose presence, culture, and sense of place are not legible or legitimized by dominant groups. For example, communities of poor, precariously housed people who may also be dealing with addictions and mental health issues, such as those that exist in Vancouver's Downtown Eastside or the "skid rows" of Los Angeles, are not typically considered real communities with true attachments to place in the same way as communities of homeowners or other privileged groups.

How we talk about gentrification matters. Although it is important to be clear about the violence of displacement and redevelopment, there is a fine line between diagnosing harm and offering a prognosis of unavoidable demise. The titles of popular books critiquing gentrification sometimes trip over this line: *Hollow City, How to Kill a City, Vanishing New York: How a Great City Lost Its*

Soul, St. Mark's Is Dead.[11] It is difficult to find a glimmer of hope, let alone comprehensive case studies of successful struggle. We have to be aware of the danger of ceding the cause, which ultimately lets those in power off the hook and solidifies the apparent inevitability of capitalist modes of development and the inequalities it produces.

Not only is this bound to create a sense of hopelessness, assumptions of inevitability also ignore long histories of tenacity, perseverance, and growth. Indigenous cultures have survived centuries of the ultimate form of displacement, colonization, and its ongoing forms of dislocation and dispossession, including gentrification. Black communities carry the strength of ancestral struggles against displacement through land theft, segregation, environmental racism, urban renewal, and more. Immigrant and working-class communities have fought back against being un-homed through squatters' movements, direct action, and political organizing. Declaring gentrification unstoppable renders previous resistance movements ineffective and risks the loss of knowledge passed down within communities about how to stay put.

It only takes one example of successful resistance to show that gentrification is not inevitable. Luckily, we have a lot more than one. Regardless of whether there is consensus on the degree of success, we can, and must, learn from the examples that exist to figure out what worked and why. Unfortunately, no single chapter or book can do justice to the range of resistance stories, strategies, and successes around the globe. Still, looking at examples across continents provides a glimpse into cases of pushback that aim to stop, reverse, mitigate, or change the course of gentrification in a variety of ways.

Some are bold grassroots initiatives and others are state-led policy interventions that attempt to institutionalize the right to stay put. In all cases, people are working in context-sensitive, locally appropriate ways to create opportunities for a future for themselves and their communities. The following seven ways that communities resist gentrification is not meant to be an exhaustive accounting of resistance strategies, but to highlight global examples where people have refused to accept the conclusion that gentrification is unstoppable.

TAKE CONTROL

How does a community stop housing, commercial properties, and land from being sold to newcomers, bought up by developers, or used by the city for redevelopment initiatives? In places where private property is king, there is no way to stop your neighbour from selling to the highest bidder. Neighbourhoods are starting to challenge this norm by doing property differently, namely, through forming community land trusts and other communal or cooperative ownership regimes. These provide ways to take control of the fate of the neighbourhood, at least for some period of time.

The objective of a CLT is to keep housing affordable in areas where it is vulnerable to speculation and precipitous increases. In Buffalo, New York, the historically Black Fruit Belt neighbourhood was facing gentrification pressure as the nearby campus of the Buffalo Niagara Medical Center—with some 17,000 employees—expanded. The area is home to some of the nation's oldest housing stock in various states of repair.

Speculation started to take off. Rent began to rise. Homeowners took advantage of market increases to sell and move on. Gentrification was starting. Eager to protect the neighbourhood, organizers set up the city's first CLT in 2017. Interestingly, and promisingly for the city, the recent Democratic candidate for mayor of Buffalo, the "socialist" India Walton, was the CLT's first executive director.[12]

The non-profit CLT is "designed to give residents control over the land within the neighborhood boundaries and keep housing there affordable."[13] The city of Buffalo, which owns two hundred lots in the Fruit Belt, dedicated an initial twenty lots to the CLT and placed a moratorium on the sale of the rest while a strategic plan for the neighbourhood was developed. The land trust stipulates that for at least ninety-nine years, the land cannot be sold privately, effectively locking out developers, wealthy homeowners, and speculators.

"Land trust, not land rush," is the new motto. Although still in its early days and in need of additional funding, the Fruit Belt CLT offers hope that the historic community can be preserved in a way that makes sense for the residents who are already there.

In Montreal, the Milton Park Community (CMP for Communauté Milton Parc) is an early example of social mobilization to prevent gentrification through the formation of a large-scale housing cooperative. Adjacent to the campus of McGill University, the historic area, full of unique housing stock, was under direct threat of gentrification when a developer bought 90 percent of the housing in the 1970s, with the intention of demolishing it for modern high-rise apartments.

The community sought a stable and long-term solution that would protect the housing stock and most importantly, its affordability, for many decades to come. Spurred on by direct-action protests and attempts to negotiate with the developer, the project received the support of Canada's federal housing agency, which purchased the buildings from the developer. Eventually, a condominium-type ownership structure was created where the buildings are owned by fifteen housing co-ops and six non-profit housing corporations. The CMP holds the lands and buildings in trust, and individual units cannot be bought or sold. It is the largest cooperative housing project in North America, and has successfully allowed low- and very low-income households to remain in the central city.[14]

The Evergreen Cooperative Initiative in Cleveland starts from the premise that local economic development fostered by green, living-wage jobs at employee-owned businesses in low-income neighbourhoods is integral to neighbourhood stabilization.[15] Responding to historical and racialized disinvestment in industrial cities, what became known as the Cleveland Model draws on "anchor institutions" like hospitals and universities to foster alternative wealth-building and sharing and alternative community-investment models.

This project scales up the typically small workers' co-op through large-scale worker-owned businesses that are also networked together to support the community. Notably, Evergreen has a home ownership program. Evergreen sells formerly foreclosed or abandoned properties to worker-owners, keeping them in the community and offering an avenue toward wealth building. Weekly payroll deductions, no down payments, and no need to apply through a traditional lending institution make it possible for workers, who may have bad credit or a history of incarceration, to become homeowners in four to six years.[16]

MAKE POLICY

Forming CLTs or cooperatives, acquiring property, and maintaining some kind of community control take a lot of time and resources, as well as partnerships across non-profit and government sectors. It is not easy to wrest some control of the housing market from the jaws of the capitalist economy, which eschews regulation. Nonetheless, anti-gentrification efforts often turn to legal and policy-oriented strategies to prevent or impede gentrification.

Tools here include zoning, by-laws, municipal legislation, and planning policy. Many of these have proven tricky to employ, since a variety of unintended consequences can create unexpected pathways for gentrification. In the context of neoliberal urbanism, which prefers deregulation, it is usually intense grassroots mobilization that leads to public policy interventions, rather than an urge toward equity from the state itself. Of course, as affordability plummets and the term "housing crisis" ripples through cities around the world, government actors are increasingly pressured to use their regulatory powers to counter the havoc wrought by decades of neoliberal policy.

———

In Buenos Aires, geographers María Carla Rodríguez and María Mercedes Di Virgilio found that in three working-class or industrial neighbourhoods in the southern part of the city displacement was happening through urban renewal programs, infrastructure projects, and neoliberal public-private ventures in the 1990s. Neighbourhood-based social movements were instrumental in pushing the government to pass Law 341 in 2000.[17] This law allows a city institute to provide loans to social organizations for new or rehabilitated housing projects for low-income households.

Local organizations insisted that housing is a human right, and that communities should have the ability to self-manage their housing plans. By 2012, researchers found that organizations representing over ten thousand families had been registered in the new programs, over a hundred cooperatives had been able to buy plots of land in the city, and overall, low-income housing had found a foothold within gentrifying areas.

———

Trying to enshrine a right to housing, a right to stay put, or a right to community in law has been an uphill battle. As geographers Phil Hubbard and Loretta Lees maintain, legal regimes are typically tilted in favour of property owners and the state (as the ultimate arbiter of property rights).[18] In London, a massive wave of "estate regeneration"—demolition or renovation of public housing—has been displacing low-income, racialized residents as private developers are given contracts to regenerate these estates while simultaneously developing private housing.

Hubbard and Lees note that some are calling this a process of social cleansing, as residents are cleared out and dispersed all over the city. However, the tenants of the Aylesbury Estate were able to secure a legal victory blocking their displacement, and the decision notably highlighted the unacceptable "dislocation from family life" as well as disproportionate impacts on racialized residents. Hubbard and Lees suggest that this decision recognized that people not only have a right to housing, but a right to community; that is, not just any old housing in any neighbourhood will do. The context matters.

While this decision has not halted the overall progression of estate regeneration across London, it provides an avenue for future challenges and an opening for the right to stay put to find expression in law.

———

Community benefit agreements can be useful tools for trying to secure affordable housing, jobs, green space, and other amenities as part of development packages. In these agreements, developers take on the cost of providing benefits to the community in exchange for local support of their project.

In some cities, like Detroit, activists have been successful in creating community benefit ordinances (CBOs) that actually codify community benefits negotiations into law. As planning researchers Lisa Berglund and Sam Butler note, Detroit's 2016 CBO is one of the first of its kind and offers hope that communities can leverage some real power in planning processes that typically favour developers.[19] Early research indicates that challenges in terms of inclusive community representation remain, and that CBO negotiation timelines still privilege the developer. However, the "CBO offers the potential for a city-wide process to create more inclusive, consistent benefits, rather than project-based campaigns that largely benefit residents of a specific project area."[20]

———

Facing rapid and extreme gentrification over the last decade or so, Berlin has seen growing support for what many consider to be radical policy interventions. In 2020, a five-year rent freeze was passed, a measure that could help over 1.5 million households in the city. However, in 2021 the courts overturned the decision. This controversial move has broadened support for an even more drastic plan: expropriating housing from major private housing companies and placing it under the control of the municipality.[21]

Right-to-the-city activists—who have been protesting gentrification, evictions, and displacement for a long time—have the support of almost 50 percent of Berliners for what is known as the "Expropriate Deutsche Wohnen and Co" movement, referring to one of the city's largest private landholders. In a city where about 85 percent of residents rent, placing control of large amounts of housing into the hands of publicly owned companies would potentially protect wide swaths of the city from gentrification.

———

The Expropriate campaign gathered momentum through 2021 and activists secured a non-binding referendum on the issue in the September German federal election, a vote that some felt could send "shockwaves" across Europe.[22] On September 26, the vote tally showed that the measure had passed with over 56 percent voting in favour of nationalizing thousands of units of housing owned by real estate companies.[23]

This movement is illustrative of the wide range of ways that activists are pushing the state to use its powers. As cities find themselves unable to ignore the housing crises at their doors, they are reaching into the dusty toolbox of regulatory strategies that can impede gentrification. These include regulations around short-term rentals like Airbnb in cities such as San Francisco, Toronto, and many others. Vancouver is taxing empty properties and foreign-owned investment properties.

Rent control and freezes on evictions made a comeback during the pandemic; as these emergency measures expire, there may be increased pressure to find ways to keep people housed. Inclusionary zoning by-laws that insist on decent percentages of affordable housing in or near new market-rate developments are in use in cities around the world.[24] Strengthening tenant protections in legislation and protecting public housing are also critical elements of state-led strategies for countering gentrification.

The story of gentrification being inevitable ignores the fact that governments are not powerless in the face of gentrification. Their refusal to intervene has been a choice. Grassroots mobilization can, however, prod states to employ measures designed to protect housing as a right, not an asset class.

GET CREATIVE

Anti-gentrification work also happens in the cultural realm, where artists use creative strategies to protest and raise awareness. In Seoul, researchers Seon Young Lee and Yoonai Han profiled the role of art activism in standing up against commercial gentrification.[25] The proposed eviction of the Takeout Drawing café in the Hannam area, a place that provided exhibition and working space for artists, mobilized widespread artist support and prompted the city to consider the dangers of commercial gentrification for vulnerable groups like artists.

Takeout Drawing squatted in the café for about a year, and was eventually successful in staying put despite attempts at forceful removal from the landlord. Over the course of the protest, musicians, artists, photographers, journalists, researchers, and others were involved in staging events, interventions, and exhibitions that brought multi-faceted attention and support not only for the café but also for anti-gentrification efforts more widely. The language of "social disaster" and the loss of the "legacy of the city" spread and allowed people to collectively articulate opposition and make displacement visible. Lee and Han insist, "art activists are shaking the unchallenged engines for speculative urbanisation, creating a meaningful political moment for a coalition."

In the suburbs of Sydney, where rapid gentrification threatens the Aboriginal community in Redfern and Waterloo, a piece of "aesthetic activism"—the Redfern-Waterloo Beauty Tours—highlighted sites that were threatened by revitalization plans. Organizers known as SquatSpace asked: "What was to be lost and what was to be gained by the process of urban transformation? How could it be done better? And how would it affect people on the ground?"[26]

Local housing and social justice organizations gave tourists a "complex but concrete experience of urban social and architectural dynamics." The tours also catalyzed conferences, exhibitions, festivals, and solidarity among Indigenous and non-Indigenous residents. Artist and tour guide Lucas Ilhein reflects that the tours were designed to offer a somewhat unsettling visit to Redfern, one that resisted neat narratives, homogeneity, and closure to a place with a very complex history.[27]

———————

Performance is another site of creative resistance. Feminist geographer Heather McLean performs in drag as the character Toby Sharp, a self-professed "urban horse whisperer" who mobilizes marginalized communities to spark "generative" urban renewal. Whether Toby is trying to turn a pulp and paper mill into a green arts hub and competitive yoga studio in Kamloops, British Columbia, or encouraging sex workers to forage for wild weeds in urban alleys to sell at the local farmers' market in Toronto, he is always using women, queer folks, and others to generate a "buzz in his hub."

McLean created Toby as an outlet for her frustrations with "the patriarchal practice of creative city discourses and their effect on women artists, community workers, and low-income, underrepresented residents. [. . .] But why wallow in bitterness when there is performance?" says McLean.[28] The subversive cabaret space of drag creates a "counter-public" that can "nurture oppositional politics and foster solidarities with other arts and activist scenes."[29] Drawing on the long history of queer performance that challenges what we take for granted as normal and good, McLean uses Toby to spark conversations about art, urban politics, displacement, and power.

These examples of creative interventions disrupt the smooth inevitability of gentrification by calling our attention to the people, places, and histories that are being exploited, lost, and displaced. They also allow artists to challenge and undermine their own complicity in gentrification processes.[30] Ilhein reflects on the Redfern Tour of Beauty as an intervention that, by focusing on the community, is also complicit in its commodification: "The Tour of Beauty is no doubt playing its own small part in this process. However, it could do more. It could, precisely, begin to cast the spotlight right back onto artists' spatial transformations of Redfern."[31]

BE DISRUPTIVE

Disruption is the name of the game for many grassroots and direct-action campaigns that aim to keep people in their housing, prevent problematic developments, and create policy that protects neighbourhoods over time. Very few significant changes in these areas happen without first putting visible, vocal community pressure on those in power. Taking over space is a central tactic in direct action.

In Redfern, activists set up The Aboriginal Tent Embassy in 2014 to protest commercial redevelopment plans for the site.[32] The words "Sovereignty never ceded" stand in large letters at the entrance to the embassy, described as a "last stand" against the Aboriginal Housing Corporation's attempts to build commercial developments in an area that is supposed to guarantee long-term, affordable housing for Aboriginal people.

Encampments are a way of claiming space that simply cannot be ignored, in much the same way as squatters' movements like Oakland Moms 4 Housing. They also bring greater visibility to problems such as homelessness, and tend to prompt visceral reactions from city officials and police who often use force in removing "tent city" sites and dispersing people into unsafe shelters.[33]

Grassroots organizing has been critical in many of Chicago's gentrifying immigrant communities. In Pilsen, the Pilsen Alliance has successfully mobilized the community to oppose new developments and city ordinances that they believe would allow gentrification. One organizer told me in 2015 that they did not necessarily believe they could stop gentrification, but they could "pump the brakes" by making it extremely tiresome and costly for any developer who proposed something in the neighbourhood.[34]

In Humboldt Park, Chicago, a grassroots campaign by the Puerto Rican Cultural Center called No Se Vende (Not for Sale) "claims that Puerto Ricans, even those who are renters, are the legitimate owners of Humboldt Park."[35] Researcher Ivis García describes how the youth-led campaign worked directly with community members to educate them about speculative buying and predatory real estate agents:

> The campaign started because speculators were targeting elderly people, asking them to sell and cash in their properties. They were, of course, buying low and selling high. Often elderly homeowners did not realize the rising value of their properties and fell prey to unscrupulous realtors.[36]

Similarly, the Pilsen Alliance uses door-to-door methods to help elderly and non-English-speaking residents understand their property tax bills and apply for discounts to which they are entitled to help them stay in their homes amid rising costs.

The grinding day-to-day work of reaching out to residents and raising awareness is a key part of grassroots organizing. Unfortunately, these actions do not attract the media or generate wider support for the community's concerns. This is where protest actions like squats, encampments, and demonstrations come in.

In Philadelphia, a six-month direct-action campaign in 2020 brought a victory for organizers seeking fifty vacant city-owned houses for affordable housing. The action included "many months of housing takeovers, protest encampments, eviction defense of the houses, barricaded and blockaded streets and mass mobilizations to defend the encampments." Responding to a housing crisis in the city, mothers and children experiencing homelessness took over vacant housing to push the city to take strong actions to prevent further homelessness, especially during the pandemic.

The city agreed to transfer the fifty homes to a CLT set up by Philadelphia Housing Action, a coalition of "housing activists who have all experienced either homelessness or institutionalization."[37] The plan is for the properties to be permanently designated for extremely low-income housing. Activists note that "this is only the beginning," as there is a need for thousands more units of housing for very low-income residents. Nonetheless, it is a "landmark agreement" that shows that activism can spur cities to use their powers to protect housing.

———

Activists may also target private corporations and people who are seen as responsible for gentrification and displacement. The Google Bus Blockades in San Francisco from 2013 to 2018 saw tenants facing eviction, seniors, disabled residents, and community organizers physically blocking the routes taken by the private buses that shuttle Google employees from gentrifying neighbourhoods like the Mission to corporate offices.

Geographer Manissa Maharawal calls this tactic infrastructural activism, wherein interrupting the functioning of infrastructure like transportation draws attention to interlinked issues such as "the privatisation of public transportation, the regional housing crisis, environmental gentrification, the technology industry and city government in the city's crisis of housing affordability."[38]

Protesters connected the structural violence represented by the buses to police violence, such as the killings of Alejandro Nieto and Amilcar Perez-Lopez, by blocking a Google bus outside the San Francisco Police department station in the Mission, carrying a banner that read "gentrification = violence." Maharawal's research insists that while direct actions are often fleeting, their effects can be deeply transformative for the people involved, offering a sense of empowerment and a space to "forge new political collectivities."

COME TOGETHER

These moments of victory typically happen because multiple organizations, individuals, and institutions come together to share resources, expertise, and social capital. Discussing the threat of gentrification to Chrisp Street Market in London's Tower Hamlets as well as other historic trading spaces in the city, geographer Oli Mould describes how coalitions of traders, community organizations, students, and activists supported one another to successfully mobilize against displacement. Mould notes that their wins hinged on coming together early in the planning process, "to share information, legal advice and tactics for navigating confusing consultation exercises."[39] Local collective action also halted developments in Haringey, and Elephant and Castle, where strategic mobilization forced developers to pause or reconsider their plans.

In the context of what has been called hyper-gentrification in San Francisco, resistance has required "collective cohesion" among anti-poverty, housing, mental health, and immigrant organizations in order to face the dire crises of homelessness, displacement, opioid addiction, and more.[40]

The San Francisco Anti-Displacement Coalition (SFADC) includes anti-eviction groups, the Tenants Union, Housing Rights Committee, Our Mission No Eviction, Just Cause, and more. While individual groups have their own specific projects and focuses, the Coalition has enabled city-wide efforts such as a ballot initiative to limit speculative flipping in 2014 and a bill at the board of supervisors designed to increase relocation fees for evicted tenants. While the ballot proposition was not successful, the ability to generate enough momentum to get the measure on the ballot at all signals the strength that comes from broad coalitions.

Activist coalition building requires an intersectional understanding of power in the city, and the ability to see that there really are no single-issue battles, just as there are no single-issue lives (to paraphrase Audre Lorde).[41] An inability to find nutritious affordable food is connected to the lack of safe spaces for drug users is connected to the glut of Airbnb rentals on the block, and so on. Increasingly, anti-gentrification struggles are interwoven with other concerns, whether these are sex workers' rights, safe injection sites, reparations, abolition, or climate change.

DRAW FROM THE PAST

Un-homing is an experience that echoes across generations. The dislocations of modern-day gentrification may feel like nothing new. However, the past can be mobilized as part of present-day claims to the right to stay put and as pushback against gentrifier businesses and practices.

Cape Town's historic Bo-Kaap district was inhabited by enslaved people from Asia in the 1760s. During South Africa's apartheid era, it was designated a Muslim-only zone. With its "picture postcard pastel-coloured houses, rich cultural heritage and beautiful location overlooking Cape Town's city centre," Bo-Kaap has long been a tourist hot spot, but more recently is facing a wave of high-priced new developments and climbing housing prices as wealthy newcomers and foreign investors take an interest.[42]

The community insists that preserving the history of Bo-Kaap, as a place built by enslaved people and as a site of apartheid-era segregation, is crucial. They are also fighting against their own cultural exclusion. Newcomers have demanded that the volume of Muslim prayer calls from mosques be lowered, while new restaurants serve alcohol and pork. Youth-led movement Bo-Kaap Rise! is working to block new high-rise developments through protest actions, and other community groups are trying to secure a heritage designation for the area.[43]

———————

The movement for housing policy-related reparations in the United States is another example where the injustices of the past are being brought to bear on claims today. Financial compensation coupled with policy changes that limit future displacement via speculation, evictions, and predatory lending are meant to allow Black communities to protect themselves from gentrification. By recreating the wealth and stability that were stolen through generations of racist policy, reparations may stave off displacement and prove to be an effective anti-gentrification tactic going forward.

In Canada, the restitution of stolen wealth from Indigenous people is the focus of the First Nations-led Yellowhead Institute's "Cash Back" report. It argues that Canada's economy "has been built on the transformation of Indigenous lands and waterways into corporate profit and national power."[44] Redress for the suppression of Indigenous institutions and culture, compensation for land theft, and restitution of Indigenous economies are presented as core principles behind "Cash Back."

Like reparations, these principles recognize that Indigenous peoples are not living in dire housing conditions (in both urban and rural spaces) due to any fault of their own. Rather, the ability to maintain sustainable economies has been ripped away through colonization. Given that gentrification affects great numbers of Indigenous people who are dealing with housing unaffordability, displacement, and homelessness, "Cash Back" is a justice-focused anti-gentrification tactic as well.

CREATE ALTERNATIVES

Halting displacement and fixing a housing shortage are not the same thing. Gentrification is driven by both demand (the kinds and locations of housing that middle-class people want) and supply (little housing supply drives up prices). Even if activists are successful in, for example, stopping the development of a luxury residential tower, the needs of unhoused people or those without affordable housing have not been met. The same could be said about other kinds of development.

Pushing back against luxury retail, exclusive amenities, and industries that do not serve the community is good, but people still need somewhere to buy food, somewhere to go with their children, and somewhere to work. For many activists and organizations, a big part of the anti-gentrification struggle is the creation of alternatives in housing, public space, consumption, and more.

In response to what geographer Juan Velásquez Atehortúa calls the urban "elitization" of Caracas, women in the barrios organized to not only stop elitist urban renewal plans, but to practise their own "insurgent urbanism," creating a new community for some six hundred families.[45] In Chacao, the smallest and richest municipality in the Caracas metropolitan region, gentrification in recent decades has been driven by a combination of neoliberalism, enhanced consumption capabilities as oil revenues trickle through the population, and privatization. At the same time, farm workers have been pushed off their rural land and are migrating to urban areas. Their presence in informal settlements and need to, essentially, create their own urban homes, work, and governance, has sparked high levels of activity and organization among new residents, especially women.

Autonomous organizations developed to address issues like evictions, rent increases, squatters' rights, and environmental concerns. Coming together as a Settlers' Movement with a unified platform in 2007, the movement embraced a manifesto with three pillars:

> Defending housing as a human right; [. . .] turning the neoliberal city into a socialist one by contesting the privatisation of the features necessary for its construction [. . .]; and [. . .] stressing the role of the people in contesting the commoditisation of housing and urban space.[46]

Barrio women in Chacao went beyond participation in what Atehortúa (following Faranak Miraftab[47]) calls the "invited" spaces of the state (such as government projects to provide housing for the poor); they contributed to generating "invented" spaces with control over the entire process of building and managing new housing for settlers. Local and self-managed communes were developed and physically built by women. Atehortúa characterizes this as a process in which barrio women put into practice the ideas behind the Bolivarian revolution in order to concretize the right to the city for those in informal settlements.

It is not only in the global south where city dwellers need to organize to make up for the many gaps in what the state provides. Mutual aid, rooted in Black and immigrant social, political, and economic traditions, is a way of resourcing one another outside of the limited, invasive, and often punitive social welfare institutions of the state. During the pandemic, mutual aid groups grew in size and number in communities around the world as strained-at-the-best-of-times social services flailed.

As a strategy in the anti-gentrification toolkit, mutual aid is about finding ways to provide things that gentrification threatens, and about creating robust, community-centred systems that help people get what they need to help them stay in place. In Brooklyn, mutual aid groups like Equality 4 Flatbush are working with organizations like the Brooklyn Anti-Gentrification Network to connect people for grocery deliveries, medication pickups, tenant and rent strike support, and police accountability organizing support.[48] They also offer small "emergency cash grants" to people to help with rent and other expenses.

Unlike charity or state-funded, needs-based services, mutual aid is not a one-way redistribution of resources that solidifies existing power relations of race, gender, ability, and class. It recognizes that everyone has something to contribute and that we are all interdependent on one another. No one is required to prove their neediness, pass a sobriety test, fill out endless paperwork, be put under state surveillance, or pray that changing political regimes will not eliminate the services they rely upon.

Mutual aid is about creating alternative systems for sharing resources.[49] In this way, it can function as an anti-displacement safeguard by helping those who are vulnerable to displacement— because of the price of food, rent, and child care—have their needs met within their community.

Helping others in a mutual exchange also strengthens neighbourly bonds and develops the kind of solidarity that helps mobilize people in the face of more acute crises. Legal scholar and mutual-aid enthusiast Dean Spade maintains that mutual aid projects "help people develop skills for collaboration, participation, and decision-making."[50] As people help one another through eviction proceedings, for example, they are learning how the system works and how to fight it, as well as developing practical skills like facilitation and conflict resolution. They are empowering themselves to make the changes they want to see: "both building the world we want and becoming the kind of people who could live in such a world together."[51]

Too often, the alternatives that people build for themselves are derided as too small, too experimental, too cost-inefficient, too unsustainable, too niche. Meanwhile, the consistently experimental, costly, and unsustainable plans generated by corporate "innovators" and "disruptors" that now replace the mega-projects once conceived at city hall are viewed as "just what we need." The devastation wrought by innovations (such as Airbnb and citizen surveillance apps) is unfortunately often done before the state recognizes the potential for harm and tries to intervene. We must push back against the idea—which only upholds the status quo—that we cannot come up with anything better or different, or that we have not already done so. That is a narrative that only serves the powerful.

The truth is that no one is going to hand us the gentrification-proof city we want. We have to imagine it, we have to believe in it, and we have to do it. Even if the doing is simply an action that saves one family from displacement, keeps one affordable food supplier open, or maintains one bench where seniors can gather, it is a necessary piece of the puzzle. The story that we have been fed—that gentrification is natural, that it is inevitable, that there are no good alternatives—is false and designed to make us feel powerless. It is not always easy to notice or learn about the local, everyday sites and practices of resistance around the world, but they are there if we care to look. Another city is possible.

CHANGE THE STORY, CHANGE THE ENDING

Throughout this book, we have engaged with many ways of telling the story of gentrification. Some of these are fables we are better off forgetting; others, partial stories that have obscured the role of forces like colonialism and sexism and hidden the effects of gentrification on groups like seniors and disabled people. Organizing this book as an intervention in those stories is my way of insisting that how we talk and think about gentrification matters.

It matters very much. After all, every story has its arc and leads us toward certain conclusions. How we frame the problem of gentrification shapes the kinds of solutions we might come up with. If our frame ignores or minimizes race, sexuality, gender, colonialism, or ability, chances are our solutions will not form adequate barriers against the forces that drive gentrification or protect those vulnerable to displacement.

The good news about recognizing the limitations of certain

ways of understanding gentrification is that the story can always be changed. Nothing is written in stone. Even if it were, we have chisels and jackhammers and a lot of spray paint. And by "we" I mean all of us, not just the academics, researchers, reporters, and policymakers who have been granted the unfair privilege of having their stories deemed most legitimate.

Although some have feared that intellectual chaos will result from an expanded concept of gentrification, I would rather risk chaos than reproduce exclusion, erasure, and ignorance by not listening to multiple voices and experiences. I am convinced that this fertile messiness is actually the starting point for broader, more intersectional anti-gentrification movements.

This is what I think intersectional, twenty-first-century anti-gentrification politics can look like through three lenses: a feminist, queer anti-gentrification politics; an anti-racist anti-gentrification politics; and a decolonial anti-gentrification politics. As ever, these are incomplete stories. I offer a set of principles under each label that, taken together, form a provisional manifesto for a different story, an enhanced anti-gentrification perspective. Finally, I invite everyone to imagine their own role in anti-gentrification practices with suggestions for places to start this work in your own life.

A FEMINIST, QUEER ANTI-GENTRIFICATION POLITICS

Gentrification has always been a feminist issue. However, feminist and queer perspectives have largely remained peripheral to the dominant stories about gentrification and what we might do about it. At the same time, it is clear that some women and some queer people have benefited from gentrification, which perpetuates the false idea that gentrification is an uplifting process for women and queer folks in general. As Morgan Bassichis, Alexander Lee, and Dean Spade remind us, there is no liberation in accepting benefits and rights that throw the most marginalized among us under the bus.[1]

In *Feminism, Interrupted*, Lola Olufemi spells out the dangers of a white, liberal feminism that defines success for women as being able to wield the same kinds of exploitative power as men: "A feminism that seeks power instead of questioning it does not care about justice."[2] Consolidating economic, cultural, and social power through gentrification is not "revolutionary work, [which] means that nobody is left behind, nobody's exploitation goes unseen."[3] So where does a feminist, queer anti-gentrification politics begin?

The Black feminist concept of intersectionality is critical to understanding the simultaneous operation of multiple systems of power, including those that drive gentrification. This approach can move us beyond the tired and exclusionary framing of "gentrification is a class-based process," not by eliminating class, but by developing a richer recognition of class as always intertwined with race, gender, sexuality, and colonialism, among other power relations.[4] An intersectional anti-gentrification politics does not prioritize one problematic system over another. Rather, it enables a context-specific analysis of the forces behind gentrification and displacement as well as the group-differentiated outcomes of these processes.

Queering the story of gentrification is another way of challenging hegemonic narratives and the damage they do. By queering, I do not simply mean adding queer people and queer perspectives to the story, although that continues to be necessary. Queering is a mode of analysis that reads systems of oppression in terms of the sexual and gender norms that are operating. It aims to show what work those norms do in upholding power relations. It also tries to destabilize norms by, for example, challenging binaries, unearthing different histories, and fighting against normalization itself.

A queer reading questions the normative values that fuel gentrification: ideas about the home and family, the relationship between property and social acceptance, and what is required for liberation and empowerment. Queering also pushes an anti-gentrification politics to interrogate its own normative assumptions. These could include the unquestioned valorization of working-class identities and spaces, the notion of community, and the foundations of the right to the city.

In addition to their theoretical contributions, feminist and queer perspectives inform several principles that I believe are core to an anti-gentrification politics. This list is not exhaustive, and every reader should feel free to add their own ideas. As a starting point, though, let me extend the following. A feminist, queer anti-gentrification politics holds that:

Urban environments matter for feminist and queer justice movements. There is a reciprocal relationship between the spaces we inhabit and the societies we create. For too long, cities have been deeply sexist, cis-normative, and heterosexist, both reflecting and reproducing social norms.[5] Nonetheless, they have remained potent sites for queer and feminist activism.

Gentrification does not advance this cause, although a select few will profit from it. An anti-gentrification politics has to consider both the harms of gentrification and the improvements that we envision through intersectional queer and feminist lenses. It is no good advocating for housing if that housing does not offer alternatives to the traditional nuclear family, the gendered division of care labour, or the dangers of domestic violence.

Housing and neighbourhoods must be valued as part of an infrastructure of care. Homes and neighbourhoods are typically spaces where much of the feminized care labour of looking after people happens. The commodification of these spaces via gentrification ignores the value (economic and emotional) of this work by turning places of care into sites of asset accumulation.

While feminist and queer theory critique the unequal burdens of care work across genders, they also insist that care matters. Housing scholars Emma Power and Kathleen Mee argue that care is "threaded through the housing system" but rarely considered as such.[6] Care in the city is either an afterthought or assumed to happen "naturally" in the home with little support. As the pandemic exposed, our privatized and individualized spaces of care

are woefully inadequate for sharing, collectivizing, and valuing care. An anti-gentrification politics needs to attend to the ways that care networks get hollowed out by gentrification and to how "housing might be better governed to support a flourishing of human life and domestic care."[7]

Gentrification is a form of violence that exacerbates ongoing gender- and sexuality-based violence. Feminist anti-violence work has, over many decades, contributed to an expanded definition of violence that encompasses a range of actions and outcomes not limited to the physical. The loss of home, broadly conceived, can be experienced as an act of violence. It is also the case that the fear of displacement and housing precarity in general place or keep people living in situations that may be abusive and dangerous, or force them into the streets or shelter system (also dangerous).

Queer youth and trans people are overrepresented amongst the unhoused, while domestic violence is a major contributing factor to homelessness for women.[8] A queer feminist anti-gentrification politics takes the links among these forms of violence seriously and understands them as more than coincidental. Opposing the violence of displacement means opposing gender- and sexuality-based violence and vice versa.

Women, non-binary, trans, and queer people are crucial contributors to neighbourhood networks. The oversimplified figure of the first-wave gentrifier, including single moms, lesbians, and gays, has produced a story where these groups are viewed with suspicion and ignored another, and maybe truer, story: that these groups are central to neighbourhood cohesion, identity, creativity, and political mobilization.

As Sarah Schulman demonstrates in *The Gentrification of the Mind*, the loss of a diverse queer community is a blow to the city as a whole.[9] The care networks and community relationships that are developed and sustained by women are blown apart by displacement, to which women are more vulnerable. Jen Jack Gieseking's research on lesbian-queer spaces in areas like Brooklyn's Park Slope insists that even though these spaces are sometimes fleeting and fragmented, they create a world of mutual recognition and the possibility for a thriving queer life.[10] An anti-gentrification movement has to consider the protection of these kinds of networks as central to the rationale for the right to stay put.

Gentrification upholds and reinforces male and heterosexual power and privilege. Whether it is through the interpersonal (but also systemic) violence of men against women that makes women vulnerable to displacement, or through the consolidation of economic and political power via property ownership and asset accumulation, men, primarily cis-het men, are the beneficiaries of the spoils of gentrification. Thus, gentrification has to be seen as part of the system of patriarchal, heterosexist domination. Anti-gentrification movements should take care to articulate the struggle as more than an anti-capitalist or class-based fight.

Anti-gentrification requires solidarity across movements. What Olufemi calls "the power of refusing to remain divided" has, she says, "always underpinned radical feminist movements" around the globe.[11] Solidarity can be fraught when it relies on the false idea that we all face the exact same forces of oppression or that these operate in the same ways everywhere. Nonetheless, we can share a vision of the future and coalesce strategically to support one another via the sharing of energy, knowledge, and resources.

In anti-gentrification work, this means recognizing that the fight against gentrification is connected to, for example, Black Lives Matter, Indigenous sovereignty, anti-globalization, sex workers' rights, environmental and climate justice, and more. Showing up for one another across these causes is part of the hard but necessary work of imagining and creating the world we want to live in.

AN ANTI-RACIST ANTI-GENTRIFICATION POLITICS

Acknowledging and really working with the fact that racism and white supremacy are central to gentrification is long overdue in the field. While race and racialization function differently around the world and will affect gentrification dynamics in locally specific ways, it is not possible to simply assume that race is irrelevant or a secondary factor.

Bringing race to the centre means interrogating whiteness, both in the process of gentrification and in the world of gentrification research and writing. The story of gentrification has largely been told by white people, especially in early accounts that remain foundational in the literature. An anti-racist perspective requires an excavation of the oversights, assumptions, and racial biases permeating the scholarship. For me and other white scholars, this requires, at the very least, a humble recognition that the stories we tell about gentrification are not definitive.

Geographers David Roberts and Minelle Mahtani argue that most work on neoliberalism has not attended to race except to analyze "moments of eruption of racial discrimination from processes of neoliberalization," while ignoring how "neoliberalism is thoroughly imbued with race."[12] This has shaped gentrification research as well, particularly since neoliberalism is a core aspect of the political-economic analysis of gentrification.

Increasingly, the concept of racial capitalism is being used to deepen our grasp of the ways that racial differentiation and hierarchization structure capitalism itself. International relations scholar Ida Danewid points out that gentrification is "typically underpinned by a set of racialised assumptions about who belongs in certain spaces and who does not."[13] The city operates on a racial logic developed during colonialism and expressed today via geographies of racialized valorization (white spaces) and disposability (Black and other non-white spaces).

Bringing racial capitalism to the heart of gentrification theory leads to the uncomfortable but inevitable conclusion that gentrification is a tactic of white supremacy. Following environmental justice scholar Laura Pulido, I will not soften this by using the term white privilege. Pulido argues that as a development in thinking about racial power, white privilege was useful in highlighting "how the individual decisions of whites were not necessarily driven by racial animus, but often were simply a desire to create the best opportunities for themselves and their families, which, in a highly racialized society, reproduced racial inequality."[14]

Part of the appeal of white privilege as a concept, however, is that it does not assign anyone real responsibility for racist outcomes. Pulido maintains that white privilege is a passive formulation that overlooks the actions involved in "the process of taking or appropriation, including the taking of land, wages, life, liberty, health, community, and social status."[15] White supremacy can be seen in white people's "awareness, taking, and an attitude of racial superiority"[16] expressed in "white's sense of ownership and the right to exclude."[17]

Although Pulido is writing about the actions of polluting industries, she could easily be writing about gentrification. An anti-racist anti-gentrification politics must be willing to face the fact that in being aware of the racial harms of gentrification, taking space, and acting on a perceived right to exclude, white gentrifiers are enacting white supremacy.

Racial capitalism and white supremacy are critical concepts to bring to bear in anti-gentrification work. I humbly offer, with the understanding that as a white person my perspective is limited, several more principles toward an anti-racist anti-gentrification politics, including the beliefs that:

Gentrification is almost always connected to racist displacement policies and practices of the past. Many communities have faced serial displacement in and from urban neighbourhoods over the course of multiple generations.[18] Prior displacements are not just distinct iterations of dispossession. They lay the groundwork for current and future displacement by dismantling structures of wealth, destroying social networks, and wreaking havoc on community cohesion.[19] Still, these experiences have engendered strategies of resistance and survival that constitute crucial knowledges for anti-gentrification struggles. An anti-racist anti-gentrification politics acknowledges and connects these histories to the present day.

Reparations are a necessary step in addressing gentrification. In places where slavery, apartheid, and legalized racial discrimination kept racialized people from building social and economic assets, establishing long-term communities, or holding on to their assets and wealth, reparations are needed to make up for a profoundly unlevel playing field. Gentrification proceeds in part because of the stripping of wealth and the chance to accumulate it from racialized communities. Combatting gentrification from an anti-racist perspective, then, requires a commitment to supporting various forms of reparations in recognition of the role of reparations in both redressing past harms and in helping people to stay put now.

Anti-gentrification is also a fight against environmental racism. The environmental justice movement as we know it today originated in Black American communities, like Afton, North Carolina, that fought to prevent toxic dump sites and other forms of environmental harm being located in or near their homes, schools, and workplaces.[20] In urban areas, low-income communities of colour are disproportionately exposed to everything from lead in the water to diesel bus fumes.[21]

A lack of affordable housing and displacement pushes families into, or keeps them in, these hazardous locations. Like many iterations of racism, this has intergenerational and wide-reaching impacts. Chronic and acute illnesses result in lost days of school and work. Lead poisoning affects child brain development. The costs of health care in many places keep people in debt and struggling to afford basics like housing and good food. All of this means that the chances of escaping the situation shrink with every year.

Gentrification is certainly not the only force to blame for urban environmental racism, but it contributes to the problem and cannot be fully combatted without advocating for environmentally sustainable communities for everyone.

Abolishing the police and the criminal justice system is integral to fighting gentrification. The racist, classist, and colonialist system of criminal punishment contributes to gentrification and displacement by tearing people out of their communities to imprison them, while leaving behind families that bear the emotional as well as economic burden of having a loved one incarcerated. Police also act as shock troops of gentrification by harassing, arresting, and sometimes even killing poor people, disabled people, people with mental illnesses, and people of colour in gentrifying neighbourhoods. Bloated policing budgets siphon resources away from services that would actually mitigate the housing crisis and toward the use of state violence to secure private property for the already wealthy.[22]

Abolitionist Mariame Kaba maintains that abolishing the police is just part of the picture because carceral attitudes and practices have become embedded in everyday life, among everyday people.[23] Gentrifiers, especially white gentrifiers, feel empowered to act *as police* as well as to call on the police.

An anti-racist anti-gentrification politics recognizes that "most criminalized harms are rooted in social and economic inequities."[24] In order to do something about that, we have to tackle those inequities rather than lock people up. In fighting against gentrification, then, we are fighting to address inequities in areas such as housing in order to address the root causes of harm.

Displacement is a form of racialized violence. Although overt and sensational forms of violence against Black and Indigenous people and people of colour are receiving more attention and condemnation, countless forms of slow, everyday, and systemic violence continue to, as Ruth Wilson Gilmore puts it, "produce group-differentiated vulnerability to premature death."[25]

Displacement—as un-homing, uprooting, domicide—is one of those forms of violence. The health impacts, physical and mental, of displacement are significant and layered on top of the stress of many other experiences of racism and injustice. This surely contributes to racialized disparities in health and longevity.[26] Anti-gentrification movements must consider the racialized impacts of displacement and frame displacement as a form of racist violence.

Racialized communities are not in need of saving either by gentrification or by white progressive movements. Katherine McKittrick and other Black geographies scholars insist that despite every attempt to sever and deny Black connections to place, Black people continue to create, sustain, and imagine place.[27] Still, communities of colour are seen as empty, neglected, troubled, and dangerous; in other words, in need of saving.

Cities often see gentrification as a solution, believing that any influx of money is a good thing. Obviously an anti-racist anti-gentrification movement would oppose this. However, I caution urban progressives, especially white people, to guard against participating in similar narratives that cast racialized communities as problems in need of solutions.

The racialized vocabulary of a lot of gentrification writing (jungles, pioneers, settlers) is an example. Many so-called progressive movements in cities are white-dominated and guilty of reproducing racist tropes, racist exclusions, and white normativity.[28] It is important that an anti-gentrification politics refuses to participate in discourse or practices that locate racialized communities as agency-less victims in need of white expertise.

A DECOLONIAL ANTI-GENTRIFICATION POLITICS

Perhaps most destabilizing to the familiar old gentrification stories is the need for decolonization. I write from the settler colonial context of Canada, where colonial occupation of Indigenous land is ongoing. However, decolonization must be attended to no matter where you are located. As anti-racist education scholar George

J. Sefa Dei puts it, "decolonization is all we do around Land, places and spaces with the goal towards transformation."[29] Dei continues:

> Decolonization is action-oriented. [. . .] It derives from an awareness of the violence and genocide perpetrated under colonialism and settler colonialism. Decolonization also marks an attempt by Indigenous and colonized bodies to take control of our own thought processes and to act in concrete ways to address colonialism, patriarchy and other forms of social oppression.

Decolonization is a process, rather than a singular destination. An anti-gentrification politics can and should be part of that process by interrogating its own colonial narratives and practices and by actively participating in tangible decolonization projects.

As a first step, we have to recognize that a western, Eurocentric epistemology—a way of knowing—structures mainstream ways of thinking about the city and processes of urban planning.[30] Global-north, English-language perspectives have dominated academic urban theory, and gentrification theory is no exception.[31] Not only does this mean that a lot of people and places are marginalized in this body of work, but a particular worldview infuses how and what we know (or think we know) about the subject.

A western worldview is shaped by particular religious, intellectual, and political traditions that form one way of making sense of the world. But it is not the only way. Colonization tried to stamp out (while still managing to steal from) Indigenous and colonized peoples' worldviews, yet they have survived.[32] Of course, these knowledges have not been widely accepted in western scholarship. The result is that a limited range of concepts, questions, and visions about city life shape our perception of problems such as gentrification.

At a minimum, non-Eurocentric worldviews offer different ways of thinking about land, rights, justice, harm, relationships, community, accountability, and responsibility.[33] For example, geographer, planner, and Indigenous methodologist Laura Harjo explores how multiple iterations of community among the Mvskoke people "build networks of relationality" that not only preserve culture, but form the grounds for Indigenous futurity (an anti-colonial form of planning).[34]

At several points in this book, I have highlighted how western ways of understanding land as property (private or otherwise) infuse both capitalist, pro-gentrification views and anti-capitalist anti-gentrification views.[35] Many anti-gentrification strategies rely on alternative ways of owning and controlling property and land, but the assumption that land can and should be owned is still operating in these approaches.

This is antithetical to many Indigenous and other non-western worldviews that posit a reciprocal relationship with the land based on mutual responsibilities.[36] Figuring out how, or if, we can reconcile these worldviews is a thorny topic. Nonetheless, we have to begin by at least being aware of the assumptions underlying our political strategies and their implications for questions of decolonization.

Decentring western worldviews and radically questioning how we think about land and property are critical to a decolonial anti-gentrification politics. As a non-Indigenous occupant of a settler colonial state, I suggest the following principles as invitations to the predominantly non-Indigenous community of gentrification scholars and activists to help us take the first steps on the path of decolonization. My modest invitation to a decolonial anti-gentrification politics holds that:

Gentrification is a manifestation of ongoing processes of colonialism and dispossession. Anishinaabe environmental scholar and activist Winona LaDuke asserts that control of land is the foundation from which social control and all other forms of power flow under a system of colonial conquest.[37] Gentrification can be understood as a recent spin on colonial, capitalist modes of controlling land and resources in order to shore up hegemonic power.

For colonized and Indigenous peoples, the displacements of gentrification are contiguous with the forced displacements of colonial policy, such as mass relocation and the establishment of reserves. The connection is not only in the repetition of similar removal processes, however. Gentrification itself, with its cherished principle of private land ownership and goal of accumulating wealth from that ownership and its eventual transfer, is part of the way that settlers occupy and maintain control of colonized lands.[38] A decolonial anti-gentrification politics must be clear on what controlling land and property means and how it consolidates colonial power.

Colonization is not a metaphor. Following from the first principle, we cannot view the relationship between colonization and gentrification as a metaphorical one. Too often, the language of gentrification mirrors the language of imperialism, discovery, and conquest but in ways that elide, rather than illuminate, the colonial structures underlying the process. In a similar fashion, the narrative of reclaiming or occupying the city, and the claim to the right to the city, ignores ongoing Indigenous claims to urban space.

Thus, anti-gentrification research and activism needs to reconsider its vocabulary and how this vocabulary structures particular ways of thinking about rights, residence, and power. It should also be emphasized that decolonization is not a metaphor either, as education scholars Eve Tuck and K. Wayne Yang write. They are wary of the relative ease with which the term decolonization is deployed as part of social justice discourse or institutional diversity and inclusion discourses, "with no regard for how decolonization wants something different than those forms of justice."[39]

In other words, decolonization is not a metaphor for other movements, nor is it a symbolic process. Tuck and Yang believe that decolonization "must involve the repatriation of land simultaneous to the recognition of how land and relations to land have always already been differently understood and enacted; that is, all of the land, and not just symbolically."[40] For anti-gentrification movements in settler colonial nations, this means that we must be prepared to be deeply *unsettled*: the solutions to gentrification cannot come at the cost of maintaining or exacerbating the material and political severance of Indigenous peoples from their lands.

Anti-gentrification must support Land Back movements. To that end, anti-gentrification efforts should be in solidarity with Land Back movements where Indigenous people occupying their traditional territories are asserting their own version of the right to stay put by implementing Indigenous jurisdiction. The Yellowhead Institute's "Land Back" Red Paper notes that Indigenous jurisdiction in Canada is a major threat to the state's legitimacy and creates "massive economic uncertainty" for a country whose power relies on resources and wealth extracted from Indigenous lands.[41] While we tend to focus on natural resource projects like logging and mining, urban space is also a site of dispossession and wealth extraction.

The city is also land, as Cree-Métis-Saulteaux writer and literature professor Lindsay Nixon states. For Indigenous people in cities:

> Land Back in the city is the embodied resurgence of street-involved and houseless youths. [. . .] Land Back is defunding the police. Land Back is taking care of our bodies. [. . .] Land Back is taking care of each other. Land Back is better harm reduction for drug users in the city, with white settlers funding these kinds of supports. Land Back is shelters for trans and queer Indigenous youth.[42]

For those who look toward a different vision of how we live on this land, Indigenous jurisdiction offers, according to the "Land Back" Red Paper's authors, perhaps our best hope for sustainable survival. A decolonial anti-gentrification movement recognizes that achieving Land Back goals is a route to achieving anti-gentrification goals.

Indigenous, colonized, and formerly colonized people are and always have been active in planning and city-building. In many places, Indigenous people and their concerns are seen as happening "over there" in rural and remote communities far from urban centres. This is both empirically and politically inaccurate, as not only are Indigenous people an increasingly urban population (over 50 percent of Indigenous people in Canada live in cities, over 70 percent in the US), but their claims, movements, and cultures have many urban connections.[43]

Anti-gentrification movements, thus, need to refrain from seeing anti-colonial struggles as geographically distinct from urban struggles. There also needs to be an explicit recognition that Indigenous, colonized, and formerly colonized peoples (those no longer under direct political colonial control) have expressed and continue to express their "rights to the city" through their formal and informal labour, community building, activism, and very ability to survive under hostile circumstances.

Indigenous peoples also have their own, centuries-old community planning practices that, while suppressed by colonialism, continue to inform Indigenous governance. Indigenous planning practices and principles are being actively reclaimed around the world and must be considered part of the toolkit of decolonial anti-gentrification movements.[44]

Anti-gentrification projects must actively co-design strategies with Indigenous, colonized, and formerly colonized people. It is more than likely that anti-gentrification projects, especially those on Indigenous land in settler colonial contexts, will conflict with or not be in accordance with the worldviews, relationship to land, and sovereignty strategies of Indigenous and colonized peoples. In order to avoid furthering the harm of dispossession, anti-gentrification work has to include meaningful engagement and co-construction.

In *Designs for the Pluriverse*, anti-colonial anthropology scholar Arturo Escobar offers an urgent but hopeful framework for a transition away from "patriarchal Western capitalist modernity" and all of its harms via a grassroots-inspired, radical-liberation approach to design.[45] A pluriversal design practice (where design refers not just to the creation of objects or buildings but to imaginative world-making projects) begins from the premise that not only is another world possible, but that multiple worlds are possible and necessary.

Collective, participatory, speculative, and relational design processes can contribute to ways of doing and thinking outside of the narrow boxes that capitalist urbanism tries to force us into. Anti-gentrification movements must understand that Indigenous claims, for example, are not obstacles or sites of conflict for anti-gentrification work, but rather sites of generative creativity that can expand possibilities for justice, sustainability, and a good life for all.

Openness to different ways of thinking about and practising our relationship to the city and all of its human and non-human inhabitants is necessary. Western political traditions, both mainstream and radical, presuppose a limited range of ways of "doing" politics, making change, achieving justice, granting rights, organizing society, and distributing resources. The deeply unimaginative way that we position ourselves at various points along a linear right-to-left political axis leaves a lot to be desired when it comes to envisioning a future, and certainly does little for decolonial thought and action.

It is also anthropocentric, or human-centred, meaning that the natural world and non-human beings do not typically have standing when we think about rights, justice, or claims to space.[46] While we must avoid the uncritical appropriation of other cultures and worldviews, a decolonial anti-gentrification movement nonetheless needs to be open to the wider range of alternative ways of relating, organizing, caring, living, and so on, that arise from different ways of making sense of the world.

WHERE DO WE BEGIN?

Take a deep breath. No one is responsible for doing all this work on their own. I certainly do not want you to put this book down feeling overwhelmed and discouraged. I want you to feel a sense of responsibility, but also empowerment. If nothing else, the take-away from this book should be that we have the power to change the story and change the outcomes of processes like gentrification. Still, you are probably wondering where to begin and what difference you might be able to make. In fact, you might be asking yourself, "Am I a gentrifier?"

When the changes happening in my old neighbourhood, the Junction, began to pick up speed, shops, bars, and restaurants that miraculously aligned with my unique personal tastes were opening everywhere. What a happy coincidence! But of course, it was nothing of the sort. My preferences for cozy cafés over sports bars, nail salons over barbershops, and organic grocers over the deli counter were structured by long-standing gender, race, culture, and class norms that were taking physical form in the built environment as the area gentrified.

The spaces frequented by older generations of working-class European immigrants were being crowded out by services that catered to another set of tastes brought in by, well, people like me. Did it matter that I could not really afford organic food or manicures?

I was certainly happy to have a smoke-free, family-friendly café to visit with other moms and their kids on rainy days. As the retail environment shifted to include coffee shops, clothing stores, yoga studios, and salons—in other words, businesses that catered largely to women—I felt more at home. However, these businesses were replacing more affordable food and recreation options, and they were doing so whether I frequented them or not. My psychic comfort was coming at the cost of material access to basic needs for others in the neighbourhood, including other women.

I share these reflections because most people have a multi-layered relationship to gentrification. Some changes might be welcome, others feared. There are some arenas where you have choices and influence, others that are beyond your control.

If you are a private property developer, a landlord evicting tenants to increase the rent, or a real estate speculator buying up properties to let them sit vacant or rake in short-term rental profits, your relationship to gentrification is not so complicated. You are actively participating in it for financial gain. I am not sure why you picked up this book, but I hope it gives you a lot to think about.

For others, there are thornier issues to contemplate. How to reconcile your measly bank balance with your white privilege in a minority neighbourhood. How to feel about the new neighbours moving onto your street who seem nice enough, but look like they have money. How to make genuine connections with people across differences. How not to participate in subtle forms of social and cultural exclusion.

Thinking about these issues means attending to questions of individual intention and responsibility and their relationship to structural, systemic factors. It also entails taking on the work of understanding positionality, marginalization, and privilege. Most importantly, we always need to think about power, especially the systemic power that operates regardless of intentions.

Urban sociologists John Joe Schlichtman, Jason Patch, and Marc Lamont Hill explore the roles, positions, and identities of gentrifiers in their aptly titled book, *Gentrifier*. They note that no matter who the newcomer is, whatever their status or financial situation, they enter "into an accumulation of previous decisions, actions, and policies that frame the current reality in the neighbourhood."[47] Thus, we are always placed in a pre-existing and ever-changing web of power when we make choices about where and how to live. How we act in that web is up to us, but our decisions will be constrained by norms and values produced by long histories of domination and oppression.

Schlichtman, Patch, and Hill caution against neat divisions between good and bad actors in gentrifying neighbourhoods. Sociologist Japonica Brown-Saracino writes about gentrifiers as people searching for a kind of authenticity in urban neighbourhoods, and who, in many cases, fight to preserve the uniqueness of those neighbourhoods in the face of corporate incursions and redevelopment schemes.[48] Geographers Trina Hamilton and Winifred Curran explore the uneasy alliances among well-connected gentrifiers and long-time residents battling environmental neglect in Greenpoint, Brooklyn, where newcomers' cultural and social capital proved valuable in the battle to secure the clean-up of toxic sites like Newtown Creek.[49] Hamilton and Curran are cautious in their endorsement here, but leave room for "the possibility for gentrifier-enhanced activism that mobilises gentrifiers to invigorate pre-existing, community-led environmental activism."[50]

The presumed binary of newcomer versus long-time resident is also an oversimplification that evades the hard work of reckoning with seemingly contradictory social locations. Newcomers could include artists, students, and working-class folks who have been freshly displaced from another gentrifying neighbourhood. Their search for affordable housing may be part of the process of transforming neighbourhoods, but they are not at the vanguard of opportunistic real estate capital searching for the next area in which to make a profit.

Long-time residents, on the other hand, are often positioned as the inevitable victims of gentrification. This assumes that everyone in a neighbourhood prior to gentrification is sitting in exactly the same social and economic position and has the same amount to win or lose. However, there are stark differences in the circumstances of owners versus renters, those who work versus those on a fixed income, and those in market housing versus social housing. Differences across race, immigration status, family type, age, ability, sexuality, gender, and more are all going to affect how people experience the impacts of gentrification.

Long-time residents are put in the unenviable position of feeling like they have to choose between gentrification or a lifetime of crumbling infrastructure and dwindling amenities. Having dealt with perhaps decades of disinvestment, though, the tangible improvements that might begin to appear as gentrification takes hold are nothing to sniff at. A new playground, working street-lights, more frequent bus service: these are the kinds of things that make a real difference in day-to-day life. The relief of finally getting much-needed service might be tinged with frustration about being ignored for so long. Still, a safe place for your children to play is not an easy thing to say no to, even if the long-term consequences of these changes run counter to your interests.

Of course, long-time residents often have divergent goals. Those who are home or business owners, landlords, or investors have the opportunity to profit from rising prices. Neighbourhood-based Business Improvement Associations are typically quite active in courting gentrification under the guise of beautification projects, festivals and events, and branding initiatives. Landlords will smell the chance to raise rents and may make use of loopholes in tenant protection legislation to attract higher-earning renters. Homeowners see the value of their properties rise, often precipitously, offering them the chance to move out or access increased home equity. Similarly, business owners can raise their prices, change their offerings, or sell the business or building for a good price.

Does selling a home or business and moving on make these long-time residents complicit in gentrification? What if they no longer feel welcome in a changing neighbourhood, yet still profit from their sales? These questions remind us that the division between newcomer and long-time resident in terms of how they are located within gentrification processes is not a neat one.

How do we do this messy work, then, of tracing the webs that catch us up in geographical and historical forces? And to what end?

For me, the purpose of this work is in shifting the focus from blame (at least at the individual level) to responsibility. Blame involves looking backwards; responsibility orients us to the now and the future. When it comes to gentrification, there are lots of factors that individuals are not responsible for: deindustrialization, globalization, centuries of racial discrimination in housing and education, to name a few.

However, individuals do make decisions about how to act

within these systems. Regardless of intentions, our choices vibrate through that web of power relations. So, if you want to move toward an answer to the "am I a gentrifier" question, you might start to consider whether you are fulfilling your ethical obligations and responsibilities to live in mutually supportive ways with your neighbours (broadly defined, human and otherwise). Although you did not create the economic system or cultural norms that you might currently benefit from, what are your capacities right now, today, to act in ways that do not cause harm, or that uplift and support others?

We all need a place to live. Unfortunately, to paraphrase a popular saying, there is no ethical housing under capitalism, and certainly not under ongoing colonialism, racialized dispossession, and gendered exploitation in the home. Thus, all of us, in different ways and with different access to forms of power, are caught up in a system that primarily values the home as a financial instrument.

Under these conditions, there is no perfect checklist for making the best choices about how to live in cities today. This does not mean you get a pass on making tough decisions. Just as none of us are completely able to live in an ecologically sustainable way but are called upon to justify our lifestyle choices and reduce our harmful footprints, so can we, as city dwellers, be called on to reconsider our gentrification footprints.

WHAT IS YOUR ROLE?

Start by identifying the roles you play in what social movement strategist Deepa Iyer calls the "social change ecosystem."[51] In this model, there are ten kinds of roles that people take on in pursuit of equity, liberation, justice, and solidarity. Namely, storytellers, guides, weavers, experimenters, frontline responders, visionaries, builders, caregivers, disruptors, and healers.

I like this approach because it recognizes that we all have different strengths, capabilities, resources, and limitations when it comes to change work. We are not all frontline activists, fundraisers, visionaries, or political influencers, and that is okay. For example, I do not live in a city right now, so building and frontline work are not very accessible to me, but I can continue to be a storyteller. Healing and caregiving work is essential to any movement, although it is often undervalued and hidden (and historically done by women, femmes, and queer people). Political and intellectual risk takers like experimenters, disruptors, and visionaries help us to imagine different worlds and reorient the movement compass when things get rough.

In other words, there are many roles, and they are all integral to the success of any social change project. I encourage you to search online for Iyer's Social Change Ecosystem Map (see endnotes for the link) and explore the pieces that resonate with you.

WHAT ARE YOUR SPHERES OF INFLUENCE?

Just as we all have roles to play, we all have areas where we exert some influence. Start thinking about the professional, personal, educational, geographical, religious/spiritual, social, and institutional spaces that you move through. These are your spheres. Some of you will have fairly obvious places where you can shift your practices toward anti-gentrification. Maybe you are a planner, urban designer, architect, or developer. Maybe you are a researcher, reporter, or writer. A business owner, property owner, or landlord. A community organizer or activist. There should be many ways to apply some of the knowledge, values, and principles you have found in this book in these roles.

However, you do not have to have a direct line to city-building, politics, or property ownership to have a relevant sphere of influence. You might be a volunteer, a neighbour, or an engaged community member who wants to protect yourself and others from displacement. You could be an educator or librarian who gets to make some choices about the stories and knowledge you share. Perhaps you are an elder in your community who has important past experiences and accumulated wisdom to pass along.

Whoever you are, wherever you are, there are places to be involved. Again, you do not have to be everywhere and do everything. Find the spaces that matter to you and start there.

SEEDING CHANGE: PRINCIPLES AND PRACTICES

If this book has you feeling at least a little bit motivated, I want to give you a few seeds so that you can act on that feeling, in at least one small way, right away. None of these will stop gentrification it its tracks. But without them, we will not make any progress at all.

Know your history: You do not need to be an expert urbanist to dig into the history of your city. You might start with the question: Whose land am I on?[52] If you do not know whether you are on colonized land or who the traditional inhabitants were, now is a great time to learn about this. You can reflect on how you or your ancestors came to be on this land. You might be a descendant of settlers and/or more recent immigrants; a member of local or non-local Indigenous groups; from a formerly colonized people; or a descendant of forced migrants like enslaved people. You could also reflect on whether you have had any relationships with local Indigenous people and what you did, or did not, learn about colonization in school.

Who built the city? is another great question. Many cities were built (and some continue to be built) using enslaved labour and indentured local and migrant labour.[53] Indigenous people, particularly Kanien'kehá:ka (Mohawk) ironworkers, built and continue to build the world's landmark skyscrapers, bridges, and buildings.[54] Working conditions were and are dangerous. Many people have died doing this work, yet most of us know little about this history. You might also investigate who the influential city planners, politicians, architects, and landscape architects were in your area, as well as who the lesser-known urban figures were (hint: they are usually women and/or people of colour). You can explore the history of planning, urban renewal, redlining, displacement, segregation, or other forces that have shaped your city over the last century.

Know your now: Even if you are interested in gentrification, you might not know a whole lot about its history, and its present, in your city. It is worth investigating the perspectives of different communities on some of the changes that have happened, whether those are luxury housing developments, new retail spaces, greening projects, and so on. In doing this, you will also probably learn about organizations that are trying to address gentrification- and displacement-related concerns, for example, housing advocacy groups, anti-poverty groups, citizen planning coalitions, anti-eviction work, mutual aid projects, and more.

Look for connections: You may not think of yourself as someone involved in anti-gentrification, but if you are active in or engaged with just about any social justice cause or urban-based work, there are almost certainly connections to gentrification-related issues. Are you working on housing, homelessness, poverty, food security, violence against women, disability, environmental protection, policing, abolition, mental health, aging, sexuality? These and many more issues are at least tangentially connected to gentrification and the work you are doing is part of the big picture.

Make good choices: If we accept that gentrification and displacement are not inevitable, we can start to see the potential to make different choices in our spheres of influence and our day-to-day lives. All of us have at least a little power to redirect or redistribute some of our resources in ways that align with our values and interests in anti-gentrification. You do not have to give it all away and become a monk (although that is cool, too). At a small scale, you can make some consumer choices about where you shop, which companies you order from, and the restaurants you frequent. You could think about which organizations you donate money to and consider redeploying some cash to anti-gentrification efforts. Your volunteer time could go to housing-related advocacy work or you could bring an anti-gentrification perspective to the organizations you are already involved with.

For those that have greater wealth and control of property, you can reconsider how you use those resources. Now, do not let me stop you from giving them all away; but, if you cannot see your way there just yet, maybe you will consider some interim steps. Can you shift your investments away from places that profit off gentrification? If your investment strategy involves property, how can you bring all or some of the profit you make back into the community? What uses can those spaces be put to that would benefit long-term or vulnerable residents? If you are a business owner in a gentrifying neighbourhood, can you offer your space or services to community organizations for events and meetings at little to no cost? If you rent property out, can you keep it in the long-term rental pool at reasonable rates rather than contributing to the rising cost of housing and low vacancies by renting on Airbnb or tourist sites?

Challenge common sense: This whole book has encouraged you to challenge the common-sense stories we hear about gentrification and to tell better stories. We all have the opportunity to push back against these and other bits of taken-for-granted "wisdom" that contribute to the keeping the status quo in place. Whether it is the orthodoxy of "growth is good," the trickle-down economics theory that just will not die, the belief that gentrification lifts everyone up, the notion that protest does not work, or the idea that there are no alternatives, do not be afraid to be the killjoy in the boardroom, at the dinner table, in the classroom, or in the design studio.[55]

Find your outside: It is popular to say there is no "outside of capitalism," and I understand the sentiment, but I also refuse to cede the entire universe to one, relatively recent, way of organizing the economy and society. The greatest trick of capitalism and its proponents has been to convince us that there are no alternatives, that everything we do is already part and parcel of this one system.

However, all of us, every day, engage in acts, relationships, and ways of thinking that are not fully predetermined by capitalism. From acts of care for others to the relationships we develop with the birds in the garden, there is always space beyond what capitalism contains in its box of exploitative power relations.

Community economies scholars like J. K. Gibson-Graham and others use the iceberg metaphor to argue that the formal, capitalist economy is only the tip, while the bulk of activities that keep society functioning are underwater and not inevitably capitalist.[56] They use the language of "the diverse economy" to acknowledge that there are already other worlds and ways of doing things all around us (a pluriverse). Finding *your* outside of capitalism, even if it is in your imagination, is part of the work of creating change and moving toward a different urban future.

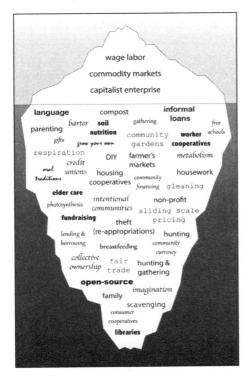

Diverse Economies Iceberg. Source: Community Economies Collective, communityeconomies.org (CC BY-SA 4.0).

Build equity in: The paradigm of design justice is an inspiring one for anti-gentrification work. After all, anti-gentrification is not just about stopping a particular process, it is about imagining and creating—designing better ways of housing people, building community, and serving people's needs in the city, for example. Communications scholar Sasha Costanza-Chock argues that designers (which can include all of us!) need to take an intersectional, equity-focused approach to problem solving and world-making. Too often, the objects, places, and systems that we live and work within encode biases across race, gender, ability, sexuality, and more. Design justice "rethinks design processes, centres people who are normally marginalized by design, and uses collaborative, creative practices to address the deepest challenges our communities face."[57]

In urban social justice movements, design justice principles remind us that people, not just planners, architects, urban designers, or other experts, have the wisdom and expertise to participate meaningfully and equitably in generating solutions to the problems that they face. The outcomes of any project, whether it is a new housing development, CLT, community space, or park, need to be controlled and managed by the community.

Furthermore, the effects of any intervention on people across different social locations and identities have to be considered at every step of the process. In design justice, equity is not just one desired outcome, it is the whole point. As you engage in projects for change, big or small, can you consider design justice principles throughout the process, from conception to realization? How can you encourage deep participation and mutual learning by and with affected communities? To learn more, the full text of Costanza-Chock's book *Design Justice* is available online, open access.

Keep the faith: Abolitionist activist and writer Mariame Kaba says "hope is a discipline." It is not a feeling that we have or do not have, that appears or disappears. It is not simple optimism or relentless positivity. Rather, hope is a practice. You choose it every day by taking actions, however small, toward creating the world you want to live in. Just because we might not live to see it fully realized is no reason not to practise hope. Kaba says that she reminds young organizers: "Your timeline is not the timeline on which movements occur." She finds freedom in letting go of the assumption that all of the work can and will be done on a knowable timeline, because then you can "do the work that's necessary as you see it and contribute in the ways you see fit."[58]

Keeping faith, practising hope: these are the ways we keep rewriting the hopeless stories of inevitability, of the impossibility of change. Kaba insists: "I understand why people feel that way. I just choose differently. I choose to think a different way, and I choose to act in a different way."

This is a power we all have. You use it every time you show up at a protest against a development that will probably happen anyway. You exercise it when you send a little money to an organization that is trying to keep people in their homes despite the churning of the eviction machine. You draw on it when you volunteer your time to go door to door talking to neighbours about their rights. The possibilities are endless, and the really amazing thing is that you are probably using that power a little bit, every day, already.

TELL A BETTER STORY

By the time this book is in your hands, the stories I weave here will have already begun to unravel and be rewoven by others. That is the nature of stories, of scholarship, of the theories we generate to explain the world. As I hope this book demonstrates, the way we construct our theories—our stories—matters. While it is impossible to tell a perfect, all-encompassing story that does justice to every voice and every nuance, it is imperative to keep being flexible and expansive.

I am committed to never getting too comfortable with the stories I hear, or the ones I write, for that matter. The story I set out to tell when I began this book is different than the one I ended up writing, because along the way I learned a lot, challenged my own thinking, and tried to respond to the rapidly changing reality of the world around me.

In some ways, gentrification began to feel like a less-urgent topic as the Covid-19 pandemic spread like wildfire, while actual wildfires and other climate-related disasters threatened the survival of so many, human and non-human. However, the logics of domination, exploitation, and power over others and the earth that have produced these crises are, at their roots, the same as those that produce gentrification and displacement.

As I noted earlier in this book, the connections between gentrification and the pandemic and gentrification and climate change are more than conceptual. They fuel, and are fuelled by, one another. The displacements caused by pandemic closures and economic hardship leave spaces that may be ripe for gentrification. The desire to protect one's home from climate change-induced damage is propelling gentrification and ongoing disparities in environmental justice. We do not have to dig very deep to see the ways that these issues are interconnected.

The purpose of this book is to make those and other connections between gentrification and multiple systems of power and oppression more visible by breathing a little extra space into the stories told about gentrification by researchers, policymakers, planners, reporters, and activists. I hope you set it down feeling more aware of your position with respect to gentrification and the responsibilities that position entails.

Responsibility is not a burden. It is an opportunity to use our capacities and resources, whatever form those take, to work toward building cities and neighbourhoods that support human and non-human flourishing, nurture relationships of care, and give all of us what we universally need: a home.

NOTES

1. GENTRIFICATION IS . . .

1   Michael Kaminer, "Skid Row to Hip in Toronto," *New York Times,* July 5, 2009, travel.nytimes.com.

2   Kaminer, "Skid Row to Hip in Toronto."

3   Leslie Kern, "From Toxic Wreck to Crunchy Chic: Environmental Gentrification Through the Body," *Environment and Planning D: Society and Space,* 33,1 (2015): 77.

4   Ruth Glass, "London: Aspects of Change (1964)," in *The Gentrification Reader,* eds. Loretta Lees, Tom Slater, and Elvin Wyly (London: Routledge, 2010): 7.

5   Glass, "London," 7.

6   Condominiums are a form of housing with a stratified ownership structure. A condominium corporation owns the common elements of the building or community (parking garages, walkways, gyms, lobbies, exteriors) while individuals or households own their own units within the building or community and pay monthly fees toward the maintenance of the shared elements.

7   Fenne M. Pinkster and Willem R. Boterman, "When the Spell Is Broken: Gentrification, Urban Tourism and Privileged Discontent in the Amsterdam Canal District," *cultural geographies,* 24,3 (2017): 457–72.

8   Damaris Rose, "Rethinking Gentrification: Beyond the Uneven

Development of Marxist Urban Theory," *Environment and Planning D: Society and Space,* 2,1 (1984): 47–74.

9   Da'Shaun Harrison, "Gentrification Is Not a Myth, It Is Real Violence," *Wear Your Voice Magazine,* November 20, 2019, wearyourvoicemag.com.

10   Tyler Fenwick, "Author Ta-Nehisi Coates Sounds Off on Reparations and Admits He's Optimistic about America," *Philadelphia Tribune,* May 20, 2019, phillytrib.com.

11   Winifred Curran, *Gender and Gentrification* (New York: Routledge, 2018).

12   Nick Estes, "Anti-Indian Common Sense: Border Town Violence and Resistance in Mni Luzahan," in *Settler City Limits: Indigenous Resurgence and Colonial Violence in the Urban Prairie West,* eds. Heather Dorries, Robert Henry, David Hugill, Tyler McCreary and Julie Tomiak (Winnipeg: University of Manitoba Press, 2019).

13   Rebecca Solnit and Susan Schwartzenberg, *Hollow City: The Siege of San Francisco and the Crisis of American Urbanism* (London and New York: Verso, 2000): 29–30.

2. GENTRIFICATION IS NATURAL

1   Philip Ball, "Gentrification Is a Natural Evolution," *Guardian,* November 19, 2014, theguardian.com.

2   Ball, "Gentrification Is a Natural Evolution."

3   Adam Satariano, "'He's Buying Up Brixton': Beloved Grocer's Eviction Sparks Gentrification Fight," *New York Times,* July 6, 2020, nytimes.com.

4   Oliver Wainwright, "Penthouses and Poor Doors: How Europe's 'Biggest Regeneration Project' Fell Flat," *Guardian,* February 2, 2021, theguardian.com.

5   Jane Jacobs, *The Death and Life of Great American Cities* (New York: Random House, 1961).

6   John Scott and Ray Bromley, *Envisioning Sociology: Victor Branford, Patrick Geddes, and the Quest for Social Reconstruction* (Albany: State University of New York Press, 2013).

7   Amy Koritz, "Urban Form vs. Human Function in the 1920s: Lewis Mumford and John Dos Passos," *American Studies,* 45,2 (2004): 101–23.

8   Júlia Todolí, "Disease Metaphors in Urban Planning," *Critical Approaches to Discourse Analysis Across Disciplines,* 1,2 (2007): 51–60.

9   Robert E. Park and Ernest W. Burgess, *The City* (Chicago: The University of Chicago Press, 2019 [1925]); Dennis R. Judd and Dick Simpson, eds.

The City Revisited: Urban Theory From Chicago, Los Angeles, and New York (Minneapolis: University of Minnesota Press, 2011).

10   Tim Cresswell, "Weeds, Plagues, and Bodily Secretions: A Geographical Interpretation of Metaphors of Displacement," *Annals of the Association of American Geographers,* 87,2 (1997): 330–45.

11   Cresswell, "Weeds, Plagues, and Bodily Secretions," 336.

12   Friendship Centres are common in Canadian cities. They are non-profit community organizations that provide support and resources for urban Indigenous people: nafc.ca/friendship-centres.

13   Victoria Freeman, "'Toronto Has No History!': Indigeneity, Settler Colonialism, and Historical Memory in Canada's Largest City," *Urban History Review,* 38,2 (2010): 21–35.

14   Sarah Launius and Geoffrey Alan Boyce, "More Than Metaphor: Settler Colonialism, Frontier Logic, and the Continuities of Racialized Dispossession in a Southwest U.S. City," *Annals of the American Association of Geographers,* 111,1 (2021): 157–74.

15   Silvano Onofri, "Colonization (Biological)," in *Encyclopedia of Astrobiology,* eds. Muriel Gargaud, Ricardo Amils, José Cernicharo Quintanilla, Henderson James Cleaves II, William M. Irvine, Daniele L. Pinti and Michel Viso, 2011, link.springer.com.

16   Jim Stratton, *Pioneering in the Urban Wilderness* (New York: Urizen Books, 1977).

17   Neil Smith, *The New Urban Frontier: Gentrification and the Revanchist City* (London: Routledge, 1996).

18   Wakíŋyaŋ Waáŋataŋ (Matt Remle), "Gentrification Is NOT the New Colonialism," *Last Real Indians,* July 29, 2017, lastrealindians.com.

19   J. K. Gibson-Graham, *The End of Capitalism (As We Knew It): A Feminist Critique of Political Economy* (Minneapolis: University of Minnesota Press, 1996).

3. GENTRIFICATION IS ABOUT TASTE

1   Katie Grant, "Cereal Killer Café Shuts Down: Owners Say 'Cheerio' and 'See You Spoon' after Closing Doors of Controversial Business," *iNews,* July 13, 2020, inews.co.uk.

2   BBC News London, "Cereal Killer Cafe Damaged in Shoreditch Anti-Gentrification Protest," September 27, 2015, bbc.com.

3   Ashok Selvam, "Bow Truss in Pilsen Again Roasted with

Anti-Gentrification Graffiti," *Eater Chicago*, October 26, 2015, chicago.
eater.com.

4   Betty Friedan, *The Feminine Mystique* (New York: W.W. Norton and
     Company, 1997 [1963]).

5   Jon Caulfield, *City Form and Everyday Life: Toronto's Gentrification and
     Critical Social Practice* (Toronto: University of Toronto Press, 1994).

6   David Ley, *The New Middle Class and the Remaking of the Central City*
     (Oxford: Oxford University Press, 1996).

7   Sharon Zukin, *Loft Living: Culture and Capital in Urban Change* (New
     Brunswick, NJ: Rutgers University Press, 1989 [1982]): 4.

8   Stuart Henderson, *Making the Scene: Yorkville and Hip Toronto in the 1960s*
     (Toronto: University of Toronto Press, 2011).

9   Damaris Rose, "Feminist Perspectives on Employment Restructuring and
     Gentrification: The Case of Montreal," in *The Power of Geography*, eds.
     Jennifer Wolch and Michael Dear (Boston: Unwin Hyman, 1989): 118–38.

10   Sam Friedman, "Why Do So Many Professional, Middle-Class Brits Insist
     They're Working Class?," *Guardian*, January 18, 2021, theguardian.com.

11   Pierre Bourdieu, "The Forms of Capital," in *Handbook of Theory and
     Research for the Sociology of Education*, ed. John G. Richardson (New York:
     Greenwood, 1986): 241–58.

12   Routledge Sociology, "Cultural Capital: Pierre Bourdieu," *Social Theory
     Re-Wired*, 2016, routledgesoc.com.

13   Routledge Sociology, "Cultural Capital."

14   Zukin, *Loft Living*.

15   Heather McLean, "Digging into the Creative City: A Feminist Critique,"
     Antipode, 46,3 (2014): 677.

16   Charles Landry and Franco Bianchini, *The Creative City* (London:
     Demos, 1995).

17   Richard Florida, *The Rise of the Creative Class* (New York: Basic Books, 2002);
     Florida, *Who's Your City?: How the Creative Economy Is Making Where to Live
     the Most Important Decision of Your Life* (New York: Basic Books, 2008).

18   Jamie Peck, "Struggling with the Creative Class," *International Journal
     of Urban and Regional Research*, 29,4 (2005): 740–70; John Paul Catungal,
     Deborah Leslie, and Yvonne Hii, "Geographies of Displacement in the
     Creative City: The Case of Liberty Village, Toronto," *Urban Studies*,
     46,5–6 (2009): 1095–114.

19   Brenda Parker, *Masculinities and Markets: Raced and Gendered Urban
     Politics in Milwaukee* (Athens: University of Georgia Press, 2017).

20   McLean, "Digging into the Creative City."

21 Allison Arieff, "Where Are All the Female Architects?," *New York Times*, December 15, 2018, nytimes.com; India Block, "'No More Excuses for All-Male Panels' Says Rebel Architette," *DeZeen Magazine*, June 2, 2020, dezeen.com; Tomoko Yokoi, "Female Gamers Are on the Rise: Can the Gaming Industry Catch Up?," *Forbes*, March 4, 2021, forbes.com.

22 Richard Florida, *The New Urban Crisis: How Our Cities Are Increasing Inequality, Deepening Segregation, and Failing the Middle Class—and What We Can Do About It* (New York: Basic Books, 2017).

23 Shirin Ghaffary, "Even Tech Workers Can't Afford to Buy Homes in San Francisco," *Vox Recode*, March 19, 2019, vox.com; Metropolitan Transportation Commission, "Housing Affordability," *Vital Signs Report*, February 2019, vitalsigns.mtc.ca.gov.

24 Elizabeth Kneebone and Emily Garr, "The Suburbanization of Poverty: Trends in Metropolitan America, 2000 to 2008," *The Brookings Institution*, January 20, 2010, brookings.edu.

25 *My Brooklyn*, directed by Kelly Anderson, USA, 2012.

26 Daniel M. Sullivan and Samuel C. Shaw, "Retail Gentrification and Race: The Case of Alberta Street in Portland, Oregon," *Urban Affairs Review*, 47,3 (2011): 422.

27 Sig Langegger, "Viva la Raza!: A Park, a Riot and Neighbourhood Change in North Denver," *Urban Studies*, 50,16 (2013): 3360–77; David Trouille, "Fencing a Field: Imagined Others in the Unfolding of a Neighborhood Park Conflict," *City and Community*, 13,1 (2014): 69–87.

28 Daniel M. Sullivan, "From Food Desert to Food Mirage: Race, Social Class, and Food Shopping in a Gentrifying Neighborhood," *Advances in Applied Sociology*, 4,1 (2014): 30–35.

29 Natalie Moore, "Signs Urging Residents to Call the Police on Chicago's Bucket Boys Spark Outrage," *WBEZ Chicago*, January 29, 2021, wbez.org.

30 Jon Betancur and Youngjun Kim, "The Trajectory and Impact of Ongoing Gentrification in Pilsen," Nathalie P. Voorhees Center for Neighborhood and Community Improvement University of Illinois Chicago, 2016, voorheescenter.uic.edu.

31 Jennifer L. Stoever, *The Sonic Color Line: Race and the Cultural Politics of Listening* (New York: New York University Press, 2016).

32 Brandi Thompson Summers, "Reclaiming the Chocolate City: Soundscapes of Gentrification and Resistance in Washington, DC," *Environment and Planning D: Society and Space*, 39,1 (2021): 32.

33 Stoever, *The Sonic Color Line*, 2.

34 Tom Slater, "The Eviction of Critical Perspectives from Gentrification Research," *International Journal of Urban and Regional Research*, 30,4 (2006): 737–57.

4. GENTRIFICATION IS ABOUT MONEY

1   Mauricio Peña and Colin Boyle, "After Old Crawford Coal Plant Smokestack Blown Up, Little Village Residents Worry About Dust During Global Pandemic," *Block Club Chicago*, April 11, 2020, blockclubchicago.org.

2   Jonathan Levy and John D. Spengler, *Estimated Public Health Impacts of Criteria Pollutant Air Emissions from Nine Fossil-Fueled Power Plants in Illinois* (Cambridge, MA: Harvard School of Public Health Report, prepared for Clean Air Task Force: 2001).

3   Julie Wernau, "Fisk, Crawford Coal Plants Had Long History, as Did Battle to Close Them," *Chicago Tribune*, September 2, 2012, chicagotribune.com.

4   Neil Smith, "Toward a Theory of Gentrification: A Back to the City Movement by Capital, Not People," *Journal of the American Planning Association,* 45,4 (1979): 538–48.

5   A Marxian approach draws and on and develops Marxist economic theories while not necessarily being ideologically or politically Marxist.

6   Smith, "Toward a Theory of Gentrification," 546.

7   Smith, "Toward a Theory of Gentrification," 545.

8   Leslie Kern and Caroline Kovesi, "Environmental Justice Meets the Right to Stay Put: Mobilising Against Environmental Racism, Gentrification, and Xenophobia in Chicago's Little Village," *Local Environment,* 23,9 (2018): 952–66.

9   John Greenfield, "Little Village Residents Hope Paseo Won't Be a Path to Gentrification," *Chicago Reader*, March 23, 2016, www.chicagoreader.com.

10   Alex Nitkin, "Pilsen's Own 606 Trail?: Rahm Announces New 'Paseo' Project," *DNAInfo Chicago*, March 21, 2016, dnainfo.com.

11   Harry Huggins, "Little Village Residents Welcome Diversity, Fear Rising Rents," *Medill Reports Chicago*, January 27, 2016, news.medill. northwestern.edu; Grace Wong, "Plans for Little Village Rails-to-Trails Project Discussed at Community Meeting," *Chicago Tribune*, March 17, 2016, www.chicagotribune.com.

12   Jackie Serrato, "Little Village Tenants Protest Evictions: 'We Will Not Be Gentrified!,'" *DNAInfo Chicago*, August 17, 2016, dnainfo.com; Alexandra Pacurar, "Development Boom Tempers Chicago Rent Growth," *Commercial Property Executive*, July 26, 2017, cpexecutive.com.

13   Yukare Nakayama, "Little Village Youth Protest Gentrification, Little Village Plaza New Owners: 'We're Not Gonna Let Things Get Taken Away From Us Anymore,'" *ABC Eyewitness News*, September 17, 2020, abc7chicago.com.

14 Lilia Fernández, *Brown in the Windy City: Mexicans and Puerto Ricans in Postwar Chicago* (Chicago: University of Chicago Press, 2012).

15 *Roger and Me*, directed by Michael Moore, USA, 1989.

16 Brett Story, *Prison Land: Mapping Carceral Power Across Neoliberal America* (Minneapolis: University of Minnesota Press, 2019).

17 Andrew Emil Gansky, "'Ruin Porn' and the Ambivalence of Decline: Andrew Moore's Photographs of Detroit," *Photography and Culture*, 7,2 (2014): 119–39; Brian Doucet and Drew Philp, "In Detroit 'Ruin Porn' Ignores the Voices of Those Who Still Call the City Home," *Guardian*, February 15, 2016, theguardian.com.

18 *Trainspotting*, directed by Danny Boyle, UK, 1996.

19 Winifred Curran, "'From the Frying Pan to the Oven': Gentrification and the Experience of Industrial Displacement in Williamsburg, Brooklyn," *Urban Studies*, 44,8 (2007): 1427–40.

20 Zukin, *Loft Living*, 2–3.

21 Caulfield, *City Form and City Life*; Catungal, Leslie, and Hii, "Geographies of Displacement in the Creative City."

22 David Harvey, "From Managerialism to Entrepreneurialism: The Transformation in Urban Governance in Late Capitalism," *Geografiska Annaler: Series B, Human Geography*, 71,1 (1989): 3–17.

23 Jamie Peck and Adam Tickell, "Neoliberalizing Space," *Antipode*, 34,3 (2002): 380–404.

24 David Harvey, *The New Imperialism* (Oxford: Oxford University Press, 2003). Harvey is widely known as a Marxist, rather than Marxian, geographer, as he is politically committed to Marxist socialism.

25 Raju Das, "David Harvey's Theory of Accumulation by Dispossession: A Marxist Critique," *World Review of Political Economy*, 8,4 (2017): 590–616.

26 Loretta Lees, "Super-Gentrification: The Case of Brooklyn Heights, New York City," *Urban Studies*, 40,12 (2003): 2487–509.

27 Randy K. Lippert, *Condo Conquest: Urban Governance, Law, and Condoization in New York City and Toronto* (Vancouver: University of British Columbia Press, 2019).

28 Sean Boynton, "Vacant Homes in Vancouver Continue to Dwindle Due to Empty Homes Tax: Mayor," *Global News*, February 7, 2020, globalnews.ca.

29 David Wachsmuth and Alexander Weisler, "Airbnb and the Rent Gap: Gentrification Through the Sharing Economy," *Environment and Planning A: Economy and Space*, 50,6 (2018): 1147–70.

30 Jennifer Combs, Danielle Kerrigan, and David Wachsmuth, "Short-Term

Rentals in Canada: Uneven Growth, Uneven Impacts," *Canadian Journal of Urban Research*, 29,1 (2020): 119–34.

31 Stephen Burgen, Jon Henley, and Rory Carroll, "Airbnb Slump Means Europe's Cities Can Return to Residents, Say Officials," *Guardian*, May 9, 2020, theguardian.com.

32 Sharda Rozena and Loretta Lees, "The Everyday Lived Experiences of Airbnbification in London," *Social and Cultural Geography* (2021), doi: 10.1080/14649365.2021.1939124.

33 Dustin Robertson, Christopher Oliver, and Eric Nost, "Short-Term Rentals as Digitally-Mediated Tourism Gentrification: Impacts on Housing in New Orleans," *Tourism Geographies* (2020), doi: 10.1080/14616688.2020.1765011.

34 Tom Perkins, "'Like a Ghost Town': How Short-Term Rentals Dim New Orleans' Legacy," *Guardian*, March 13, 2019, theguardian.com.

35 Lyndsey Matthews, "New Orleans Bans Airbnb-Style Rentals from Garden District, Most of French Quarter," *Afar Magazine*, August 9, 2019, afar.com.

36 Kiley Goyette, "'Making Ends Meet' by Renting Homes to Strangers: Historicizing Airbnb Through Women's Supplemental Income," *City* (2021), doi: 10.1080/13604813.2021.1935777.

37 Jasmine Tucker and Clair Ewing-Nelson, "Women of Color Would Be Hardest Hit if Eviction Protections End," National Women's Law Center Fact Sheet, June 2021.

38 Pete E. Moskowitz, *How to Kill a City: Gentrification, Inequality, and the Fight for the Neighbourhood* (New York: Bold Type Books, 2017): 18.

39 Moskowitz, *How to Kill a City*, 26.

40 Naomi Klein, *The Shock Doctrine: The Rise of Disaster Capitalism* (Toronto: Alfred A. Knopf Canada, 2007).

41 Jamie Peck, "Liberating the City: Between New York and New Orleans," *Urban Geography*, 27,8 (2006): 681–713.

42 Moskowitz, *How to Kill a City*.

43 Clinton Parks, "Hurricane Sandy May Have Worsened Gentrification in Brooklyn and Queens," Earth Institute, Columbia Climate School, October 3, 2019, blogs.ei.columbia.edu; Yung Chun, "Gentrification of Neighborhoods in New York City after Hurricane Sandy: Focusing on Housing Market Change of Three Borough Regions by Zip Code Area" (Master thesis, Columbia University, 2015); Joanne Massey, "The Gentrification of Consumption: A View from Manchester," *Sociological Research Online*, 10,2 (2005): 114–24; Jess Linz, "Where Crises Converge: The Affective Register of Displacement in Mexico City's Post-Earthquake Gentrification," *cultural geographies* (2021), doi: 10.1177/1474474021993418.

44 Hao Chen and Yunpeng Zhang, "Dancing with the Devil?: Gentrification and Urban Struggles in, Through and Against the State in Nanjing, China," *Geoforum*, 12,1 (2021): 74–82; Anna Badyina and Oleg Golubchikov, "Gentrification in Central Moscow: A Market Process or a Deliberate Policy?: Money, Power and People in Housing Regeneration in Ostozhenka," *Geografiska Annaler: Series B, Human Geography*, 87,2 (2005): 113–29.

45 Neil Smith, "New Globalism, New Urbanism: Gentrification as Global Urban Strategy," *Antipode*, 34,3 (2002): 427–50.

46 Ståle Holgerson, "The 'Middle Class' Does Not Exist: A Critique of Gentrification Research," *Antipode Online*, September 9, 2020, antipodeonline.org.

47 Leslie Kern and Heather McLean, "Undecidability and the Urban: Feminist Pathways Through Urban Political Economy," *ACME: An International Journal for Critical Geographies*, 16,3 (2017): 405–426.

48 Kern and McLean, "Undecidability and the Urban," 406.

49 Rosalind Deutsche, "Boystown," *Environment and Planning D: Society and Space*, 9,1 (1991): 5–30.

5. GENTRIFICATION IS ABOUT CLASS

1 Leslie Kern, *Sex and the Revitalized City: Gender, Condominium Development, and Urban Citizenship* (Vancouver: University of British Columbia Press, 2010).

2 Leslie Kern, "Selling the Scary City: Gendering Freedom, Fear and Condominium Development in the Neoliberal City," *Social and Cultural Geography*, 11,3 (2010): 209–30.

3 Kimberlé Crenshaw, "Demarginalizing the Intersection of Race and Sex: A Black Feminist Critique of Antidiscrimination Doctrine, Feminist Theory, and Antiracist Politics," in *Feminist Legal Theory: Readings in Law and Gender*, eds. Katherine Bartlett and Roseanne Kennedy (New York: Routledge, 1991): 57–80.

4 Alan Warde, "Gentrification as Consumption: Issues of Class and Gender," *Environment and Planning D: Society and Space*, 9,2 (1991): 223–32.

5 Liz Bondi, "Gender Divisions and Gentrification: A Critique," *Transactions of the Institute of British Geographers*, 16,2 (1991):190–98; Kim England, "Gender Relations and the Spatial Structure of the City," *Geoforum*, 22,2 (1991): 135–47; Gerda Wekerle, "A Woman's Place Is in the City," *Antipode*, 16,3 (1984): 11–19.

6 Ann R. Markusen, "City Spatial Structure, Women's Household Work,

and National Urban Policy," *Signs: Journal of Women in Culture and Society*, 5,S3 (1980): 22–44.

7   Parker, *Masculinities and Markets*.

8   World Health Organization, "Violence Against Women," March 9, 2021, who.int.

9   World Health Organization, "Violence Against Women."

10 Tara Carman, "Women, Children Turned Away from Shelters in Canada Almost 19,000 Times a Month," *CBC News*, March 5, 2020, cbc.ca.

11 Caroline Bradbury-Jones and Louise Isham, "The Pandemic Paradox: The Consequences of COVID-19 on Domestic Violence," *Journal of Clinical Nursing*, 29,13–14 (2020): 2047–49.

12 Brad Boserup, Mark McKenney, and Adel Elkbuli, "Alarming Trends in US Domestic Violence During the COVID-19 Pandemic," *American Journal of Emergency Medicine*, 38,12 (2020): 2753–55.

13 Curran, *Gender and Gentrification*.

14 Amber Jamieson, "Her Landlord Asked to Spend the Night with Her after She Lost Her Job and Couldn't Afford Rent," *BuzzFeed News*, May 14, 2020, buzzfeednews.com.

15 Jamieson, "Her Landlord Asked to Spend the Night."

16 Phil Hubbard, "Revenge and Injustice in the Neoliberal City: Uncovering Masculinist Agendas," *Antipode*, 36,4 (2004): 665–86; Marilyn A. Papayanis, "Sex and the Revanchist City: Zoning Out Pornography in New York," *Environment and Planning D: Society and Space*, 18,3 (2000): 341–53.

17 Bryce Covert, "Why Landlords Target Mothers for Eviction," *New Republic*, March 16, 2021, newrepublic.com.

18 Curran, *Gender and Gentrification*.

19 Curran, *Gender and Gentrification*, 26.

20 Citizens Housing and Planning Council, "What the F Is a Feminist Housing Plan?," 2021, chpcny.org.

21 Wekerle, "A Woman's Place is in the City."

22 Parker, *Masculinities and Markets*.

23 Nancy Fraser, *Fortunes of Feminism: From State-Managed Capitalism to Neoliberal Crisis* (London: Verso, 2013).

24 Adrienne Rich, "Compulsory Heterosexuality and Lesbian Existence," *Signs: Journal of Women in Culture and Society*, 5,4 (1980): 631–60.

25 Curran, *Gender and Gentrification*, 5.

26 Mickey Lauria and Larry Knopp, "Toward an Analysis of the Role of Gay

Communities in the Urban Renaissance," *Urban Geography*, 6,2 (1985): 152–69.

27   Heidi J. Nast, "Queer Patriarchies, Queer Racisms, International," *Antipode*, 34,5 (2002): 874–909; Dana Collins, *The Rise and Fall of an Urban Sexual Community: Malate (Dis)placed* (London: Palgrave Macmillan, 2016).

28   Curran, *Gender and Gentrification*.

29   Jen Jack Gieseking, *A Queer New York: Geographies of Lesbians, Dykes, and Queers* (New York: New York University Press, 2020): 7.

30   Erin Fitzgerald, Sarah Elspeth, and Darby Hickey, "Meaningful Work: Transgender Experiences in the Sex Trade" (Washington, D.C.: National Center for Transgender Equality, 2015).

31   Curran, *Gender and Gentrification*.

32   Julie Podmore, "Gone 'Underground'?: Lesbian Visibility and the Consolidation of Queer Space in Montréal," *Social and Cultural Geography*, 7,4 (2006): 595–625; Tamar Rothenberg, "'And She Told Two Friends': Lesbians Creating Urban Social Space," in *Mapping Desire: Geographies of Sexualities*, eds. David J. Bell and Gill Valentine (New York: Routledge, 1995): 150–65.

33   Sarah Schulman, *The Gentrification of the Mind: Witness to a Lost Imagination* (Berkeley: University of California Press, 2012): 26.

34   Schulman, *The Gentrification of the Mind*, 38.

35   Julie Bosman, "Chicago Suburb Shapes Reparations for Black Residents: 'It Is the Start,'" *New York Times*, March 22, 2021, nytimes.com; Brentin Mock, "What It Actually Means to Pass Local 'Reparations,'" *Bloomberg CityLab*, April 15, 2021, bloomberg.com.

36   Deborah Ralston, "Home Ownership and Super Are Far More Entwined than You Might Think," *Conversation*, December 10, 2020, theconversation.com; J. David Hulchanski, "A Tale of Two Canadas: Homeowners Getting Richer, Renters Getting Poorer" (Toronto: Centre for Urban and Community Studies, 2001).

37   Keeanga-Yamattha Taylor, *Race for Profit: How Banks and the Real Estate Industry Undermined Black Homeownership* (Chapel Hill, NC: University of North Carolina Press, 2019); Natalie Y. Moore, *The South Side: A Portrait of Chicago and American Segregation* (London: St. Martin's Publishing, 2016).

38   Linda Gartz, *Redlined: A Memoir of Race, Change, and Fractured Community in 1960s Chicago* (Berkeley: She Writes Press, 2018); Richard Rothstein, *The Color of Law: A Forgotten History of How Our Government Segregated America* (New York: Liveright, 2017).

39   The G.I. Bill is the popular name for the Serviceman's Readjustment

Act of 1944, which enabled a variety of social programs and benefits for soldiers returning from the Second World War, including low-cost mortgages and low-interest loans.

40   The Fair Labor Standards Act was part of President Roosevelt's New Deal designed to improve working conditions, including pay, benefits, and safety standards, in many industries. However, Black-dominated occupations were excluded from the legislation, leaving Black Americans behind as workers and without the benefit of improved wages and buying power.

41   David Callahan, "How the GI Bill Left Out African Americans," *Demos*, November 11, 2013, demos.org; Kriston McIntosh, Emily Moss, Ryan Nunn, and Jay Shambaugh, "Examining the Black-White Wealth Gap," *Brookings Institution*, February 27, 2020, brookings.edu.

42   Ta-Nehisi Coates, "The Case for Reparations," *Atlantic*, June 2014, theatlantic.com.

43   McIntosh, Moss, Nunn, and Shambaugh, "Examining the Black-White Wealth Gap."

44   Darrick Hamilton and William J. Darity, "Can 'Baby Bonds' Eliminate the Racial Wealth Gap in Putative Post-Racial America?," *Review of Black Political Economy*, 3,3–4 (2010): 207–16.

45   Cedric J. Robinson, *Black Marxism: The Making of the Black Radical Tradition* (Chapel Hill, NC: University of North Carolina Press, 1983).

46   Robin D. G. Kelley, "What Did Cedric Robinson Mean by Racial Capitalism?," *Boston Review*, January 12, 2017, bostonreview.net.

47   Jodi Melamed, "Racial Capitalism," *Critical Ethnic Studies*, 1,1 (2015): 76–85.

48   Katherine McKittrick, "Plantation Futures," *Small Axe*, 17,3-42 (2013): 1–15.

49   Lance Freeman, *There Goes the Hood: Views of Gentrification From the Ground Up* (Philadelphia: Temple University Press, 2011).

50   Jonathan Glick, "Gentrification and the Racialized Geography of Home Equity," *Urban Affairs Review*, 44,2 (2008): 280–95; Cameron Hightower and James C. Fraser, "The Raced-Space of Gentrification: 'Reverse Blockbusting,' Home Selling, and Neighborhood Remake in North Nashville," *City and Community*, 19,1 (2020): 223–44.

51   Robert D. Bullard, *Dumping in Dixie: Race, Class and Environmental Quality* (New York: Routledge, 1990).

52   Kathryn Vasel, "You Can Buy a House in Flint for $14,000," *CNN*, March 4, 2016, money.cnn.com; Daniel Goldstein, "Lead Poisoning Crisis Sends Flint Real-Estate Market Tumbling," *MarketWatch*, February 17, 2016, marketwatch.com.

53 Jeremy McDonald, Menna Elnaka and Asha Tomlinson, "It Pays to Get a 2nd Home Appraisal, Especially if You're a Black Homeowner, Hidden Camera Investigation Shows," *CBC News*, March 5, 2021, cbc.ca.

54 Brentin Mock, "A Neighborhood's Race Affects Home Values More Now than in 1980," *Bloomberg CityLab*, September 21, 2020, bloomberg.com.

55 Junia Howell and Elizabeth Korver-Glenn, "Race Determines Home Values More Today than It Did in 1980," *Rice Kinder Institute for Urban Research*, September 24, 2020, kinder.rice.edu.

56 Listen Chen and Lama Mugabo, "Is 'Revitalizing' Hogan's Alley Black Racial Justice?: Tensions Between Real Estate and Redress in Black Vancouver's Community and Housing Development, An Interview with Lama Mugabo," *Volcano*, May 21, 2019, thevolcano.org.

57 Craig Wilder, *A Covenant with Color: Race and Social Power in Brooklyn* (New York: Columbia University Press, 2000).

58 Amanda Parris, "Remembering Little Jamaica: This New Film Pays Tribute to a Disappearing Toronto Neighbourhood," *CBC News*, September 27, 2019, cbc.ca.

59 Parris, "Remembering Little Jamaica."

60 Tarry Hum, "Black Dispossession and the Making of Downtown Flushing," *Progressive City*, n.d., progressivecity.net.

61 Amanda Boston, "Gentrifying the City: From Racialized Neglect to Racialized Reinvestment," *Insights from the Social Sciences*, September 1, 2020, items.ssrc.org.

62 Boston, "Gentrifying the City."

63 Christopher Mele, "Neoliberalism, Race and the Redefining of Urban Redevelopment," *International Journal of Urban and Regional Research*, 37,2 (2013): 598–617.

64 Nadia Rhook, "What's in a Grid?: Finding the Form of Settler Colonialism in Melbourne," *Global Urban History*, February 11, 2016, globalurbanhistory.com.

65 Nicholas Blomley, *Unsettling the City: Urban Land and the Politics of Property* (London: Routledge, 2004): xv.

66 Robyn Maynard, *Policing Black Lives: State Violence in Canada from Slavery to the Present* (Black Point, NS: Fernwood Publishing, 2017).

67 Rinaldo Walcott, *On Property: Policing, Prisons, and the Call for Abolition* (Windsor, ON: Biblioasis, 2021).

68 Nickita Longman, Emily Riddle, Alex Wilson, and Saima Desai, "'Land Back' Is More than the Sum of Its Parts," *Briarpatch Magazine*, September 10, 2020, briarpatchmagazine.com.

69 *Vanishing City*, directed by Fiore Derosa and Jen Senko, USA, 2009.

70 Joseph Tunney, "Sandy Hill Rowhouse Residents Face 'Renovictions,'" Advocates Say," *CBC News*, April 18, 2021, cbc.ca.

71 Ivis García and Mérida M. Rúa, "'Our Interests Matter': Puerto Rican Older Adults in the Age of Gentrification," *Urban Studies*, 55,14 (2018): 3169.

72 Stacy Torres, "'For a Younger Crowd': Place, Belonging, and Exclusion among Older Adults Facing Neighborhood Change," *Qualitative Sociology*, 43,1 (2020): 2.

73 H. Shellae Versey, "A Tale of Two Harlems: Gentrification, Social Capital, and Implications for Aging in Place," *Social Science & Medicine*, 214 (2018): 1–11.

74 Torres, "'For a Younger Crowd,'" 9.

75 Lidia Domínguez-Parraga, "The Effects of Gentrification on the Elderly: A Case Study in the City of Cáceres," *Social Sciences*, 9 (2020): 154.

76 Versey, "A Tale of Two Harlems."

77 Earni Young, "The Issues That Can Divide a Changing Neighborhood," *Philadelphia Inquirer*, October 23, 2014, inquirer.com.

78 Versey, "A Tale of Two Harlems."

79 Sandra Edmonds Crewe, "Aging and Gentrification: The Urban Experience," *Urban Social Work*, 1,1 (2017): 1.

80 Crewe, "Aging and Gentrification."

81 Crewe, "Aging and Gentrification."

82 Sarah Adjekum, "We Need to Talk About Gentrification and Public Health," *Hamilton Spectator*, February 11, 2018, thespec.com.

83 Centers for Disease Control and Prevention, "Health Effects of Gentrification," October 15, 2009, cdc.gov.

84 Sungwoo Lim, Pui Ying Chan, Sarah Walters, Gretchen Culp, Mary Huynh, and L. Hannah Gould, "Impact of Residential Displacement on Healthcare Access and Mental Health Among Original Residents of Gentrifying Neighborhoods in New York City," *Plos One*, 12,12 (2017): e0190139.

85 James Iveniuk and Scott Leon, "An Uneven Recovery: Measuring COVID-19 Vaccine Equity in Ontario," *Wellesley Institute*, April 16, 2021, wellesleyinstitute.com; Rudayna Bahubeshi, "Inequality in the COVID Recovery, from Infection Rates to Vaccine Access," *Policy Magazine*, June 15, 2021, policymagazine.ca.

86 Jessica M. Parish, "The Vital Politics of Gentrification: Governing Life in Urban Canada into the 21st Century" (PhD diss., York University, 2018).

87 Michael J. Dear and Jennifer R. Wolch, *Landscapes of Despair: From*

Deinstitutionalization to Homelessness (New Haven: Princeton University Press, 1987).

88   Thomas Fuller, "Life on the Dirtiest Block in San Francisco," *New York Times*, October 8, 2018, nytimes.com.

89   Fuller, "Life on the Dirtiest Block in San Francisco."

90   Kern, "From Toxic Wreck to Crunchy Chic."

91   Tom Slater, "Municipally Managed Gentrification in South Parkdale, Toronto," *Canadian Geographer*, 48,3 (2004): 303–25.

92   David Sibley, *Geographies of Exclusion: Society and Difference in the West* (London: Routledge, 1995)

6. GENTRIFICATION IS ABOUT PHYSICAL DISPLACEMENT

1   UNHCR The UN Refugee Agency, "Flagship Reports: Forced Displacement in 2020," unhcr.org.

2   Sukari Ivester, "Removal, Resistance and the Right to the Olympic City: The Case of Vila Autodromo in Rio de Janeiro," *Journal of Urban Affairs*, 39,7 (2017): 970–85.

3   Mindy Thompson Fullilove, *Root Shock: How Tearing Up City Neighborhoods Hurts America, and What We Can Do About It* (New York: New Village Press, 2004).

4   Neil Brenner, Peter Marcuse, and Margit Mayer, eds., *Cities for People, Not for Profit: Critical Urban Theory and the Right to the City* (New York: Routledge, 2012).

5   Elvin Wyly, Kathe Newman, Alex Schafran, and Elizabeth Lee, "Displacing New York," *Environment and Planning A*, 42,11 (2010): 2602–23.

6   Rowland Atkinson, "Measuring Gentrification and Displacement in Greater London," *Urban Studies*, 37,1 (2000): 149–65.

7   Wyly et al., "Displacing New York."

8   Mark Davidson, "Displacement, Space and Dwelling: Placing Gentrification Debate," *Ethics, Place and Environment: A Journal of Philosophy and Geography*, 12,2 (2009): 219–34.

9   Davidson, "Displacement, Space and Dwelling."

10   Yi Fu Tuan, *Space and Place: The Perspective of Experience* (Minneapolis: University of Minnesota Press, 2001 [1977]).

11   Mindy Thompson Fullilove and Rodrick Wallace, "Serial Forced Displacement in American Cities, 1916–2010," *Journal of Urban Health: Bulletin of the New York Academy of Medicine*, 88,3 (2011): 381–89.

12 Mariame Kaba, *We Do This 'til We Free Us* (Chicago: Haymarket Books, 2021).

13 Domicide and topocide refer the killing of the home and of place, respectively. Urbicide is the killing of the city.

14 Versey, "A Tale of Two Harlems," 5.

15 Rachel Pain, "Chronic Urban Trauma: The Slow Violence of Housing Dispossession," *Urban Studies*, 56,2 (2019): 393, 395.

16 Ade Kearns and Phil Mason, "Regeneration, Relocation and Health Behaviours in Deprived Communities," *Health and Place*, 32 (2015): 43–58.

17 Adam Elliott-Cooper, Phil Hubbard, and Loretta Lees, "Moving Beyond Marcuse: Gentrification, Displacement and the Violence of Un-homing," *Progress in Human Geography*, 44,3 (2020): 503.

18 Belinda Crawford and Peter Sainsbury, "Opportunity or Loss?: Health Impacts of Estate Renewal and the Relocation of Public Housing Residents," *Urban Policy and Research*, 35,2 (2017): 137–49.

19 Elliott-Cooper, Hubbard, and Lees, "Moving Beyond Marcuse," 501.

20 Henri Lefebvre, *Critique of Everyday Life: Foundations for a Sociology of the Everyday* (London: Verso, 1991 [1977]).

21 Versey, "A Tale of Two Harlems," 5.

22 Domínguez-Parraga, "The Effects of Gentrification on the Elderly," 9.

23 Tine Buffel and Chris Phillipson, "Ageing in a Gentrifying Neighbourhood: Experiences of Community Change in Later Life," *Sociology*, 53,6 (2019): 995.

24 Sociologists call these "weak ties." See Mark S. Granovetter, "The Strength of Weak Ties," *American Journal of Sociology*, 78,6 (1973): 1360–80.

25 Freeman, *There Goes the Hood*.

26 Princess McDowell, "They Are Gentrifying My Neighborhood in Silence," *Rebellious Magazine*, n.d., rebelliousmagazine.com.

27 Gretchen Brown, "How Discussions of 'Neighborhood Character' Reinforce Structural Racism," *Rewire*, July 17, 2020, rewire.org.

28 Versey, "A Tale of Two Harlems," 5.

29 Schulman, *The Gentrification of the Mind*.

30 McDowell, "They Are Gentrifying My Neighborhood in Silence."

31 Jaime Guzmán, "The Whiteness Project of Gentrification: The Battle over Los Angeles' Eastside" (PhD diss., University of Denver, 2018).

32 Guzmán, "The Whiteness Project of Gentrification," 67.

33 Katie M. Mazer and Katharine N. Rankin, "The Social Space of Gentrification: The Politics of Neighbourhood Accessibility in Toronto's Downtown West," *Environment and Planning D: Society and Space,* 29,5 (2011): 831.

34 Lam Thuy Vo, "As Wealthy Residents Moved in, These Business Owners Found Themselves Raided by Police," *Buzzfeed News,* August 27, 2020, buzzfeednews.com.

35 Lam Thuy Vo, "They Played Dominoes Outside Their Apartment for Decades: Then the White People Moved in and Police Started Showing Up," *Buzzfeed News,* July 18, 2018, buzzfeednews.com.

36 David Helps, "The Police: Gentrification's Shock Troops," *Public Books,* November 3, 2020, publicbooks.org.

37 Mark Jay and Philip Conklin, *A People's History of Detroit* (Durham: Duke University Press, 2020).

38 Rebecca Solnit, "Death by Gentrification: The Killing That Shamed San Francisco," *Guardian,* March 21, 2016, theguardian.com.

39 Phillip M. Bailey and Tessa Duvall, "Breonna Taylor Warrant Connected to Louisville Gentrification Plan, Lawyers Say," *Courier Journal,* July 5, 2020, courier-journal.com.

40 Bailey and Duvall, "Breonna Taylor Warrent."

41 Henry-Louis Taylor Jr., "Breonna Taylor's Death and Racist Police Violence Highlight Danger of Gentrification," *NBC News Think,* July 22, 2020, nbcnews.com.

42 Luanda Vannuchi and Mathieu Van Criekingen, "Transforming Rio de Janeiro for the Olympics: Another Path to Accumulation by Dispossession?," *Articulo: Journal of Urban Research,* 7 (2015), journals. openedition.org; Constance G. Anthony, "Urban Forced Removals in Rio De Janeiro and Los Angeles: North-South Similarities in Race and City," *University of Miami Inter-American Law Review,* 44,2 (2013): 337–64.

43 Elliott-Cooper, Hubbard, and Lees, "Moving Beyond Marcuse."

44 By formerly colonized people I mean those whose nations and/or ancestors were once under direct colonial rule but are now politically independent.

45 Carol Martin and Harsha Walia, "Red Women Rising: Indigenous Women Survivors in Vancouver's Downtown Eastside," Downtown Eastside Women's Centre, 2019, dewc.ca.

46 Martin and Walia, "Red Women Rising," 97.

47 Martin and Walia, "Red Women Rising," 97.

48 Anne Bonds and Joshua Inwood, "Beyond White Privilege: Geographies of White Supremacy and Settler Colonialism," *Progress in Human*

Geography, 40,6 (2016): 715–33; Adam Barker and Emma Battell Lowman, "Settler Colonialism," *Global Social Theory*, globalsocialtheory.org.

49   *Reclaiming Power and Place: The Final Report of the National Inquiry into Missing and Murdered Indigenous Women and Girls* (Canada, 2019), mmiwg-ffada.ca.

50   Martin and Walia, "Red Women Rising," 129.

51   Wendy Shaw, "Ways of Whiteness: Harlemising Sydney's Aboriginal Redfern," *Australian Geographical Studies*, 38,3 (2000): 291–305.

52   Liza Kim Jackson, "The Complications of Colonialism for Gentrification Theory and Marxist Geography," *Journal of Law and Social Policy*, 27 (2017): 69.

53   Alexander Baker, "From Eviction to Evicting: Rethinking the Technologies, Lives and Power Sustaining Displacement," *Progress in Human Geography*, 45,4 (2021): 796–813.

54   Matthew Desmond, *Evicted: Poverty and Profit in the American City* (New York: Crown Publishers, 2016).

55   Kriston Capps, "In California, Landlords Threaten Immigrant Tenants with Deportations," *Bloomberg CityLab*, April 5, 2017, bloomberg.com; Taylor Romine and Mirna Alsharif, "NYC Judge Recommends Landlord Pay $17,000 for Threatening to Call ICE on Undocumented Tenant," *CNN*, September 21, 2019, cnn.com.

56   Desmond, *Evicted*.

57   Annie Nova, "30 Second Trials: Judges Muting Tenants; The Problems with Virtual Evictions," *CNBC News*, May 1, 2021, cnbc.com.

58   Peter Hepburn, Renee Louis, and Matthew Desmond, "Racial and Gender Disparities among Evicted Americans," *Eviction Lab*, December 16, 2020, evictionlab.org; Kim Eckart, "UW Study Reveals Gender, Racial Disparities in Evictions," *UW News*, February 10, 2020, washington.edu.

59   Kimiko de Freytas-Tamura, "Why Black Homeowners in Brooklyn Are Being Victimized by Fraud," *New York Times*, October 21, 2019, nytimes.com.

60   Winifred Curran and Trina Hamilton, "Just Green Enough: Contesting Environmental Gentrification in Greenpoint, Brooklyn," *Local Environment*, 17,9 (2012): 1027–42.

61   Ann Dale and Lenore L. Newman, "Sustainable Development for Some: Green Urban Development and Affordability," *Local Environment*, 14,7 (2009): 669–81; Hamil Pearsall, "Superfund Me: A Study of Resistance to Gentrification in New York City," *Urban Studies*, 50,11 (2013): 2293–310.

62   Jennifer R. Wolch, Jason Byrne, and Joshua P. Newell, "Urban Green

Space, Public Health, and Environmental Justice: The Challenge of Making Cities 'Just Green Enough,'" *Landscape and Urban Planning*, 125 (2014): 234–44; see also Jennifer Foster, "Off Track, in Nature: Constructing Ecology on Old Rail Lines in Paris and New York," *Nature & Culture*, 5,3 (2010): 316–337; Darren J. Patrick, "The Matter of Displacement: A Queer Urban Ecology of New York City's High Line," *Social and Cultural Geography*, 15,8 (2014): 920–41.

63 Curran and Hamilton, "Just Green Enough."

64 Ysabelle Kempe, "House Hunters Are Fleeing Climate Change, Causing a New Kind of Gentrification," *Grist*, April 9, 2021, grist.org.

65 Phil Hubbard and Andrew Brooks, "Animals and Urban Gentrification: Displacement and Injustice in the Trans-Species City," *Progress in Human Geography* (February 2021): 2.

66 Hubbard and Brooks, "Animals and Urban Gentrification," 6; see also Fahim Amir, *Being and Swine: The End of Nature (As We Knew It)*, trans. Geoffrey C. Howes and Corvin Russell (Toronto: Between the Lines, 2020).

67 Hubbard and Brooks, "Animals and Urban Gentrification," 7.

68 Amir, *Being and Swine*.

69 Mauricio Peña, "Target Set to Hire 2,000 Employees for Controversial Little Village Warehouse," *Block Club Chicago*, April 29, 2021, blockclubchicago.org.

70 David Madden, "The Urban Process under Covid Capitalism," *City* 24,5–6 (2020): 677–80.

71 Siobhan Hughes, "How Cori Bush Put Life Story to Work in Eviction Protest at Capitol," *Wall Street Journal*, August 5, 2021, wsj.com.

72 Madden, "The Urban Process," 678.

73 Schulman, *The Gentrification of the Mind*.

74 Julia Lurie, "How PPP Loan Distribution Became the New Redlining," *Mother Jones*, May 1, 2021, motherjones.com.

75 Laura C. Morel, Mohamed Al Elew, and Emily Harris, "Rampant Racial Disparities Plagued How Billions of Dollars in PPP Loans Were Distributed in the U.S.," *Reveal*, May 1, 2021, revealnews.org.

76 Nova, "30 Second Trials"; CBC News, "Legal Clinics Raise Concerns About Virtual Eviction Hearings," November 19, 2020, cbc.ca.

77 Torres, "'For a Younger Crowd.'"

78 Buffel and Phillipson, "Ageing in a Gentrifying Neighbourhood."

7. GENTRIFICATION IS A METAPHOR

1   Karen Mizoguchi, "Beyoncé Is Prepping for Coachella 2018 by Going Vegan—and You Too Can Copy Her Meal Plan!," *People*, March 2, 2018, people.com.

2   Jamie Ballard and Amanda Garrity, "30 Celebrities You Didn't Know Were Vegan," *Good Housekeeping*, December 20, 2018, goodhousekeeping.com.

3   Karen Bettez Halnon and Saundra Cohen, "Muscles, Motorcycles and Tattoos: Gentrification in a New Frontier," *Journal of Consumer Culture*, 6,1 (2006): 33–56.

4   Joseph Brean, "From Counter-Culture to Mainstream: Why the Red-Hot Tattoo Boom is Bound to End," *The National Post*, August 16, 2013, nationalpost.com.

5   Halnon and Cohen, "Muscles, Motorcycles and Tattoos."

6   Andrija Filipović, "Drag for Everyone: Creative Industries and the Becoming-Visible of Drag in the 21st Century Belgrade," *Sexualities*, (2021), doi: 10.1177/13634607211019364.

7   Elizabeth De Michelis, *A History of Modern Yoga* (London: Continuum, 2004); Sarah Strauss, *Positioning Yoga: Balancing Acts Across Cultures* (Oxford: Berg, 2004).

8   John Philp, *Yoga Inc.: A Journey Through the Big Business of Yoga* (Toronto: Viking Canada, 2009).

9   Curran, *Gender and Gentrification*.

10 Shari L. Dworkin and Faye L. Wachs, "'Getting Your Body Back': Postindustrial Fit Motherhood in Shape Fit Pregnancy Magazine," *Gender and Society*, 18,5 (2004): 610–24.

11 Leslie Kern, "Connecting Embodiment, Emotion and Gentrification: An Exploration Through the Practice of Yoga in Toronto," *Emotion, Space and Society*, 5,1 (2012): 27–35.

12 Chelsea Vowel, *Indigenous Writes: A Guide to First Nations, Métis, and Inuit Issues in Canada* (Winnipeg: Highwater Press, 2016).

13 Van Badham, "'Mentrification:' How Men Appropriated Computers, Beer and the Beatles," *Guardian*, May 19, 2019, theguardian.com. Thank you to my editor Amanda Crocker for mentioning this term to me.

14 Kern, *Sex and the Revitalized City*.

15 Brentin Mock, "The New Urban Fried-Chicken Crisis," *Bloomberg CityLab*, May 10, 2017, citylab.com.

16 Gene Demby, "Where Did That Fried Chicken Stereotype Come From?," *CodeSwitch*, May 22, 2013, npr.org.

17 Jessica Hester, "When Food Gets Gentrified," *Bloomberg CityLab*, December 6, 2016, citylab.com.

18 East Liberty development, "History of East Liberty," 2021, eastliberty.org.

19 Alison Hope Alkon, Yuki Kato, and Joshua Sbicca, *A Recipe for Gentrification: Food, Power, and Resistance in the City* (New York: New York University Press, 2020).

20 Renee E. Walker, Christopher R. Keane, and Jessica G. Burke, "Disparities and Access to Healthy Food in the United States: A Review of Food Deserts Literature," *Health and Place*, 16 (2010): 876–84.

21 Mandy Meyer, "This Is How Many Vegans Are in the World Right Now," *VOU*, January 17, 2021, wtvox.com.

22 Davide Banis, "Everything Is Ready to Make 2019 the 'Year of the Vegan': Are You?," *Forbes*, December 13, 2018, forbes.com.

23 Vegandale, "Vegan Powered. Events Driven," vegandale.com.

24 Murray Whyte, "'My Parkdale Is Gone': How Gentrification Reached the One Place That Seemed Immune," *Guardian*, January 14, 2020, theguardian.com.

25 Lauren O'Neil, "Vegans Now Have Their Own Neighbourhood in Toronto," *BlogTO*, March 7, 2018, blogto.com.

26 Thomas Frank, *The Conquest of Cool: Business Culture, Counterculture, and the Rise of Hip Consumerism* (Chicago: University of Chicago Press, 1998).

27 Céline Chuang, "Let Us Be Water: Grieving Gentrification in the Heart of the City," *Guts Magazine*, January 19, 2020, gutsmagazine.ca.

8. GENTRIFICATION IS INEVITABLE

1 Hannah Fry and Julia Wick, "Moms Squatting in Home to Protest Bay Area Housing Crisis Are Kicked Out by Deputies," *Los Angeles Times*, January 14, 2020, latimes.com.

2 Michael Bott and Sean Myers, "Examining Wedgewood: A Look at the Home-Flipping Giant in Battle with Homeless Mothers," *NBC Bay Area*, December 31, 2019, nbcbayarea.com.

3 Sarah Holder and Brentin Mock, "A Group of Mothers, a Vacant Home, and a Win for Fair Housing," *Bloomberg CityLab*, January 28, 2020, citylab.com.

4 Loretta Lees, Sandra Annunziata, and Clara Rivas-Alonso, "Resisting Planetary Gentrification: The Value of Survivability in the Fight to Stay Put," *Annals of the American Association of Geographers*, 108,2 (2018): 346–55.

5   Sandra Annunziata and Clara Rivas-Alonso, "Resisting Gentrification," in *Handbook of Gentrification Studies*, eds. Loretta Lees with Martin Phillips (Cheltenham, UK: Edward Elgar Publishing, 2018): 393–412.

6   Annunziata and Rivas-Alonso, "Resisting Gentrification."

7   Clyde Woods, "Life after Death," *Professional Geographer*, 54,1 (2002): 62–66.

8   McKittrick, "Plantation Futures."

9   Dorries et al., *Settler City Limits*.

10 Kern, *Sex and the Revitalized City*.

11 Solnit and Schwartzenberg, *Hollow City*; Moskowitz, *How to Kill a City*; Jeremiah Moss, *Vanishing New York: How a Great City Lost Its Soul* (New York: Dey Street Books, 2017); Ada Calhoun, *St. Mark's Is Dead: The Many Lives of America's Hippest Street* (New York: W.W. Norton, 2015).

12 Luis Ferré-Sadumi, "India Walton Stuns Longtime Incumbent in Buffalo Mayoral Primary," *New York Times*, June 23, 2021, nytimes.com.

13 Lornet Turnbull, "To Combat Gentrification, One City Is Changing How Homes Are Bought and Sold," *Yes Magazine*, July 13, 2018, yesmagazine.org.

14 World Habitat Awards, "Milton Park Community," world-habitat.org; La Communauté Milton Parc, "History and Architecture of the Milton Park District," 2013, www.miltonparc.org.

15 Evergreen Cooperatives, "About Us," 2016, www.evgoh.com.

16 Yessenia Funes, "Own a Home in Just Four Years?: This Co-op Program Keeps Workers in the Neighborhood," *Yes Magazine*, August 24, 2015, yesmagazine.org.

17 María Carla Rodríguez and María Mercedes Di Virgilio, "A City for All?: Public Policy and Resistance to Gentrification in the Southern Neighborhoods of Buenos Aires," *Urban Geography*, 37,8 (2016): 1215–34.

18 Phil Hubbard and Loretta Lees, "The Right to Community?," *City*, 22,1 (2018): 8–25.

19 Lisa Berglund and Sam Butler, "Detroit's Community Benefits Ordinance: Setbacks and Opportunities to Giving Residents a Voice in Development," *Journal of Community Practice*, 29,1 (2021): 23–45.

20 Berglund and Butler, "Detroit's Community Benefits Ordinance," 39.

21 Isaac Würmann, "The Tenants' Rebellion," *Slate*, May 10, 2021, slate.com; Lukas Hermsmeier, "Berlin's Radical Housing Activists Aren't Afraid of Expropriations," *Nation*, March 27, 2019, thenation.com.

22 Dave Braneck, "Berlin Referendum: Voters Mull One of Europe's Most

Radical Ripostes to Gentrification," *EuroNews*, September 21, 2021, euronews.com.

23 Alex Berry, "Germany: Berlin Locals Vote to Expropriate Real Estate Giants," *DW*, September 26, 2021, dw.com.

24 Martine August, "Inclusionary Zoning: Six Insights from International Experience," *Plan Canada* (Winter 2018): 6–11.

25 Seon Young Lee and Yoonai Han, "When Art Meets Monsters: Mapping Art Activism and Anti-Gentrification Movements in Seoul," *City, Culture and Society*, 21 (2020), doi: 10.1016/j.ccs.2019.100292.

26 SquatSpace, "Tour of Beauty," 2019, squatspace.com.

27 Lucas Ilhein, "Complexity, Aesthetics, and Gentrification: Redfern/ Waterloo Tour of Beauty," in *There Goes the Neighbourhood: Redfern and the Politics of Urban Space*, eds. Zanny Begg and Keg De Souza (Sydney: Performance Space, 2009): 46–49.

28 Heather McLean, "Featured Video—'A Buzz in My Hub: Gender, Race, and Performing the Creative City,'" *Antipode Online*, March 28, 2013, antipodeonline.org.

29 Heather McLean, "Hos in the Garden: Staging and Resisting Neoliberal Creativity," *Environment and Planning D: Society and Space*, 35,1 (2017): 9.

30 McLean, "Hos in the Garden"; Ilhein, "Complexity, Aesthetics, and Gentrification."

31 Ilhein, "Complexity, Aesthetics, and Gentrification," 49.

32 Silvia Boarini, "Aboriginal Australians Defying Gentrification," *AlJazeera*, February 9, 2015, aljazeera.com.

33 CBC News, "Toronto Mayor to Review Clearing of Homeless Encampment from Trinity Bellwoods," June 23, 2021, cbc.ca.

34 Research field notes, interview, September 2015.

35 Ivis García, "No Se Vende (Not for Sale): An Anti-Gentrification Grassroots Campaign of Puerto Ricans in Chicago," *América Crítica*, 3,2 (2019): 35–61.

36 García, "No Se Vende," 49.

37 Philadelphia Housing Action, "Philadelphia Housing Action Claims Victory after 6 Month Direct Action Campaign Forces City to Relinquish 50 Vacant Homes to Community Land Trust," September 26, 2020, philadelphiahousingaction.info.

38 Manissa M. Maharawal, "Infrastructural Activism: Google Bus Blockades, Affective Politics, and Environmental Gentrification in San Francisco," *Antipode* (2021), doi: 10.1111/anti.12744.

39 Oli Mould, "Gutsy, Organised Londoners Have Learned to Stop

Gentrification in Its Tracks—Here's How," *Conversation*, March 1, 2018, theconversation.com.

40   Florian Opillard, "Resisting the Politics of Displacement in the San Francisco Bay Area: Anti-Gentrification Activism in the Tech Boom 2.0," *European Journal of American Studies*, 10,3 (2015).

41   Audre Lorde, *Sister Outsider* (Freedom, CA: The Crossing Press, 1984).

42   Mohammed Allie, "Cape Town Anger Over Slave Quarter Gentrification," *BBC News*, August 5, 2018, bbc.com.

43   Eoghan Macguire, "Can South Africa's 'Cradle of Islam' Survive Gentrification?," *AlJazeera*, December 11, 2018, aljazeera.com.

44   Shiri Pasternak, Naiomi Metallic, Yumi Numata, Anita Sekharan, and Jasmyn Galley, "Cash Back: A Yellowhead Institute Red Paper" (Yellowhead Institute, 2021): 5.

45   Juan Velásquez Atehortúa, "Barrio Women's Invited and Invented Spaces Against Urban Elitisation in Chacao, Venezuela," *Antipode*, 46,3 (2014): 835–56.

46   Velásquez Atehortúa, "Barrio Women's Invited and Invented Spaces," 843.

47   Faranak Miraftab, "Insurgent Planning: Situating Radical Planning in the Global South," *Planning Theory*, 8,1 (2009): 32–50.

48   Elizabeth Lawrence, "'Love and Solidarity': Amid Coronavirus, Mutual Aid Groups Resurge in New York City," *NPR*, July 26, 2020, npr.org; Equality for Flatbush, "Brooklyn Shows Love Mutual Aid Project, 2020, www.equalityforflatbush.org.

49   Dean Spade, *Mutual Aid: Building Solidarity During This Crisis (and the Next)* (London: Verso, 2020); Abigail Savitch-Lew, "Mutual Aid Movement Playing Huge Role in COVID-19 Crisis," *City Limits*, April 3, 2020, citylimits.org.

50   Spade, *Mutual Aid*.

51   Spade, *Mutual Aid*.

9. CHANGE THE STORY, CHANGE THE ENDING

1   Morgan Bassichis, Alexander Lee, and Dean Spade, "Building an Abolitionist Trans and Queer Movement with Everything We've Got," in *Captive Genders: Trans Embodiment and the Prison Industrial Complex*, eds. Eric A. Stanley and Nat Smith (Edinburgh: AK Press, 2011): 15–40.

2   Lola Olufemi, *Feminism, Interrupted: Disrupting Power* (London: Pluto Press, 2020).

3   Olufemi, *Feminism, Interrupted.*

4   Crenshaw, "Demarginalizing the Intersection of Race and Sex."

5   Leslie Kern, *Feminist City: A Field Guide* (Toronto: Between the Lines, 2019).

6   Emma R. Power and Kathleen J. Mee, "Housing: An Infrastructure of Care," *Housing Studies,* 35,3 (2020): 500.

7   Power and Mee, "Housing."

8   Chelsea Kirkby and Kathryn Mettler, "Women First: An Analysis of a Trauma-Informed, Women-Centred, Harm Reduction Housing Model for Women with Complex Substance Use and Mental Health Issues," in *Exploring Effective Systems Responses to Homelessness,* eds. Naomi Nichols and Carey Doberstein (Toronto: The Canadian Observatory on Homelessness Press, 2016): 114–31.

9   Schulman, *The Gentrification of the Mind.*

10   Gieseking, *A Queer New York.*

11   Olufemi, *Feminism, Interrupted.*

12   David J. Roberts and Minelle Mahtani, "Neoliberalizing Race, Racing Neoliberalism: Placing 'Race' in Neoliberal Discourses," *Antipode,* 42,2 (2010): 248.

13   Ida Danewid, "The Fire This Time: Grenfell, Racial Capitalism and the Urbanisation Of Empire," *European Journal of International Relations* 26,1 (2020): 299.

14   Laura Pulido, "Geographies of Race and Ethnicity 1: White Supremacy vs White Privilege in Environmental Racism Research," *Progress in Human Geography,* 29,6 (2015): 810.

15   Pulido, "Geographies of Race and Ethnicity 1," 812.

16   Pulido, "Geographies of Race and Ethnicity 1," 813.

17   Pulido, "Geographies of Race and Ethnicity 1," 812.

18   Fullilove and Wallace, "Serial Forced Displacement."

19   Taylor, *Race for Profit.*

20   Bullard, *Dumping in Dixie.*

21   Julie Sze, *Noxious New York: The Racial Politics of Urban Health and Environmental Justice* (Boston: MIT Press, 2006).

22   David Moscrop, "Fixing the Housing Crisis Will Mean Treating Shelter as a Right—Not a Commodity," *Canadian Dimension*, June 25, 2021, canadiandimension.com.

23   Kaba, *We Do This 'til We Free Us.*

24   Kaba, *We Do This 'til We Free Us.*

25 Ruth Wilson Gilmore, *Golden Gulag: Prisons, Surplus, Crisis, and Opposition in Globalizing California* (Berkeley: University of California Press, 2007).

26 Centers for Disease Control and Prevention, "Health Effects of Gentrification."

27 McKittrick, "Plantation Futures."

28 Tamika Butler, "Last Year, the Bike Industry Promised Inclusivity: But Advocacy Allies Still Don't Get It," *Bicycling*, July 1, 2021, bicycling.com.

29 George J. Sefa Dei, "Foreword," in *Decolonization and Anti-Colonial Praxis: Shared Lineages*, ed. Anila Zainub (Leiden, The Netherlands: Brill, 2019): vii–x.

30 Jennifer Robinson, *Ordinary Cities: Between Modernity and Development* (London: Routledge, 2006); Libby Porter, *Unlearning the Colonial Cultures of Planning* (London: Routledge, 2016 [2010]).

31 Linda Peake and Martina Rieker, *Rethinking Feminist Interventions into the Urban* (London: Routledge, 2013).

32 Linda Tuhiwai Smith, *Decolonizing Methodologies: Research and Indigenous Peoples* (London: Bloomsbury Academic, 1999).

33 Deborah McGregor, "*Mino-Mnaamodzawin*: Achieving Indigenous Environmental Justice in Canada," *Environment and Society: Advances in Research*, 9 (2018): 7–24.

34 Laura Harjo, *Spiral to the Stars: Mvskoke Tools of Futurity* (Tucson: University of Arizona Press, 2019): 10.

35 Dorries et al., *Settler City Limits*.

36 Winona LaDuke, "A Society Based on Conquest Cannot Be Sustained: Native Peoples and the Environmental Crisis," in *Toxic Struggles: The Theory and Practice of Environmental Justice*, ed. Richard Hofrichter (Philadelphia: New Society Publishers, 1993): 98–106.

37 LaDuke, "A Society Based on Conquest Cannot Be Sustained."

38 Jackson, "The Complications of Colonialism."

39 Eve Tuck and K. Wayne Yang, "Decolonization Is Not a Metaphor," *Decolonization: Indigeneity, Education and Society*, 1,1 (2012): 2.

40 Tuck and Yang, "Decolonization Is Not a Metaphor," 7.

41 Shiri Pasternak and Hayden King, "Land Back: A Yellowhead Institute Red Paper" (Yellowhead Institute, 2019): 36.

42 Lindsay Nixon, "This Prairie City Is Land, Too," *Briarpatch Magazine*, September 10, 2020, briarpatchmagazine.com.

43 Evelyn Peters and Chris Anderson, *Indigenous in the City: Contemporary Identities and Cultural Innovation* (Vancouver: UBC Press, 2014).

44   Ryan Walker, Ted Jojola, and David Natcher, eds., *Reclaiming Indigenous Planning* (Montreal: McGill-Queen's University Press, 2013).

45   Arturo Escobar, *Designs for the Pluriverse: Radical Interdependence, Autonomy, and the Making of Worlds* (Durham: Duke University Press, 2017).

46   McGregor, *"Mino-Mnaamodzawin."*

47   John Joe Schlichtman, Jason Patch, and Marc Lamont Hill, *Gentrifier* (Toronto: University of Toronto Press, 2017): 89.

48   Japonica Brown-Saracino, *A Neighborhood That Never Changes: Gentrification, Social Preservation, and the Search for Authenticity* (Chicago: University of Chicago Press, 2010).

49   Trina Hamilton and Winifred Curran, "From 'Five Angry Women' to 'Kick-Ass Community': Gentrification and Environmental Activism in Brooklyn and Beyond," *Urban Studies*, 50,8 (2013): 1557–74.

50   Hamilton and Curran, "From 'Five Angry Women,'" 1558.

51   Deepa Iyer, "The Social Change Ecosystem Map (Building Movement Project)," 2018, buildingmovement.org.

52   Celia Haig-Brown, "Decolonizing Diaspora: Whose Traditional Land Are We On?," *Cultural and Pedagogical Inquiry*, 1,1 (2009): 4–21.

53   Michelle Buckley, "From Kerala to Dubai and Back Again: Construction Migrants and the Global Economic Crisis," *Geoforum*, 43,2 (2012): 250–59; National Park Service, "African Burial Ground: History and Culture," April 26, 2019, nps.gov.

54   David Weitzman, *Skywalkers: Mohawk Ironworkers Build the City* (New York: Macmillan Publishers, 2010).

55   Sara Ahmed, *Living a Feminist Life* (Durham: Duke University Press, 2017).

56   J. K. Gibson-Graham and Kelly Dombroski, *The Handbook of Diverse Economies* (Cheltenham, UK: Edgar Elgar, 2020).

57   Sasha Costanza-Chock, *Design Justice: Community-Led Practices to Build the Worlds We Need* (Cambridge MA: MIT Press, 2020). Full text access: design-justice.pubpub.org.

58   Kaba, *We Do This 'til We Free Us.*

INDEX

Gibson, William, 36
Gibson-Graham, J. K., 28, 201
Gieseking, Jen Jack, 80, 81, 179–80
Gilmore, Ruth Wilson, 184
Glass, Ruth, 6–7, 8, 10, 34, 37, 68, 103
globalization, 36, 56–58, 68–69. *see also* post-industrial city
Google Bus Blockades, 167, 168
governance. *see* urban neoliberalism
Goyette, Kiley, 65
Gray, Freddie (resident), 118
green space projects, 11, 54–55, 125. *see also* environmental justice movement
Greenpoint (Brooklyn), 194
Greenwich Village (New York), 34, 81
grid layouts, colonial, 92–93
grief, 148
Guardian, 19, 140, 145
Guzmán, Jaime, 115

Halifax (Nova Scotia), 25
Halnon, Karen, 134–35
Hamilton, Trina, 194
Han, Yoonai, 163
Hannam area (Seoul), 163
Haringey (London), 168
Harjo, Laura, 186–87
Harlem: policing, 116; seniors/older adults, 96, 97, 98, 108, 112, 130; sense of belonging, 48, 108; sensory environment, 114; social networks, 112, 113
Harrison, Da'Shaun, 11
Harvey, David, 62
health inequalities, 87, 94, 95, 98–100, 127–28, 129, 184–85. *see also* environmental racism; industrial pollution
healthification, 99–100
Hernandez, Ramon (resident), 117
heteronormativity, 72, 78, 79–80
High Line Park (New York), 55, 125
Hilco Redevelopment Partners, 127
Hill, Marc Lamont, 193
Hogan's Alley (Vancouver), 85
Hogan's Alley Society, 88
Hollow City (Solnit), 14, 155
home. *see* sense of belonging; sensory environment; un-homing
home ownership: alternative models, 159; long-time residents, 194, 195;

market values, 6, 7; private property norms, 92–94; racial wealth gap, 86; speculators' pressure on seniors, 97–98; wealth creation, 83–84. *see also* redlining
home sharing, 65–66
home-flipping, 124, 151–52
homelessness and unhoused people: creative city, 45; deinstitutionalization, 100; direct-action campaigns, 152–53, 167; domestic violence, 75, 179; Indigenous, 119–20; nuisance complaints, 80; policing of, 116–17, 166; queer and trans youth, 179; seniors/older adults, 98
Hometown Hero: The Legend of New York's Chopped Cheese, 143
homogenization, 114–15
homonormativity, 80–82
House of Lancaster (Toronto), 42
housing: activism, 128, 129, 151–52; affordability, 44, 45, 120, 160, 162–63; precarity, 100–102, 179; short-term rental impact, 65, 66; speculation, impact of, 8, 19, 151–52
housing alternatives: community benefit ordinances, 161; community land trusts, 14, 88, 157–58, 159, 167; cooperatives, 158–59, 160
housing policies and practices: domestic violence, 75–76; G.I. bill, 85, 215n39; patriarchal, 72; racist, 83–84, 85, 88, 91–92, 216n40. *see also* redlining
Housing Rights Committee, San Francisco, 169
How to Kill a City (Moskowitz), 155
Hubbard, Phil, 110, 126–27, 160–61
Hum, Tarry, 90
humanistic approaches, 108–11
Humboldt Park (Chicago), 96, 166
Hurricane Katrina, 65, 66–67
Hurricane Sandy, 68
Hurst, Kelly Wickham, 48
hyper-gentrification, 168
hyperinvestment, racialized, 91–92

identity politics, 192–96
Ilhein, Lucas, 164, 165
immigrants, waves of, 2, 6–7, 23, 52, 55, 192

imperialism, 26, 56, 62
Indigenous peoples: design justice, 190–91; displacement, 13, 26–27, 105, 120–21, 187–88; reparations, 170–71; rights to the city, 190
Indigenous women, housing discrimination and, 120
individual actions, 197–203. *see also* anti-gentrification politics
industrial pollution, 40, 51, 54–57, 124–25, 127, 182. *see also* deindustrialization; post-industrial city
inevitability narrative, 14–15, 154, 155, 156, 174. *see also* naturalization
informal settlements, women's, 171–72
insurgent urbanism, 171
intensive parenting, 138
interdisciplinary approaches, 109
intersectional perspectives, 12–13, 72–74, 92, 102, 169, 202
investors/speculators, 8, 19, 52, 55, 56–58
Iyer, Deepa, 196
Iyer's Social Change Ecosystem Map, 197, 231n51

Jackson, Liza Kim, 121
Jacobs, Jane, 21, 33–34
Jay, Mark, 116
Jay-Z (a.k.a. Shawn Carter), 92
Jim Crow laws, 12, 47, 86
Junction (Toronto), 1–4, 42, 101, 192
Just Cause, 169

Kaba, Mariame, 184, 202–3
Kamloops, 164
Kanien'kehá:ka (Mohawk), 198
Kat Von D, 135
Keery, Alan and Gary, 31
Kelley, Robin D. G., 86
Klein, Naomi, 67
knowledge economies, 43, 58–59. *see also* creative city
Kucenic, Adam, 142

LA Ink, 135
LaDuke, Winona, 187
Land Back movements, 93–94, 189
landlords: delinquent, 101; pressure on seniors, 97; rent gap, 55; sexual harassment, 76; tenancy-law

loopholes, 94–95, 122–23, 128, 129. *see also* evictions
Landry, Charles, 42
Las Vegas, 129
Last Real Indians Media Movement, 27
Latinx communities: cultural appropriation, 48; environmental justice, 124–25, 127; Mexican immigrant, 32, 48, 51–52, 54–55; policing, 117–18; whiteness/whitening, 115
Law 341 (Buenos Aires), 160
Lee, Alexander, 176
Lee, Seon Young, 163
Lees, Loretta, 110, 160–61
Lefebvre, Henri, 111
legal and policy interventions, 159–63
Ley, David, 34, 35, 37
LGBTQ communities/spaces, 76, 80–81, 114, 117, 179–80
Liberty Village (Toronto), 60
lifestyle gentrifiers, 32, 34–35, 52
Little Jamaica (Toronto), 89–90
Little Village (Chicago), 51–52, 54–55, 124–25, 127
loft living, 26, 34, 35, 36, 38, 60. *see also* deindustrialization
Logan Square (Chicago), 95
London (England): Battersea, 19–20; Brixton, 19; Chrisp Street Market, 168; early gentrifiers, 37; garment district, 56; Islington, 5–8; Notting Hill, 6; post-industrial city, 58–59; right to housing activism, 160–61; Shoreditch, 31–32; super-gentrification, 63
London Underground, 5
Longman, Nickita, 94
long-time residents, 39, 95, 112–13, 194–96. *see also individual gentrifiers*
Lorde, Audre, 169
Los Angeles (California), 129, 145, 155
Louisville (Kentucky), 118
low-income community builders, 35, 36–37, 78
Luminato festival, 45. *see also* creative city

Macedonia AME Church (Queens), 90

ABOUT THE AUTHOR

Leslie Kern is the author of two books on gender and cities, including *Feminist City: Claiming Space in a Man-Made World*. She holds a PhD in women's studies from York University. Currently, Leslie is an associate professor of geography and environment and women's and gender studies at Mount Allison University. Her research has earned a Fulbright Visiting Scholar Award, a National Housing Studies Achievement Award, and several national multi-year grants. Leslie is also an academic career coach, where she helps academics find meaning and joy in their work. Originally from Toronto, Leslie now resides with her partner and two cats in Mi'kma'ki, Sackville, New Brunswick, Canada.